Schenker's Interpretive Practice is the first comprehensive study of this century's most influential music theorist, Heinrich Schenker (1868–1935). Since the 1960s, American theorists and musicologists have focused almost exclusively on analytical methods distilled from Schenker's writings. Breaking from that tradition, Robert Snarrenberg returns to Schenker's text and to the humanist roots of his approach, situating Schenker's work in the broader context of his desire to portray the richness and particularity of musical experience. Snarrenberg concentrates on four aims that Schenker hoped to achieve: to present a theoretical account of musical effects encountered in European music of the eighteenth and nineteenth centuries, to represent the mindset shared among composers of that music, to convey the expressive interaction of musical effects in individual artworks, and to promote continued creative and re-creative participation in the musical tradition. Snarrenberg also reveals that the center of Schenker's interpretive practice lies in the interweaving of technical analysis with metaphor and imagery.

CAMBRIDGE STUDIES IN MUSIC THEORY AND ANALYSIS

GENERAL EDITOR: IAN BENT

SCHENKER'S INTERPRETIVE PRACTICE

TITLES IN THIS SERIES

SCHENKER'S INTERPRETIVE PRACTICE

ROBERT SNARRENBERG

Associate Professor, Department of Music, Washington University in St. Louis

CAMBRIDGE
UNIVERSITY PRESS

Published by the Press Syndicate of the University of Cambridge
The Pitt Building, Trumpington Street, Cambridge CB2 1RP
40 West 20th Street, New York, NY 10011-4211, USA
10 Stamford Road, Oakleigh, Melbourne 3166, Australia

First published 1997

Printed in the United Kingdom at the University Press, Cambridge

A catalogue record for this book is available from the British Library

Library of Congress cataloguing in publication data

Snarrenberg, Robert
Schenker's interpretive practice / Robert Snarrenberg
p. cm. – (Cambridge Studies in Music Theory and Analysis; 11)
Includes bibliographical references and index
ISBN 0 521 49726 4 (hardback)
1. Schenker, Heinrich, 1868–1935. 2. Schenkerian analysis.
3. Music – Philosophy and aesthetics. I. Title. II. Series.
MT6.S674S3 1997
781.1'7–dc20 96–25104 CIP MN

ISBN 0 521 49726 4 hardback

AH

TO MILDRED KIMMICK,

JAMES EATON, AND MARION GUCK,

WHO TAUGHT ME THE

WAY OF MUSIC

CONTENTS

FOREWORD BY IAN BENT

Theory and analysis are in one sense reciprocals: if analysis opens up a musical structure or style to inspection, inventorying its components, identifying its connective forces, providing a description adequate to some live experience, then theory generalizes from such data, predicting what the analyst will find in other cases within a given structural or stylistic orbit, devising systems by which other works – as yet unwritten – might be generated. Conversely, if theory intuits how musical systems operate, then analysis furnishes feedback to such imaginative intuitions, rendering them more insightful. In this sense, they are like two hemispheres that fit together to form a globe (or cerebrum!), functioning deductively as investigation and abstraction, inductively as hypothesis and verification, and in practice forming a chain of alternating activities.

Professionally, on the other hand, "theory" now denotes a whole subdiscipline of the general field of musicology. Analysis often appears to be a subordinate category within the larger activity of theory. After all, there is theory that does not require analysis. Theorists may engage in building systems or formulating strategies for use by composers; and these almost by definition have no use for analysis. Others may conduct experimental research into the sound-materials of music or the cognitive processes of the human mind, to which analysis may be wholly inappropriate. And on the other hand, historians habitually use analysis as a tool for understanding the classes of compositions – repertories, "outputs," "periods," works, versions, sketches, and so forth – that they study. Professionally, then, our ideal image of twin hemispheres is replaced by an intersection: an area that exists in common between two subdisciplines. Seen from this viewpoint, analysis reciprocates in two directions: with certain kinds of theoretical inquiry, and with certain kinds of historical inquiry. In the former case, analysis has tended to be used in rather orthodox modes, in the latter in a more eclectic fashion; but that does not mean that analysis in the service of theory is necessarily more exact, more "scientific," than analysis in the service of history.

The above epistemological excursion is by no means irrelevant to the present series. Cambridge Studies in Music Theory and Analysis is intended to present the work of theorists and of analysts. It has been designed to include "pure" theory – that is, theoretical formulation with a minimum of analytical exemplification; "pure" analysis – that is, practical analysis with a minimum of theoretical underpinning; and writings that fall at points along the spectrum between the two extremes. In these capacities, it aims to illuminate music, as work and as process.

However, theory and analysis are not the exclusive preserves of the present day. As subjects in their own right, they are diachronic. The former is coeval with the very study of music itself, and extends far beyond the confines of Western culture; the latter, defined broadly, has several centuries of past practice. Moreover, they have been dynamic, not static fields throughout their histories. Consequently, studying earlier music through the eyes of its own contemporary theory helps us to escape (when we need to, not that we should make a dogma out of it) from the preconceptions of our own age. Studying earlier analyses does this too, and in a particularly sharply focused way; at the same time it gives us the opportunity to re-evaluate past analytical methods for present purposes, such as is happening currently, for example, with the long-despised methods of hermeneutic analysis of the late nineteenth century. The series thus includes editions and translations of major works of past theory, and also studies in the history of theory.

The present book follows soon after the completion of two other Schenker projects in this series, Leslie D. Blasius's *Schenker's Argument*, and the three volumes of Schenker's yearbook *The Masterwork in Music*, translated. Where Blasius charted the location of Schenker's theoretical work within the Western intellectual tradition, Robert Snarrenberg takes us deep inside the mind of this influential theorist.

The reader's attention will be engaged again and again by this volume's fascinating inquiries: by, for example, the revelatory opening-up in chapter 3 of Schenker's world of metaphor, his creation of "analytical fictions"; or the probing examination in chapter 2 of the economies that Schenker employed in his arguments, and the reconstructing of the undeclared steps of reasoning, and filling-in of the elided levels of graphs; or the deep and subtle exploration in chapter 4 of how Schenker viewed the sustaining of a musical tradition, and of the role that listener and performer play in that sustaining – an exploration that reveals a deep-seated ambivalence on Schenker's part. Snarrenberg touches each of the principal facets of Schenker's work, illuminating it brilliantly and creatively.

Along the way, he provides countless fascinating snippets of information about Schenker's life, career, and publication history, many of them researched for the first time from Schenker's papers in the Ernst Oster and Oswald Jonas Memorial Collections. These include important insights into the chronology of Schenker's thought during that melting-pot period between 1915 and early 1921, when he was writing commentaries on two late Beethoven piano sonatas, completing the second volume of *Counterpoint*, drafting portions of what would become *Free Composition*, and possibly some of the material later to appear in *Der Tonwille*, and at the same time preparing his complete edition of the Beethoven sonatas. The volume is also studded with searching and superbly executed definitions of crucial terms in the Schenkerian vocabulary – terms such as *Durchgang*, *Zug* and *Ursatz*.

However, this is no assemblage of separate inquiries, or assortment of facts and definitions: it is a compelling single argument that drives from first page to last. It delves into the deepest elements of Schenker's theoretical construct, scrutinizes his motivations and intentions, and inspects his methods of realization, his modes of presentation. One of the products of this examination of "interpretive practice" is the vividness with which Schenker's own voice emerges, not only in discussions of his sense of the dramatic, his appeal to the "life" of musical tones, his harnessing of rhetoric, and his deployment of programs and imageries, but also in Snarrenberg's own striking translations, which unleash the full force of Schenker's utterances.

PREFACE

In the tumultuous artistic and political context of the waning Habsburg Empire, Heinrich Schenker (1868–1935) proclaimed himself the saviour of a dying art. Cultural rejuvenation was both his passion and his despair. Like the hero of so many operettas produced by Alexandrine von Schönerer at the Theater an der Wien, Schenker longed nostalgically for a time when "a marvelous nobility will be reclaimed against all vulgar resistance."[1] In a letter to Baron Alphons von Rothschild, a former piano student and later benefactor who bore the publication costs of *Harmonielehre* and the first book of *Kontrapunkt*, he wrote:

Dear Herr Baron! The noble-minded deed of your participation in my great work provides me the most joyful occasion to express to you my most cordial thanks and heart-felt gratitude. In an epoch like the present, in which the world is visited by the "plagues" of obscurity, ignorance, lack of character, deceit, and the like, as Egypt was once visited by the notorious "10 plagues," it is doubly rewarding to welcome a strong hand that supports and promotes one who is resolved to bring light into the darkness and to free the land of plagues.[2]

Schenker styled himself as a Moses, a prophet who would lead Austro-German musicians out of their bondage to Progress and Demos, into a musical culture that was their rightful inheritance; but unlike Moses, Schenker saw himself as blessed with the gift of speech, a prophet who would proclaim a monotriadic creed and inscribe the eternal laws of the cultus.

Though he gave his all to bring about "a renaissance of music" (*NTB* 24), to recover the spirit of the Austro-German tradition which was in serious decline, even just a few short years after the death of Brahms, he held out little hope that his efforts to re-create a musical aristocracy could succeed in the face of the overwhelming leveling forces of democracy and capitalism.[3] With zealous dedication to Austro-German tonal music of the eighteenth and nineteenth centuries that was purchased at the price of rejecting the future of Strauss, Mahler, Debussy, Schoen-

---

[1] Frederic Morton, *A Nervous Splendor* (Harmondsworth: Penguin, 1980), 74.

[2] Draft dated Feb. 1911; OJ 5 f. 34 and *NTB* 24.

[3] Schenker was by no means alone in desiring to save a dying Germanic culture or in believing that he could define what was its Germanic essence; see Pamela Potter, "The Music of a Nation: Attempts to Define 'Germanness' in Music in the Eighteenth, Nineteenth, and Twentieth Centuries," paper presented at Washington University in November 1995, and *German Musicology and Society from the Weimar Republic to the End of Hitler's Reich* (New Haven, Conn.: Yale University Press, forthcoming), chapter 7.

berg, and Stravinsky, a future that he regarded as no future insofar as the history of artistic spirit was concerned, Schenker battled to preserve the Austro-German musical spirit, if not as a living compositional tradition, then at least as a force that would enable listeners and performers to participate re-creatively in the tradition and so nourish their spirits with the products of music's world-historical individuals.

At a time when musicologists are redefining the nature of their pursuits, calling for historically sensitive criticism, for interpretation mindful of the situated listener's role in the musical event, for consideration of non-Western musics as well as of Western music that lies outside the canon of Germanic high art – at such a time it must seem curiously backward to write a book about Schenker, who for so many is the very embodiment of outmoded scholarship: a man reputedly concerned only with the technical dimension of a small handful of German (or at least Germanic) male composers of the eighteenth and nineteenth centuries, haughtily dismissive of any music that lay outside a tradition that was born with J. S. Bach and died with Johannes Brahms, and insensitive to the changing cultural contexts within which his revered masters produced their works. There is no disputing the fact that the historical and stylistic scope of Schenker's project is narrow; if the attempts of others to expand its scope have severely strained the application of his central concepts, that only confirms the bond between Schenker's project and that one musical tradition. That is one of its principal strengths, for few if any have as yet produced so penetrating an account of the Austro-German musical tradition.

When he embarked upon his career in the early 1890s, Schenker participated in virtually every facet of that tradition. He composed, worked as a critic for various Vienna weeklies, gave piano lessons, appeared in recitals as both soloist and accompanist, wrote essays on musical theory and culture, edited performing editions, and published a practical treatise on ornamentation. As the new century began, he abandoned the careers of composer, pianist and critic, and focused his energies on writing and private instruction. It was a career choice that bespeaks an intense, personal motivation, for the profession most suited to fostering such pursuits – an academic position – was closed to him (he lacked the imprimatur of a certificate from the Vienna Conservatory and did not endear himself to people in the academy who could help him obtain a position on the strength of his accomplishments).[4] The rather solitary pursuits of writing and private piano instruction were undoubtedly better suited to his self-image and his desire to remain free of obligations that might encumber his intellectual labors. He felt most at home, it seems, being a lone prophetic voice in a cultural wilderness. And yet it was a rather prolific voice: one

---

[4] His piano teacher Ernst Ludwig sent him some piano students but did nothing else to further his career (*NTB* 7), and Schenker's published remarks about Bruckner were sure to sour any feelings the latter may have had for his one-time student. Moreover, as we know from Hans Weisse's reports to Schenker on his musicological studies at the University of Vienna, the influential Guido Adler did what he could to check Schenker's influence, for a time even keeping Schenker's writings out of his seminar reading-room (*NTB* 50–55).

hundred essays and reviews written for periodicals between 1891 and 1901; performing editions of works by Handel, C. P. E. Bach, and Beethoven; five books; eight extensive commentaries on works by Beethoven; more than seventy essays on theoretical, analytical, and miscellaneous topics; and several projects that were never completed.[5]

When the great conductor Wilhelm Furtwängler looked back over the twenty years he had known Schenker, he wrote that he "came to know an author who, as a person, had at his disposal experiences incomparably richer and more lively than his theoretical utterances led one to expect."[6] Furtwängler meant to convey both that Schenker's private reporting of musical experiences outstripped the public reports recorded in his writings and that he was a keen observer of nonmusical experiences besides. Furtwängler's remark is a caution against several sorts of errors. No analysis by Schenker is an exhaustive account of his experience of the work or of its content. No theoretical text, not even the posthumously published *Der freie Satz*, ought to be regarded as Schenker's definitive statement about tonal music.[7] And no utterance, analytical or theoretical, should be assumed to be a straightforward reporting of his musical experiences. Schenker's public speech is a trace – albeit richer than most, but no less partial – of experiences that invariably outran his attempts to communicate them.[8]

My aim in this book is to reconstruct the structure and content of the musical experiences reported by Schenker. To do so I have had to pay close attention to the verbal traces of that rich, lively musical life that Furtwängler encountered in Schenker. Complicating matters is the fact that the perception of Schenker's musical imagination has been warped in the process of translation and assimilation into late twentieth-century America.[9] Under the pressure of a post-Sputnik ideology that valued the application of scientific approaches to all intellectual endeavors, American music theorists appropriated only the portion of Schenker's interpretive practice that seemed most technical, eschewing anything that might be perceived as overtly metaphorical.[10] One recent writer put his finger on the problem:

[5] The latter include treatises on musical form and performance, an essay "On the Decline of Music," and plans for numerous analyses. Most of these materials are preserved in OC and JC.

[6] Wilhelm Furtwängler, *Ton und Wort*, 4th edn (Wiesbaden: F. A. Brockhaus, 1955), 200.

[7] In the preface to *NS*, which is by far the longest analytical text Schenker ever wrote (if not the most perspicuous), Schenker paralleled himself with C. P. E. Bach, who had written, 'it will be seen that I have [not only] said nothing unnecessary, but have not yet said all there is to say' (*NS* xxiii/16).

[8] That the relation between musical experience and reporting is frequently, if not typically, indirect is argued by Stephen Peles in "Musical 'Meaning' and Talk About It," a paper presented at the special session on Analysis and Meaning in Music at the annual meeting of the Society for Music Theory, New York City, November 1995.

[9] On the reception of Schenker in post-war America, see William Rothstein, "The Americanization of Schenker," *ITO* 9 (1) (1986), 5–17 (reprinted in *Schenker Studies*, ed. Hedi Siegel [Cambridge: Cambridge University Press, 1990], 193–203). See also my essay "Competing Myths: The American Abandonment of Schenker's Organicism," in *Theory, Analysis and Meaning in Music*, ed. Anthony Pople (Cambridge: Cambridge University Press, 1994), 30–58.

[10] As Marion A. Guck has suggested, the turn toward science in music theory can be traced to Milton Babbitt's writings in the early 1960s; Guck insightfully defends the claim that whereas American music theory adopted

We have become quite content to think of [the *Ursatz*] as a "theoretical construct," or as a "hypothetical substructure," or as an "axiom." In other words, we speak of the *Ursatz* in terms that sound scientific, perhaps because the atmosphere of science has a reassuring bouquet of scholarly rationality about it, or, at any rate, because we breathe it more easily than the atmosphere of organicism, life forces, and the will of the tones.[11]

Though seldom voiced so explicitly, the same testimony is no less clearly expressed by American theorists in their crafting of analytical and theoretical utterances: Schenker's rhetorical habits have been perceived as irrelevant, unintelligible, or uncomfortable. All but the most recent translations calcified Schenker's lively rhetoric, choosing technical sounding, Latinate words to render densely resonant German terms.[12] The time has come, I believe, when the crass linguistic pressure of that scientistic ideology has abated, when many musicologists and theorists now desire to represent music's place in the larger weave of human life – the time has come to turn a fresh ear to Schenker's rhetoric and listen for the traces of the music Furt-wängler must have come to know as a result of his encounters with Schenker. That is why this book focuses on Schenker's analytical writings, in which prose – vivid, engaging, and reflective of why music matters to him so deeply – is indispensable in the portrayal of musical experience. Situating Schenker's theories and analyses in the context of his desire to portray musical experience as fully as possible returns us to the humanist roots of Schenker's approach.

I have fashioned this text for an audience of music theorists, musicologists, and aestheticians. For theorists and musicologists the book can serve as a general introduction to Schenker's interpretive practice, one not skewed exclusively toward production of "the graph." Much of the technical content of Schenker's so-called theory is presented in chapter 1. Chapters 2 through 4 introduce the wider scope of Schenker's interpretive practice and deal with aspects of the practice that are not reflected in existing theoretical literature. Along the way I hope to remedy some prevalent misconceptions of Schenker's analytical practice.

Aestheticians will, I hope, find this a fascinating case study in aesthetic interpretation, for Schenker rationalizes the use of psychological and expressive interpretants for classically tonal music by connecting them directly to the composer's activity of arranging tones.

Much of the book's content is difficult: Schenker's writings are difficult in themselves, and the musical artworks that were the objects of his concern are among the

---

the language but not the methods of science, Babbitt in practice depends more on the empirical requirements of scientific method and less on the formal requirements of scientific language; see "Rehabilitating the Incorrigible," in *Theory, Analysis and Meaning in Music*, ed. Pople, 57–73.

[11] William A. Pastille, "The Development of the *Ursatz* in Schenker's Published Works," in *Trends in Schenkerian Research*, ed. Allen Cadwallader (New York: Schirmer Books, 1990), 71.

[12] The parallel with American translations of Freud are too obvious to overlook: id and ego for "das Es" and "das Ich," for example; on this see Bruno Bettelheim, *Freud and Man's Soul* (New York: Random House, Vintage Books, 1984), esp. 52–60.

most difficult and complex works of Western music. It is difficult, too, because it situates the ideas of concern to current musicologists and aestheticians – musical criticism and hermeneutics, musical meaning or affect – within an interpretive practice devoted to detailed analytical understanding of those works and the behavior that produced them and sustains them.

ACKNOWLEDGMENTS

I thank Rieko Terai, my partner, without whose wonderful o-bento or long-suffering and patience I would never have completed this book. Thanks to my daughters, to Shana for allowing me to relearn the art of music with her and to Karina for keeping my play-impulse active.

I owe a special debt to Marion A. Guck for her careful questioning of ideas and interpretations that led to significant improvements in this book, and even more for her generous friendship and encouragement. Ian Bent supported this project nearly from its inception and exercised his keen editorial eye all along the way. William Drabkin provided helpful criticism of an earlier version of chapter 1. Joseph Dubiel, Stephen Peles, Craig Monson, and William Rothstein also made various contributions to the content and development of ideas expressed in this book. For all this assistance I am most grateful. I also happily acknowledge the students in my first-year theory course, who bore with interest and patience my attempts to clarify Schenker's ideas about rhythm, harmony, and phrase; Sarah Stoycos, who helped me with research in 1993–94; Washington University in St. Louis, which provided a sabbatical leave in 1994 so that I could do the initial research and a Faculty Research Grant in 1995 to help with expenses; and the National Endowment for the Humanities, which granted me a Fellowship for University Teachers in 1995 that allowed me to complete the book.

Finally, I would like to thank the proprietors and staffs of three St. Louis coffee-shops, Ibid's, Kaldi's, and Aesop's, where much of this book was written and mulled over.

ABBREVIATIONS

All translations in the text are my own, but published English translations have been consulted and, where they exist, are cited with English pagination following German pagination, separated by a slash. All works are cited by page number unless indicated otherwise.

SCHENKER'S PUBLISHED WRITINGS

BO   *Ein Beitrag zur Ornamentik*. Neue revidierte und vermehrte Auflage. Vienna: Universal Edition, 1908.
         "A Contribution to the Study of Ornamentation." Trans. Hedi Siegel. (Based on a preliminary draft by Carl Parrish.) *MF* 2 (1976), 1–139. New York: Columbia University Press.

CPF   J. S. Bach. *Chromatische Phantasie und Fuge (d moll): Kritische Ausgabe mit Anhang.* Vienna: Universal Edition, 1910.
         J. S. Bach's Chromatic Fantasy and Fugue: *Critical Edition with Commentary.* Trans. Hedi Siegel. New York: Longman, 1984.

EK   *Heinrich Schenker als Essayist und Kritiker: Gesammelte Aufsätze, Rezensionen und kleinere Berichte aus den Jahren 1891–1901.* Ed. Hellmut Federhofer. Hildesheim: Georg Olms, 1990.

Erl   "Erläuterungen." First published in *Tw* 8–9: 49–51 and subsequently reprinted in *Tw* 10, *Mw* 1, and *Mw* 2.

FS   *Der freie Satz.* Vol. 3 of *Neue musikalische Theorien und Phantasien.* Vienna: Universal Edition, 1935. Figures in the supplement are cited by figure number, the number of the part of the figure (if any), and the letter assigned to the relevant section of the figure (if any). E.g., *FS* fig. 123-5a.
         Free Composition. Vol. 3 of *New Musical Theories and Fantasies.* Trans. and ed. Ernst Oster. New York: Longman, 1979.

FS²   *Der freie Satz.* Vol. 3 of *Neue musikalische Theorien und Phantasien.* Ed. Oswald Jonas. 2nd edn. Vienna: Universal Edition, 1956.

FUT   *Fünf Urlinie-Tafeln (Five Analyses in Sketch Form).* Vienna: Universal Edition; New York: David Mannes Music School, 1932.
         Five Graphic Analyses. Reprint of original edition, with an introduction by Felix Salzer. New York: Dover, 1969.

Hl   *Harmonielehre*. Vol. 1 of *Neue musikalische Theorien und Phantasien*. Stuttgart: Cotta, 1906.

       Harmony. Vol. 1 of *New Musical Theories and Fantasies*. Ed. Oswald Jonas. Trans. Elisabeth Mann Borgese. Chicago: University of Chicago Press, 1954.

Kp1   *Kontrapunkt*. Vol. 2 of *Neue musikalische Theorien und Phantasien*. 1st half-volume. *Cantus Firmus und Zweistimmiger Satz*. Stuttgart: Cotta, 1910.

       Counterpoint. Vol. 2 of *New Musical Theories and Fantasies*. Book 1. *Cantus Firmus and Two-Voice Counterpoint*. Trans. John Rothgeb and Jürgen Thym; ed. John Rothgeb. New York: Schirmer, 1987.

Kp2   *Kontrapunkt*. Vol. 2 of *Neue musikalische Theorien und Phantasien*. 2nd half-volume. *Drei- und Mehrstimmiger Satz, Übergänge zum freien Satz*. Vienna: Universal Edition, 1922.

       Counterpoint. Vol. 2 of *New Musical Theories and Fantasies*. Book 2. *Counterpoint in Three and More Voices, Bridges to Free Composition*. Trans. John Rothgeb and Jürgen Thym; ed. John Rothgeb. New York: Schirmer, 1987.

LfS   *Die letzten fünf Sonaten von Beethoven*. Lacking an autograph for op. 106, Schenker ultimately published commentaries on only four of the last five sonatas: opp. 101, 109, 110, and 111. Citations include opus and page number. Page references to passages retained in Jonas's second edition follow those of the original edition, separated by a superscript 2. E.g., *LfS101* 46^{2}58.

LfS101 *Die letzten fünf Sonaten von Beethoven: Kritische Ausgabe mit Einführung und Erläuterung*. [Sonate A dur Op. 101.] Vienna: Universal Edition, 1921.

       Beethoven: Die letzten Sonaten, Sonate A dur Op. 101: Kritische Einführung und Erläuterung. Ed. Oswald Jonas. 2nd edn. Vienna: Universal Edition, 1972.

LfS109 *Die letzten fünf Sonaten von Beethoven: Kritische Ausgabe mit Einführung und Erläuterung*. [Sonate E dur Op. 109.] Vienna: Universal Edition, 1913.

       Beethoven: Die letzten Sonaten, Sonate E dur Op. 109: Kritische Einführung und Erläuterung. Ed. Oswald Jonas. 2nd edn. Vienna: Universal Edition, 1971.

LfS110 *Die letzten fünf Sonaten von Beethoven: Kritische Ausgabe mit Einführung und Erläuterung*. [Sonate As dur Op. 110.] Vienna: Universal Edition, 1914.

       Beethoven: Die letzten Sonaten, Sonate As dur Op. 110: Kritische Einführung und Erläuterung. Ed. Oswald Jonas. 2nd edn. Vienna: Universal Edition, 1972.

LfS111 *Die letzten fünf Sonaten von Beethoven: Kritische Ausgabe mit Einführung und Erläuterung*. [Sonate C moll Op. 111.] Vienna: Universal Edition, 1916.

       Beethoven: Die letzten Sonaten, Sonate C moll Op. 111: Kritische Einführung und Erläuterung. Ed. Oswald Jonas. 2nd edn. Vienna: Universal Edition, 1971.

Mw   *Das Meisterwerk in der Musik*. 3 yearbooks. Munich: Drei Masken Verlag, 1925, 1926, and 1930. Cited by yearbook and page number. E.g., *Mw* 2: 35.

Figures in the text are cited with page number; figures in the supplements are identified by "suppl." E.g., *Mw* 2: 60 fig. 2 or *Mw* 3 suppl. fig. 10.

The Masterwork in Music, Vol. 1. Ed. William Drabkin, trans. Ian Bent, William Drabkin, Richard Kramer, John Rothgeb, and Hedi Siegel. Cambridge Studies in Music Theory and Analysis, ed. Ian Bent. Cambridge: Cambridge University Press, 1994.

NS   *Beethovens neunte Sinfonie.* Vienna: Universal Edition, 1912.

Beethoven's Ninth Symphony. Trans. and ed. John Rothgeb. New Haven, Conn.: Yale University Press, 1992.

Tw   *Der Tonwille: Flugblätter zum Zeugnis unwandelbarer Gesetze der Tonkunst einer neuen Jugend dargebracht von Heinrich Schenker.* 10 issues. Vienna: Tonwille Flugblätterverlag, 1921–24. Citations use the same forms as *Mw.*

OTHER SOURCES

JC   The Oswald Jonas Memorial Collection. Heinrich Schenker Archive. University of California, Riverside, Library. Cited by box and folder number, in accordance with the listing in Robert Lang and JoAn Kunselman, *Heinrich Schenker, Oswald Jonas, Moriz Violin: A Checklist of Manuscripts and Other Papers in the Oswald Jonas Memorial Collection.* Berkeley: University of California Press, 1994.

NTB   Federhofer, Hellmut. *Heinrich Schenker: Nach Tagebüchern und Briefen in der Oswald Jonas Memorial Collection, University of California, Riverside.* Studien zur Musikwissenschaft, Vol. 3. Hildesheim: Georg Olms, 1985.

OC   The Oster Collection. Papers of Heinrich Schenker. Music Division, New York Public Library. Cited by file and item number where applicable, in accordance with the finding list compiled by Robert Kosovsky.

PERIODICALS

CMS   *College Music Symposium*
ITO   *In Theory Only*
JAAC   *Journal of Aesthetics and Art Criticism*
JMT   *Journal of Music Theory*
MA   *Music Analysis*
MF   *Music Forum*
MP   *Music Perception*
MTS   *Music Theory Spectrum*
NCM   *19th-Century Music*
PNM   *Perspectives of New Music*
TP   *Theory and Practice*

INTRODUCTION

> It is instructive, and not without an involuntarily comic side-effect, to observe how all these who repudiate hermeneutics – Schenker, Halm, Pfitzner, on down to the most recent generation – themselves become hermeneuts as soon as they start to speak seriously about music.[1]

It has been said that to nineteenth-century Europeans, Beethoven's Ninth Symphony was "a reflecting glass" for the ideological vicissitudes of their century, "always present, hugely, at the center of discourse, inviting the attachment of meanings, almost as though it were a blank surface."[2]

Blank, reflecting – but what lay beneath this polished surface? What, if anything, was contained in the symphony itself? That is the question that stood before Schenker in the autumn of 1910 as he considered whether to accept an invitation to deliver a series of lectures on the Ninth Symphony to Vienna's Association of Music Critics.[3] In fact, it was the question of content that stood before him whenever he wrote of a musical work, but it was always more sharply defined when the work had become an object of discourse for critics, particularly the "hermeneutic" critics that found the surface of the Ninth Symphony so inviting.

When Schenker looked at what critics wrote of Beethoven's Ninth, he, too, saw a mirrored surface, not in the Ninth but in hermeneutic discourse itself. What he saw in that mirror was a reflection of subjective impression, a reflection that as often as

---

[1] Paul Bekker, writing in *Die Musik* (January 1925). Schenker saved a clipping of Bekker's article in a scrapbook, along with other clippings of other publications that mention Schenker by name. The scrapbook is preserved in OC 2; this clipping is found on p. 66.

[2] This is the premise of Ruth Solie's attempt to read nineteenth-century musical discourse as a microcosm of intellectual life, in "Beethoven as Secular Humanist: Ideology and the Ninth Symphony in Nineteenth-Century Criticism," in *Explorations in Music, the Arts, and Ideas: Essays in Honor of Leonard B. Meyer*, ed. Eugene Narmour and Ruth A. Solie (Stuyvesant, N.Y.: Pendragon Press, 1988), 3. Solie brackets the question of how "meanings" relate to the symphony; in fact, as far as her history of ideas is concerned, the musical work is but a scrap of paper – blank, intellectual currency.

[3] The earliest record of the invitation is a letter signed by the president and secretary of the association dated 30 September 1910 (JC 14 f. 44), though the matter probably had been raised in conversation prior to the formal invitation. This seems plausible since, according to Schenker, the invitation was the impetus for his monograph on the Ninth (NS v/3) and he had already written to his then publisher Cotta on 10 September 1910 concerning the possibility of that monograph (JC 5 f. 6). In the end it was Emil Hertzka of Universal Edition who published the work in 1912 (NTB 29–30).

not occluded the music's content. To Vienna's music critics, to hermeneutic critics, and to any who had ears to hear, Schenker proclaimed:

In the beginning was content! (*NS* vii/4)

Though the words of this proclamation never resounded through the hall where Vienna's music critics assembled (the lecture invitation ultimately fell through), their force, as portentous as the words of St. John's gospel to which they allude, pervades the nearly 400-page treatise that emerged from the would-be lectures.[4]

Above all, the proclamation confronts Wagner. Where Wagner had claimed that the notated content of the Ninth Symphony frequently failed to realize Beethoven's intentions, Schenker countered with the claim that the only reliable evidence of the composer's intentions is the content notated in the score.[5] Wagner also promoted the idea that Tone is incomplete without Word, an idea whose truth Beethoven was supposed to have expressed in the choral finale of the Ninth. Describing the first words uttered in the finale by the baritone, Wagner wrote in his program notes of 1846 that "a human voice, with the clear, sure utterance of articulate words, confronts the din of instruments." And years later, in an essay on performing the Ninth, he described the outcome of this confrontation, an outcome that he took to be a decisive step into the future of music: "Light breaks on chaos; a sure and definite mode of utterance is won . . . supported by the conquered element of instrumental music."[6] By replacing "das Wort" of St. John's proclamation with "das Inhalt," a term that signified the work's configuration of tones as notated by the composer and authentically rendered in performance, Schenker staked his interpretive practice on the claim that there is a genuine art whose medium is tone alone. That claim is the basic lesson of his textbook on counterpoint:

Contrapuntal theory . . . teaches the effect that most belongs to the tones [*die eigenste Wirkung*], the movement that is proper to them [*deren Eigenbewegung*], one might say; it liberates the apprentice of the art most assuredly from the delusion that tones, in addition to their absolute effect [*ihrer absoluten Wirkung*], must also have to signify something else, something objective, external [*was anderes, Gegenständliches, Äußerliches*]. (*Kp1* 21/14)[7]

---

[4] The first to point out the biblical allusion and the force of the statement was Leo Treitler, in his essay "History, Criticism, and Beethoven's Ninth Symphony," in *Music and the Historical Imagination* (Cambridge, Mass.: Harvard University Press, 1989), 28. Schenker uses the Johannine formula for other axiomatic concepts: for "consonance" (*Kp1* 248/184) and for the human voice as the archetypal musical instrument (*FS* 181/111).

[5] See Richard Wagner, "Zum Vortrag der neunten Symphonie von Beethoven," in *Gesammelte Schriften und Dichtungen*, 2nd edn (Leipzig: E. W. Fritzsch, 1887–88), 9: 231–51. Wagner's revisions were targeted in an early essay by Schenker, "Beethoven-'Retouche'" (*EK* 259–68). On the problematical nature of Schenker's anti-Wagnerian rhetoric, see Nicholas Cook, "Heinrich Schenker, Polemicist: A Reading of the Ninth Symphony Monograph," *MA* 14 (1) (1995), 89–105.

[6] *Gesammelte Schriften und Dichtungen*, 2: 61–62 and 9: 243, respectively. See *NS* 316/281.

[7] Rothgeb and Thym's rendering of *Eigenbewegung* as "proprieties of their movement" is misleading, since Schenker's point, amply illustrated in this first book of *Kontrapunkt*, is that the rules of strict counterpoint are not rules about tonal propriety – how tones must behave; rather, they concern tonal property – the effects that must

The force of Schenker's proclamation reached far beyond the pages of his treatise on the Ninth Symphony. Content – tones arranged in such and such a manner – was the touchstone for his interpretive practice. As a way of introducing the various aspects of interpretation that will be taken up in turn in the following chapters – effects, intentions, and synthesis – it will be useful to consider how Schenker interpreted the Ninth Symphony's opening passage and how he placed himself in relation to the so-called hermeneutics of Hermann Kretzschmar.

I

Schenker begins his "analysis of content" by stating that the symphony's opening passage of sixteen bars forms an introduction of uncertain tonal orientation in which the movement's principal motive has its origin.[8] Various aspects of the way tones are arranged in the passage are called upon in support of this interpretation. Uncertain tonal orientation, for example, is an effect of the passage's limited tonal content: the only tones are E's and A's, which, though they clearly indicate an A triad of some sort, do not indicate whether it is major or minor, much less tonic or dominant. The effect of a motive arises when the first violins, violas, and basses repeat a series of descending leaps. An effect of acceleration arises when the motive is presented for a third time at a faster pace, and then once more at an even faster pace.[9] And because each presentation of the motive is accompanied by the introduction of new instruments, there is the effect of a gradual accumulation of instrumental forces.

Schenker assumes that these configurations and their various effects were instrumental in realizing a compositional intention, the content of which he describes as "enacting the dynamic growth of the harmony." Having made that assumption, Schenker takes the intention as given and specifies the "necessities that caused the tonal content to arise in just this way and not otherwise" (NS vi/4).

Since the task at hand was to enact the dynamic growth of the harmony, it was necessary to maintain in the entry of the instruments certain proportions that would be intended to achieve the expression of that dramatic growth. Beethoven proceeded here by introducing, after the entry of the horns in D in bar 1, the remaining wind instruments . . . at ever decreasing time intervals. (NS 5/33)

---

belong to the tones. (There is also an overtone of a Hegelian theme that will figure in later discussions: music has its own specific way of realizing the concept of movement.)

[8] Throughout the monograph, Schenker's interpretation is refracted through a tripartite scheme into analysis of content, suggestions for performance, and critique of secondary literature. So one has to search at least three separate places to determine what he had to say about a particular passage. The first movement's introduction is discussed on pp. 1–6/31–34, 15–16/41, and 20–29/45–53 passim.

[9] The second, longer tone of each leap marks a reference point that coincides with the onset of the tremolo in the second violins and cellos; the regular spacing of those points creates the effect of meter (the bar). The descents of the violas and basses mark a larger metrical unit (four bars).

The desired effect of a dynamic growth of the harmony was brought about by intentionally arranging for there to be, among other things, certain proportions in the instrumental entries, namely, ever-decreasing time intervals, and a certain constancy in the pitch-class content of those entries, namely the open fifth, A–E.

"Dramatic growth" describes the cooperative synthesis of these effects. Schenker refines that description in his advice on the performance of the first movement's introduction, using the portent of stormy weather as a metaphor:

Here the wind instruments [*Blasinstrumente*], commencing singly in succession, have to enter altogether imperceptibly; their arrival ought to be just as difficult to notice as it would be in the case of swelling winds [*anschwellende Winde*], for example, to mark clearly the time points in which the accumulation of intensity proceeds. (*NS* 15/41)

In addition to a glimpse of the function that effects and intentions will play in Schenker's interpretation of content, we now have an example of the kind of conjectural language he will use to represent the quality of a combination of musical effects. The expression "swelling winds" (like the less fanciful "dynamic growth of the harmony") fuses a variety of musical aspects into a single experiential quality. The following list shows what is encapsulated in the idea of "swelling winds," presented in terms of concepts (effects) and the technical means by which they are realized (configurational aspects of the tonal content):

• an enduring state of expectation (effected by the static yet uncertain harmonic content of the introduction),
• a gradual manifestation of an event (the gradual accumulation of instrumental forces),
• an acceleration in the process of its manifestation (the decreasing time intervals between instrumental entries) that stimulates one's
• expectation for the outbreak of an event at the culmination of the acceleration (the explosive onset of the first theme in D minor), and
• a smooth, fluid transition from the onset to the culmination of the event (the imperceptibility of the entrances Schenker recommends to conductors).

Notice, however, that using "swelling winds" to focus a listener's attention on this composite of musical effects is quite different than saying the introduction *is* (or expresses or signifies or represents) that aspect of a gathering storm.[10] Schenker introduces the idea of "swelling winds" obliquely, placing it side by side with the description of technical means (gradual, imperceptible entries of wind instruments) but casting it in the potential, subjunctive mood. The oblique injection of this interpretant into the discussion is instructive: it is not the object of musical experience. At most, Schenker places the experience of swelling winds alongside that of the

---

[10] Craig Monson (personal communication) pointed out that Rothgeb's translation of the "anschwellende Winde" as "a gathering storm" gives the impression that Schenker may have had programmatic effects such as thunder and rain in mind, even though these would be ill-suited as descriptions of the Ninth's introduction; unlike peals of lightning, crashes of thunder, and the onset of rain, swelling winds are elusive, arising without perceptible shifts in intensity.

introduction, apparently hoping that the familiar meteorological occurrence would train his readers' attention on the unfolding dynamics of Beethoven's introduction.

II

In Schenker's view, the verbal or literary meaning ascribed to music by hermeneutic critics failed to meet the standards of "signification" or "representation." His view, however, did not rule out everything but so-called technical language. Schenker allowed himself to use images and programmatic ideas in representing or communicating the effects of tones. Such images and ideas are not descriptive names for those effects; they are often something more like pointers or hints that assist with the sharing of complex experiences. Of the Ninth Symphony, for instance, Schenker might have said the following: "Here are the basic effects of the introduction: . . . Now, if you imagine what it's like to experience the swelling of winds that portend a storm you'll have some idea of what it is like for me to hear the beginning of Beethoven's Ninth." His frequent recourse to the sort of conjectural, *ad hoc* imagery exemplified by "swelling winds" suggests that the experience of musical content – particularly the synthesis of effects – regularly outstripped his capacity for technical description.[11]

Schenker demands that the relation between tonal content and interpretive images like "swelling winds" be demonstrated. Whatever the experience or meaning of music is believed to be, it must be traced back to composed arrangements of tones and their effects. Schenker's insistence on establishment of the purely factual (*das rein Sachliche*) as the basis for adjudicating interpretation is likely due, in part, to his training in civil law.[12] But it is a principle he regarded as binding upon all interpretive activity, not just musical or judicial. Not long after the publication of the Ninth Symphony monograph, for instance, he wrote in his diary that "relation to the facts [*die Beziehung zur Sache*] ought to be desired as the true religion of the future." He goes on to wonder "whether Feuerbach means by 'sense perception' [*Anschauung*] the same as I mean by redeeming devotion to the demands of the facts" (*NTB* 333, entry dated 22 October 1913). The passage of Feuerbach's *Principles of the Philosophy of the Future* to which Schenker undoubtedly alludes is this:

[T]hought for itself alone cannot bring about any positive distinction and opposition to itself; but for this very reason it also has no criterion of truth other than that nothing should contradict the idea or thought; thus, it has only a formal and subjective criterion that does not decide whether the ideated truth is also a real truth. The criterion that decides this is solely perception [*Anschauung*]. . . . [J]ust as only perception that is determined by thought is

---

[11] This is very much in the spirit of Treitler's critique, for he, too, believes that the musical experience outruns the verbal or the literary: quoting T. S. Eliot, he says it is a "feeling which we can only detect, so to speak, out of the corner of the eye" ("History, Criticism, and Beethoven's Ninth Symphony," 36).

[12] At his father's insistence, Schenker left his native Galicia for Vienna in order to study law (*NTB* 345). He received his degree in 1889, not long after his father's death, but never actually entered the profession (a record of his legal studies is preserved in OC B-435).

true perception, so conversely only thought that is broadened and opened by perception is true thought corresponding to the essence of reality.[13]

The manifestation of that devotion was a demonstration of the factual basis of interpretation. It was on this point that Schenker rejected what the critics of his day presented as their interpretations of musical works.

Take, for example, his response to Kretzschmar's interpretation of Beethoven's Ninth that was published in his widely read concert guide, *Führer durch den Concertsaal*.[14] Kretzschmar describes the opening of the first movement as follows:

The depiction of a situation lacking in joy is the essential idea of the first movement. With the formal freedom that typifies the works from Beethoven's last period, he begins at first without a theme. It surges in a mist, chaotically and indistinctly, over the famous empty fifths. Then, after only sixteen bars, the heroic shape of this allegro arises in its murky majesty, full of power and defiance, yet marked by a trait [*Zug*] of suffering: what a heroic entry, how long and measured the way – but how singularly troubled the outcome!

And Schenker remonstrates:

How much more useful it would have been, instead of a "trait of suffering," to speak of the actual musical traits [*Züge*] of the principal idea, which alone – especially in a "guide" – are the point! (*NS* 25/49)

The issue here is whether mentioning a "trait of suffering" serves the purpose at hand. According to what Schenker says here, a musical guidebook ought to introduce readers to music's content, and for that reason any mention of a "trait of suffering" would be beside the point. But look at what Schenker goes on to say:

---

[13] Ludwig Feuerbach, "Grundsätze der Philosophie der Zukunft," in *Gesammelte Werke*, ed. Werner Schuffenhauer, vol. 9, *Kleinere Schriften II (1839–1846)* (Berlin: Akademie-Verlag, 1970), 329–30; translated by Manfred Vogel as *Principles of the Philosophy of the Future* (Indianapolis, Ind.: Hackett, 1986), 64–65.

[14] In *NS* Schenker quotes all but the two introductory paragraphs from the second edition of Kretzschmar's *Führer durch den Concertsaal* (Leipzig: Breitkopf und Härtel, 1890). Kretzschmar wrote two essays on hermeneutics: "Anregungen zur Förderung musikalischer Hermeneutik," *Jahrbuch der Musikbibliothek Peters der 1902*, 45–66, and "Neue Anregungen zur Förderung musikalischer Hermeneutik: Satzästhetik," *Jahrbuch der Musikbibliothek Peters der 1905*, 73–86; both essays are reprinted in vol. 2 of Kretzschmar's *Gesammelte Aufsätze* (Leipzig: Breitkopf und Härtel, 1911), 168–92, 280–93. Schenker's critique of these essays appears in *LfS109* 56–57. Kretzschmar sought to revive the Baroque "doctrine of affects," claiming that there is a "spiritual content" (namely, affect) contained within musical forms. In the first essay, he writes: "The task of hermeneutics consists in loosening the affects from the tones and giving the skeletal structure of their development in words" and that hermeneutics "seeks the soul within the body." "The notion that music works only musically must be laid aside, and pleasure in 'absolute music' must be recognized as an aesthetic obscurity. In the sense of a purely *musical* content, *there is no absolute music*!" Affective content is "embodied in motives, themes, and tonal figures," but these tonal entities are but "husks and rinds." The implication, perhaps unintended but certainly inescapable, is clear: tones are not the object of musical experience, tones are not part of music's "spiritual content." They are a dispensable medium in which a listener feels the reflected warmth of an affective state, and not that of the composer but rather one that emanates from listeners themselves. Kretzschmar even admits that interpretation amounts to a "shadowplay" and that the shadows are cast not by the musical object but by the listening subject: "If a person has imagination and the degree of proper artistic talent that every engagement with art assumes, then he will not fail to animate subjectively the skeleton of affect with forms and events drawn from his own memory and experience, or from the worlds of poetry, dream and intuition." Schenker's response is to reject such subjective contributions to the extent that they are not warranted by the tonal content.

What good is a "guide" if it offers the reader nothing more than what he himself already perceives and knows ...? "Long and measured the way" is undoubtedly the impression that everyone receives from the principal idea; wasn't Kretzschmar's task rather at least to indicate correctly the technical means that led to such an effect ...?

Schenker does not object to Kretzschmar's characterization on the grounds that it is out of place, or unwarranted, or even inept, even though that is his usual line of attack against hermeneutic writings. He objects to it because Kretzschmar fails to demonstrate how it is grounded in the tonal content of the introduction. What the readers of a guidebook presumably cannot know readily from their own experience – and what Schenker is convinced readers ought to desire to know – is how the arrangements of tones crafted by a composer can result in anything like a "trait of suffering."

Failure to meet this demand puts the credulity of interpretation at risk. Kretzschmar and his ilk "drift about on the most barren stock of phrases, empty words and pictures!" (NS 54/72). Their words lack the substance of musical content, that is, the substance of tones that alone can give "living content" to mere concepts. Later in his commentary Schenker displays phrases from Kretzschmar's verbal stock beside a few from his own:

Kretzschmar would undoubtedly have fared better if, instead of the plethora of words – "brief moment," "happy frolic," "elements of weary longing," "stifled," "cheered on," "forceful strokes" – he had, while maintaining the same brevity, provided concepts of truly orientational value, such as "modulatory idea," "second idea," and so forth. (NS 163/159)

Given what Schenker said about the task of a guidebook he evidently does not mean that Kretzschmar's stock of words has no place in writing that is purportedly of use to laymen or professionals. What he must mean is more like this: given the need to maintain a certain brevity in a concert guide, and, for that reason, faced with a choice between unsubstantiated interpretants and "truly orienting concepts," one should choose the latter. The reason implied is twofold: the former, if true, are already known to readers; and, without the substantiation of conceptual analysis, the former risk being false. Readers who need a concert guide in the first place are left in the end without the knowledge of the specific factual situation they would need to verify the author's interpretation (assuming they ought to desire verification).

III

Schenker conceives of music as a form of communication in the broadest sense. Composition and interpretation are complementary activities centered on tonal content. Composers intend to produce effects or responses in others by means of configuring tones in such and such a manner. Listeners hear (or imagine hearing) the presented configuration of tones and respond appropriately. The perceptual act of interpretation (the psycho-physical response) may be followed up and enriched by a reflective act in which the response is analyzed (the effects of tones described) and the requisite intentions imputed to the composer. For this complementary relation to hold, composers and listeners must be disposed to respond in similar ways to tonal configurations. The point of Schenker's interpretive practice is just to bring about that sharing of mental disposition, to do so by bringing noncomposers' minds into line with what he believed to be the mental disposition of the great German composers of the eighteenth and nineteenth centuries. Schenker makes the content of that belief plausible by deriving it from the disciplines of strict counterpoint and thoroughbass in which those composers were schooled.

Schenker's interpretive practice rests on the hypothesis that an authentic specification of the musical artwork's tonal arrangements (a score) expresses the means for realizing the effects intended by the composer. It also rests on the assumption that the intended effects can be perceived without independent confirmation of the initial hypothesis; the plausibility of this assumption depends on there being a congruence between the cognitive dispositions of perceivers and composers.[15]

Schenker's written interpretations of musical artworks include at least the first and sometimes all of the following phases:

- analysis of the effects produced by the work's tonal arrangements structured in terms of intentions imputed to the composer, proceeding from the most general to the most specific,
- verbal adumbration of the individual quality projected by the resulting complex of effects,
- advice to performers on how to render the intended effects,
- critique of other authors' misrepresentation of effects,
- discussion of manuscripts or sketches to the extent that they impinge upon the initial hypothesis, and
- a performing edition of the score (or emendations to a modern edition).

The first two of these phases are the subject of this book. In chapter 1 I present an overview of musical effects, their paradigmatic realizations, and their application in individual cases. In chapter 2 I examine the way in which Schenker's inference of composers' intentions contributes to the structure and content of his interpretations. In chapter 3 I examine the metaphorical and conjectural language that Schenker uses to characterize the individual sound of synthesis. And in chapter 4 I discuss the purpose of Schenker's practice – namely, increased participation in the Austro-German tradition – and the rhetorical posture that compromised that end.

---

[15] Schenker thinks his own mind is in the right state, so in practice perceived effects are assumed to be intended.

1

EFFECTS

Schenker never attempted a comprehensive account of all the effects that could be produced by tonal configurations. He did not do so, I expect, primarily because the repertory of basic effects is large enough to make the combinatorial possibilities enormous, probably infinite. But he did develop an astounding repertory of musical ideas that, for its scope and inventiveness of implementation, knew no precedent. Which is not to say that he did not borrow components of this repertory from other writers, some of whom he acknowledged (C. P. E. Bach and Fux), most of whom he did not (for example, Rameau, Riemann, Kurth). All of the basic concepts were part of the musical discourse that he learned from others – passing, delay, *Stufe*, and repetition, for instance. His ingenuity lay in realizing the possibility of extending these concepts to nonparadigmatic tonal configurations, ones more complex than simple passing tones, suspensions, vertical chords, and melodic motives. Schenker never attempted, however, a comprehensive account of all the tonal configurations that could realize these concepts, perhaps because doing so, as Joseph Dubiel puts it, would have limited in advance a domain of compositional invention.[1] The extension of effects (their prolongation) was accomplished by means of a set of relational concepts (transformations) under which relatively complex configurations of tones can be interpreted in terms of relatively simple configurations. This, too, is not new; precedents abound in eighteenth-century composition manuals. What is distinctive, again, is the scope and inventiveness of Schenker's implementation.

The following exposition provides an overview of the basic genera of effect, loosely organized into three families: passing, delay, and entity.

I

I begin with an effect of cardinal significance for Schenker's theory of triadically tonal music, the effect of "transience" or "passing" (*Durchgang*). The effect of transience cannot be produced independently of quiescent effects (the converse, however, is false). The paradigmatic realizations of quiescence and transience are the classes of

---

[1] Joseph Dubiel, " 'When You are a Beethoven': Kinds of Rules in Schenker's *Counterpoint*," *JMT* 34 (2) (1990), 327.

tonal configurations we know as consonance and dissonance. A consonant configuration is complete, "at rest in its euphony," sufficient in and of itself, both "beginning and end," able to sustain itself, to endure and persist, in short, able to be permanent. The effect of a dissonant configuration is the negation of quiescence: incomplete, restless, never sufficient in and of itself, "pointing urgently beyond itself"; it is, in short, transient (*Kp1* 153/111).[2]

A study of the "passing" effect must begin, then, with a preliminary consideration of the terms consonance and dissonance. The effect of "passing" is important enough to warrant paying rather close attention to Schenker's working definitions of consonance and dissonance and to a variety of rather simple variations on the effect.

In traditional accounts, consonance and dissonance describe the intervallic relation between two tones. An interval is consonant if it can be formed between two tones of a major or minor triad; dissonant, if the interval cannot. Traditionally, consonances are defined extensionally as a list of intervals. To understand Schenker's interpretive practice, we will have to take a different approach to defining consonance and dissonance. Rather than referring intervals to triads, Schenker's working definitions refer the constituent tones themselves to a triadic concept. This approach extends the domain of the terms to include single tones and configurations of many tones; it also allows a distinction to be made between what I will call absolute and contextual types of consonance and dissonance.

The classes of consonant and dissonant configurations are defined in terms of an axiomatic concept of "triad" that embraces both the "natural" major triad and an "artificial" variant in which a minor third is substituted for the major third of the "Chord of Nature" found in the overtone series.[3] Example 1.1 presents a sample of tonal configurations and identifies specific triadic concepts to which the tones can be referred. The class of consonances comprises all configurations whose constituent tones can be collectively referred to at least one specific triadic concept (ex. 1.1a–d).[4] If all the tones of a configuration can belong to a single triad, the configuration is absolutely consonant; reference to a specific triad is not mandated in cases where the configuration can be referred to more than one triad. In other words, it is an important feature of this definition that it does not resolve ambiguities. The

[2] My discussion of Schenker's *Kontrapunkt* owes much to Peter Westergaard's excellent pedagogical reformulation in *An Introduction to Tonal Theory* (New York: Norton, 1975) and Dubiel's thoughtful essay, " 'When You are a Beethoven' "; Westergaard's debt to Schenker is the subject of Marion A. Guck's "The Schenkerian Roots of Westergaard's Counterpoint" (paper presented at the annual meeting of the Society for Music Theory, Cincinnati, Ohio, November 1991). For a coherent, concise, and extremely faithful introduction to *Kontrapunkt*, see John Rothgeb's "Strict Counterpoint and Tonal Theory," *JMT* 19 (2) (1975), 260–84.

[3] See *Hl* 32–42/20–29 and 64–65/50; see also *Erl* and *FS* 30/10. The axiomatic status of the concept in Schenker's theory is marked by his resort to irrational justifications for its conceptual priority: first, he reduces the *Naturklang* to a major triad by ignoring all but the first five partials of the overtone series, appealing to the number five as a mysterious limit in human consciousness (*Hl* 37–39/25–26) and, second, he grants the minor triad identical status within the system, notwithstanding his assertions about the natural quality of the major and the artificial quality of the minor.

[4] I.e., a specific pitch-class instance of the triadic concept. See *Hl* 134–35/131.

Ex. 1.1

single tone, whose absolute consonance is tautological, can be referred to as many as six different triads. Only the invocation of an independent principle such as "If possible attribute root-status to contextual tones" can reduce (and in some cases eliminate) this type of ambiguity. If a single tone is consonant by this definition, then dissonant configurations must contain two or more tones. The class of dissonances comprises all configurations of two or more tones that contain at least one tone that cannot be referred to the same specific triadic concept as its mates (ex. 1.1e–f). It is important, again, to note that nothing in the definition specifies a particular referent triad as the definitive referent for the entire configuration. Given only these definitions and the configuration in *e*, we have no reason to decide whether to prefer F's consonance to G's, much less to choose among the twelve possible referents; again, ambiguity can be reduced only by invoking independent principles: if we invoke the root-status principle given above, we can narrow the field to four triads, and if we invoke a second root-status principle such as "If possible attribute root-status to the contextually lowest tone," we can reduce it even further and at the same time attach the dissonant effect to F. In cases like ex. 1.1*g*, where two of the three tones can be referred to a single triad, we might invoke something like the democratic principle of majority rules.[5]

Tonal life would be relatively simple if this were all there was to consonance and dissonance. But Schenker tacitly operates with another, more constrained definition of consonance and dissonance, which I will call "contextual," in contrast to what we might call the "absolute" version sketched above.[6] Our first definition brought brute

[5] The adjudication of dissonant configurations in fact always requires the invocation of an independent principle, even in species counterpoint; when dissonances are formed against the cantus firmus, it is in part the postulated consonance of the cantus firmus that permits attaching the dissonant effect to the tone in the counterpointing line. In free composition the harmonic idea (*Stufe*) assumes a similar role in adjudicating effects of consonance and dissonance (see *Kp1* 154/112).

[6] Schenker is not the only author to operate with this distinction. Rudolf Louis and Ludwig Thuille, co-authors

Ex. 1.2

tonal facts under the most general concept of triad and did not require that we bring anything to bear upon the situation other than a perception of tones and the ability to refer those tones to triads (though we saw how several independent principles could affect interpretation). The contextual sort, by contrast, requires the exercise of greater interpretive judgment; it involves the interpretation of a particular configuration in terms of a specific triadic concept relative to a particular time span and thus rests on a harmonic interpretation of the configuration's context. The judgment as to which triadic concept to use may be determined by the nature of the configuration itself, but often it is a matter of considering the configurations in adjacent time spans. The contextual definition runs as follows: a tone is contextually consonant (dissonant) if it belongs (does not belong) to the triad that is in play during a particular span of time.[7]

And now to a definition of "transience": if tones are configured in such a way as to produce the succession of effects – consonance–dissonance–consonance – the total configuration will produce the effect of "transition" from one place of stability to another. That, in short, is the effect of passing.

II

In a single melodic line, the effect of passing is most simply produced by stepwise motion through the consonant interval of a third.[8] The interval of a second between adjacent tones in this configuration produces an unambiguously dissonant effect, in that two tones which form that interval cannot under any circumstances belong to the same triad.[9] Schenker describes the formation of this simple passing effect in the opening of Fux's Dorian cantus firmus (ex. 1.2).

of a *Harmonielehre* (Stuttgart: C. Grüninger, 1907) that Schenker knew well, termed the contextually dissonant absolute consonance (e.g., some six-four chords) a "conceptual dissonance" (*Auffassungsdissonanz*) (pp. 29–30); for discussion of Louis and Thuille, see Robert W. Wason, *Viennese Harmonic Theory from Albrechtsberger to Schenker and Schoenberg* (Ann Arbor, Mich.: UMI Research Press, 1985), 125. If there is anything noteworthy in Schenker's use of the distinction, it is his realization of the concept of conceptual "levels" that arises in the very cases covered by Louis and Thuille's term.

[7] In the contextual definition, the concept of triad is slightly broader than in the absolute definition, which recognizes only major and minor triads. The context in question is the diatonic system of a particular tonic and thus includes a "dissonant" diminished triad (VII in major systems, II in minor) (see *Hl* 54–55/40). (Augmented triads in Schenker's practice are always interpreted as absolutely and contextually dissonant configurations.)

[8] Why a neighboring motion is not paradigmatic for the effect will be explained below in connection with example 1.5.

[9] As Schenker explains in *Kp2*, this horizontal dissonance is the root of the passing effect even in second species, where the effect is supported in most cases by a vertical dissonance; theorists writing about strict counterpoint

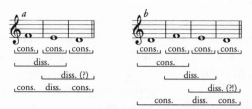

Ex. 1.3

The tone E in bar 3, as a second between F and D (bars 2 and 4), forms a bridge, as it were, on which these two tones meet one another to make the effect of a third. Inferring from the resultant third, we of course suppose the triad on D; yet this triad still lacks its fifth, A, and so the melody progresses on. In bar 5 appears the fourth, G, hence the lower fifth of the initial tone D, and already suggests a new triad, namely G–D, even before the first third sum D–F found its further completion and fulfillment; but it is again precisely a second, F (in bar 6), which immediately leaves the apparently new triad that was suggested a moment ago and leads back into the region of the first one (D–F). But finally, because the tone A appears in bar 7, the ear realizes the full triadic sum which it has obtained, D–F–A: from here on the ear fully comprehends not only the role of the fourth, G, but also that of the seconds in bars 3 and 6, and also those in bars 8 and 9. (*Kp1* 116–17/83)

According to Schenker's account, a triad (D–F–A) is posited as the particular triadic concept that defines the consonance of an interval (D–F). The effect of a melodic second, as he states explicitly with respect to the F in bar 6, is that of being contextually dissonant *vis-à-vis* the triadic concept in play (G–[B(♭)]–D). The fact that Schenker says that D–G "suggests" an "apparently new triad" indicates that the G triad is not fully realized; the D triad suggested by D–F has the same conceptual status until the appearance of A in bar 7, which confirms the initial inference. Now consider the effects of two consecutive steps as in bars 2–4. If we isolate these bars (ex. 1.3*a*) and consider the various time spans that have differentiated pitch contents (indicated by the brackets beneath the staff), it is a fairly simple matter to read off the effects: F by itself is consonant; E is dissonant with respect to whatever triad defines F's consonance and vice versa. Because the F comes first, Schenker probably would not accord much weight to the "vice versa"; the principle here is a psychological one articulated by Peter Westergaard: given two successive events, it is easier to think of the second in terms of the first, "presumably because the listener can refer back to his memory of the first while experiencing the second."[10] The D in Fux's cantus firmus is dissonant with respect to whatever triad defines E's consonance, but if you

prior to Schenker invested the vertical dissonance with the responsibility of securing the passing effect. The sustaining voice keeps us apprised of the consonance on the downbeat, while the (in most cases) dissonant interval formed against it by the melodically dissonant tone in the second-species line is a byproduct of the dissonant melodic step. See *Kp2* 57–59/56–58 and also *Kp1* 247/183 and *Mw* 2: 24 ff.

[10] *An Introduction to Tonal Theory*, 228–29.

don't lose touch with F, if you keep it in play, D is also consonant with F, an effect that counteracts its dissonance against E (whose consonance is dubious for the reason given above). The dissonant effect of D recedes even further if you keep both bars 1 and 2 in play (ex. 1.3*b*), for then D in bar 4 consonates with both D and F in bars 1–2 (or, we might say, it reasserts or confirms the consonance spanning bars 1–2).[11] Taking bars 1–4 as a whole, then, it seems that E is the cause of the only incontrovertibly dissonant effect and that the sequence of effects in these bars is consonance–dissonance–consonance relative to the triad in play (D–F–A).

To convey the synthesis of this sequence of effects, Schenker invites us to imagine a bridge: a connection that spans between two stable points and across (*durch-*) which one can go or pass (*-gehen*) from one to the other. It is not coincidental, I think, that Schenker only rarely uses the expression *Durchgangston* for a tone that has an effect like that of E. Instead, he prefers the term *Durchgang*. This term refers not to the effect of a single tone E in isolation, but rather to its effect in the context that spans from F to D. The effect of "passing" is in a sense distributed across the three bars (or at least across two bars plus the downbeat of the third). By using *Durchgang* instead of *Durchgangston* Schenker avoids localizing the effect in one component of the broader configuration (see *Kp1* 247/183–84).

Only the dissonant step is paradigmatic for the passing effect. Dissonant leaps are not paradigmatic, because they produce effects in addition to the effect of transience. Schenker's explanation of this rests on the premise that effects of tonal configurations are, to a great extent, gauged in terms of human vocal capacity. In this respect, there is a difference in absolute character between a second and a seventh: "Better than any other instrument, the human voice reveals that, besides the dissonance which it has in common with the second, the seventh also contains the difficulty of the larger leap" (*Kp1* 76–77/52–53). This additional effect is part of the seventh's "psychological content." In general, dissonant leaps have a more intensely expressive effect deriving from the greater difficulty of producing that interval with the human voice. Dissonant leaps may also create the effect of a compound line (see *Kp1* 86/59 and 89–90/61–63); the seventh may, given contextual indicators, have the effect of being a substitute for a second (see *Kp1* 91–95/63–66).[12]

The effect of passing within a melodic line will be intensified if there is another against which it moves and in relation to which it produces the succession of consonance–dissonance–consonance. Before examining configurations of this sort, let us first consider the range of effects produced by absolutely consonant configurations formed by two tones sounding simultaneously. A representative sample is given in example 1.4. Schenker carefully distinguishes among the effects produced by each

---

[11] Milton Babbitt was right on the mark when he observed that "the remarkable aspect of Schenker is what it tells you about musical memory and the way in which you can take in a piece, because obviously you can't take in a passage unless you chunk it and relate it and parallel it in a variety of ways. I think that his is a most efficient description of the process" (*Words about Music*, ed. Stephen Dembski and Joseph N. Straus [Madison, Wisc.: University of Wisconsin Press, 1987], 145).

[12] For another use of the vocal premise, as well as his claim that it is a general principle, see *LfS109* 32–33[2]17–18.

Ex. 1.4

two-tone configuration (*Kp1* 169–71/124–25). Unisons produce the effect of complete agreement between two different vocal or instrumental lines; octaves produce
a combined effect of identity and difference by presenting identity of pitch class
with a differentiation of actual pitch; and perfect fifths produce the effect of delimiting a triadic concept in which the status of each tone in the fifth is unambiguous
(root and fifth). This might seem to be an advantage that fifths have over unisons and
octaves, since the latter could be referred to six different major or minor triads or to
four different triad roots. In the absence of any additional indications, however,
Schenker thinks we ought to refer the tones of a unison or octave to a triad in which
they represent a root. Owing to the fact that unisons, octaves, and fifths do not stand
in the way of attributing root-status to the lowest sounding tone, these intervals
produce the effect of stability. Thirds, by the same token, have the effect of stability,
but not the effects of agreement or delimiting a particular triad. The lower tone of a
sixth, by contrast, cannot be imagined as a root tone without at the same time
canceling the consonant effect of the upper tone; hence sixths cannot have the effect
of stability. The consonant effect of sixths is always admixed, therefore, with the
effect of mobility. Perfect fourths, though triadic, are unstable as vertical intervals
because the effects they produce are strongly contradictory: the fourth and fifth
share the effect of delimiting a particular triad, but the fourth, by not expressing the
triad's root in the lower voice, lacks the stability of the fifth; moreover, it emphasizes
that lack by expressing the stability-defining tone in the upper voice, thus effectively
denying the roothood tendency of the lowest tone (see *Kp1* 155–58/112–14). By
itself, then, the fourth does not have a clear consonant effect; only the contribution
of other effects by other tones can tip the scale in favor of consonance or dissonance
(see *Kp1* 158–63/114–19).

Differentiating the effects of vertical consonance is taught in the first species of
strict composition. First species also teaches the effects produced by the various
ways in which two melodic lines can move in relation to one another: motion in the
same direction has the effect of agreement of purpose; motion in the opposite
direction excludes agreement and instead has the effect of independence (the same
effect follows if one line moves while the other remains stationary). Vertical dissonance is introduced in the second species of strict composition. The tones initiated
together must, as in first species, be consonant, but the second tone of the faster line
may be dissonant with the sustained tone of the other voice; if so, it must be approached and left by step (that is, it must produce an unambiguously passing dissonance in the melodic line as well).

To the extent that each of the configurations in example 1.5 presents the succes-

Ex. 1.5

sion consonance–dissonance–consonance (in the rhythmic guise of second species),
each produces the effect of transition or passage. Other effects produced by the
configurations, however, differentiate their transitional effects. The effect of transience produced in *a* and *d*, for instance, where the upper voice returns to the tone it
started from, is distinguishable from the others, in which the starting and ending
pitches in the upper voice are different. In all cases there is the effect of passing
through a transient state, but in *b*, *c*, and *e* there is additionally the effect of moving
from one place to another within the upper voice. The effect of transition is thus
stronger in these two cases. It is not coincidental that the type of configuration
represented by the upper voice in *b*, *c*, and *e* is paradigmatic for the concept of
passing, for the step motion is at once dissonant, gradual, and direct (because it is
primarily responsible for the passing effect, the mediating tone in the upper voice is
commonly called a "passing tone"). In *a* and *d*, where the upper voice does not leave
the vicinity from which it began, and so does not pass away, the effect is more like,
for lack of a better word, "neighboring"; the mediating tones in these cases are
"passing" only in an extended sense of the term.

The rhythmic guise of second-species counterpoint is not just a pedagogical
expedient. Schenker's idea of passing has an essential rhythmic aspect that is expressed in its simplest form in second species, where the tones of the cantus firmus
represent contextual consonances during the time of which the second voice passes
from the consonance of one bar to that of the next. Dubiel aptly describes Schenker's expansion of the concept:

The nature of this "expansion" is to identify the attribute of being "passing" not with the
pitch-structural definition "stepwise in between," but with: an essentially *rhythmic* definition
that generalizes it: "within the time of: that is, not yet displacing – and inferably on the way
to a successor entity on the same level as."[13]

The simplest, paradigmatic realization of the effect (simplest in respect of the number of side effects) is a unidirectional stepwise motion between two tones that are
consonant with one another. But the concept can also be extended to other configurations of tones so long as the succession of effects essential to this definition is
realized. Some confusion inevitably arises from the fact that Schenker uses the same
term "Durchgang" for both extended transient effects and its paradigmatic species.

The configurations in example 1.5 also differ with respect to the effect produced

[13] Dubiel, "'When You are a Beethoven'," 327.

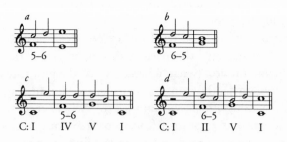

Ex. 1.6

by the sum of the two boundary sonorities. In *a–d*, the boundary sonorities can both be referred to the same triad and are thus consonant with one another. The dissonant sonority mediating the two thus produces the effect of passing "within" an entity. Though *a–d* are all closed configurations in this respect, the absence of the triadic root in the final sonority's lower voice in *c* and *d* attenuates the effect of closure. In *e*, by contrast, the boundary sonorities are dissonant with one another, and thus the configuration as a whole has the effect of incompleteness, restlessness, and dependence on a larger context. The mediating sonority in *e* has the effect of passing "between" the two boundary sonorities as well as the effect of being on the way from but not yet displacing the first sonority.

Now take the case shown in example 1.6*a*. Given what has been said, the upper line's d^2 has the hallmarks of the passing tone (as a stepwise bridge uniting two tones that are absolutely consonant with one another) but at the same time it is consonant with the sustained lower voice. Its consonant effect mitigates its passing character. Strict composition, says Schenker, does not have sufficient resources to tip the scales in favor of one of these effects; given only the absolute definition of consonance that is operative in strict counterpoint and the configuration itself, there is nothing that could shift the balance between the competing effects. Only the interpretive contribution of a referential triadic concept, and hence the presence and influence of other tonal configurations (real or imagined), can give a dissonant effect to an interval that is absolutely consonant. And even then, the consonant effect is only attenuated, not eliminated.[14] So, for example, if the first bars of *a* and *b* were placed in the context of *c* and *d*, and if these contexts were interpreted in terms of an evenly paced succession of triads, the second tone of the upper line in each bar 2 would be dissonant with respect to the triad in play (indicated by the Roman numerals beneath the example); in addition to their absolute consonance with the sustained lower voice, each of these tones has a contextually defined transient effect. In *c*, d^2

[14] This is the line of interpretation he takes with respect to the perfect fifth on the downbeat of bar 5 in the first movement of Haydn's Piano Sonata no. 43, where the upper tone is interpreted as absolutely consonant with the bass but nevertheless contextually dissonant with respect to the I chord that the harmonic progression brings into play; on this interpretation, see Dubiel, " 'When You are a Beethoven'," 314–16.

has an additional effect because it is identical in pitch to its consonant goal; it has the effect of "anticipating" the goal.

The assumption of a contextual triad in free composition is powerful enough, says Schenker, to "emancipate" the passing dissonance from the requirement of unidirectional stepwise motion (what Schenker calls "the postulate of the second"), so that any tone foreign to the contextual harmony has, first and foremost (but rarely exclusively), a passing effect (*Kp1* 248/184).[15] Schenker regarded this emancipation of the dissonance as a cardinal feature of free composition, as attested by repeated reference to this passage elsewhere in the first book of *Kontrapunkt* and in later writings.

Before going on let me summarize what has been said about the effect of passing within a musical line:

- "transience" or "passing" is an effect synthesized from a succession of effects;
- side effects of a passing configuration serve to differentiate various subtypes of "passing";
- to some of the subtypes Schenker gave (or inherited) specific names: passing, neighboring, anticipating; to most he did not;[16] and
- effects sometimes support, sometimes compete with one another.

III

Starting in the early 1920s, Schenker theorized another passing effect, the effect of passing *between* two lines. His term for this effect is *Zug*, a term so rich with meanings that it is virtually untranslatable. Derived from the verb *ziehen*, "to pull, draw," Zug has the sense of drawing a connection or a line between two points; it is not far, therefore, from *sich beziehen*, "to relate, refer," and *Beziehung*, "relation" (the latter connection did not escape Schenker's ear; see, for example, *FS* 121–22/74). One of its most common denotations is "train, locomotive," as in a series of cars "pulled"

---

[15] By overlooking the possibility that Schenker imagined such free dissonances could have effects in addition to the effect of passing, Rothgeb rejects Schenker's description of emancipated passing tones; see pp. 354–55, note 4, in the English translation. See below, section VII.

[16] In general, Schenker gives more or less determinate descriptions only of effects that are of relatively low orders of complexity (reaching-over being one of the most complex). Dubiel has pointed out that this lack of determinate verbal labels is still with us and has made it difficult for psychologists to test the cognitive reality of musical effects; "How Do You Know You Hear It That Way?" (paper presented at the Fifteenth Annual Meeting of the Society for Music Theory, Kansas City, Missouri, 1992). In *Kontrapunkt*, for instance, Schenker often points to slight differences in the basic effect produced by two or three similar configurations; his assistance to the reader in such cases is usually limited to ranging the effects along one or more continua: good to poor, simple to complex, more to less natural, and more to less comprehensible. (This is the list provided by Rothgeb in his preface to the English translation [p. xiii].) Rothgeb astutely notes that "what is strikingly unique about Schenker's *Kontrapunkt*," in contrast to the works of other authors, "is that his prescriptions and restrictions" derive "from a connected and systematic set of direct observations of the effects that necessarily accompany each of the basic ways of combining tones both simultaneously and in succession." Also distinctive, as Dubiel notes in "'When You are a Beethoven'" (298), is the fact that Schenker devotes so much of his discussion to effects and configurations that are excluded from the discipline of strict counterpoint.

along a path from a point of departure to a destination; it also sometimes denotes static linear arrangements of discrete entities, as in *Gebirgszug*, "mountain range." The linear connotation comes to the fore when Zug is used to mean a "line" of type or text. It can also mean "facial line" and, by extension, "trait" or "characteristic." The association with trains also contributes a sense of motion, of cars being drawn somewhere. Zug also denotes a single, uninterrupted gesture, as in the "drawing of a breath," a "drag" (on a cigarette), a "move" in chess, and the phrase *in einem Zug*, "at a stretch, in one fell swoop." Directness comes to the fore when Zug means a passageway (*Durchgang!*) or conduit, as in a chimney flue.

The core of its meaning appears to be "a direct, unimpeded motion from one place to another." In Schenker's technical sense, the Zug is a set of tones drawn out of a diatonic collection and arranged in a line between two voices. The standard translation of Zug as "linear progression" captures this as well as any short English expression might, but it fails to have the crucial goal orientation associated with trains or resonances with "relation" or "trait," the latter a resonance that often gives Schenker occasion for puns.[17] Schenker first uses Zug in its technical sense in his commentary on Beethoven's Piano Sonata op. 101 (1921), though he continues to use it in its customary senses as well. For example, at one point, just before it appears in its restricted technical sense, he uses it in the looser sense of "a series of like entities" when he writes that "a series [*Zug*] of half notes is attached to $b\flat^2$ in bars 88–90" of the second movement (*LfS101* $42^2$49). The content of this "series" is a succession of half-note chords played by the right hand, but none of the component voices in these chords is arranged as a direct passing motion.

In that a Zug is a motion between voices, it depends upon a polyphonic conception of a given tonal configuration. A "voice" is either a triadic tone or a series of consecutive tones all lying within a range roughly equal in compass to that of the human voice and capable of being sounded without gaps over a certain span of time. A voice, then, may be a component tone in a mentally posited harmony (*Stufe*) or a line in an imagined species-counterpoint setting (*Satz*). Given the multiple senses in which Schenker conceives of "voice," any stretch of tonal music more involved than a single sustained tone or a neighbor-note configuration is susceptible to a multivoice conception. Passages like those represented in example 1.7*a* or *b*, for example, will have the effect of passing between two component tones in the harmony, assuming that one has reason to think of them in terms of a C-major harmony or in terms of the three-voice setting shown in *c* (the sustained C in the lowest voice could be interpreted as expressing the perdurance of the harmony). The stepwise motion draws a connecting line, a Zug, between the two voices; it is a line in its own right and also a connection between two lines (*Erl*). The Zug is one of several ways to create this compound effect. Any so-called polyphonic melody blends the effects of one and many voices. Even the complex polyphonic melody of a Bach solo

---

[17] Schenker's puns on the figurative use of Zug are noted by William Drabkin in his entry on "Zug" in *The New Grove* (reprinted in a glossary to Ian Bent's *Analysis* [New York: Norton, 1987], 141–42).

Ex. 1.7

sonata can be understood as an extension of the concept of voice (cp. *Mw* 1: 89/ 48–49).

Schenker stipulates that the Zug pass through a space larger than a second. Usually the interval is consonant, as in the case of passing within a harmony (ex. 1.7), but not necessarily. When the imagined background of the Zug is, say, a second-species setting, there is the possibility of connecting a consonant tone of the cantus firmus to a dissonant passing tone in another voice. It is important, if only because it has been the source of some confusion, to observe that Schenker does not require a consonant relation between the initial and final tones, either in the absolute or contextual sense.[18] What is required is that the two tones have a "genuine relation" and that depends on how the two tones are situated in the larger interpretive context; some contexts, such as the most basic contrapuntal setting of a tonal work (see section IV), contain no dissonant intervals through which a Zug could pass; other contexts admit more possibilities.

A Zug will have other effects besides the essential ones of passing between two lines and of creating a single line between an origin and goal, but these are all contingent on particular features of its execution. The effect of completion that attaches to any Zug by virtue of its attaining a goal, for instance, may be mitigated or strengthened by the nature of the role played by the goal tone in its own line, the actions of other voices, the timing of the goal tone, or the direction in which it moves. Take the last of these considerations, for example. The effect of the Zug's direction is dependent upon a vocal interpretation of tonal motion. As has long been recognized, the effect of a vocally executed tone varies according to its location within vocal register. For instance, two eleventh-century copies of the important treatise *Scolica enchiriadis* (orig. *c*. A.D. 900) include a diagram that divides the universe of tones for singing into two zones – the "relaxed" and the "intense" (*remissum* and *intensum*) – presumably because tones we would call higher require more vigor to vocalize than do lower tones.[19] Schenker extended this conception to instrumental lines and incorporated it into his theory of tonal effects: if a Zug falls in tonal space, it has the effect of decreasing in tension, of aiming toward quiescence; if

---

[18] Allen Forte and Steven E. Gilbert (*Introduction to Schenkerian Analysis* [New York: Norton, 1982], 237) are wrong, then, to claim that "the test for the validity of a linear progression [Zug] rests ... on whether the interval between its starting and ending points agrees with the harmonic goal of the passage." While this is true of most linear progressions, we shall see several examples where it is not. Discussions with Edward Klonoski following his paper "When Is a Line a Zug?" (presented at the Fifth Annual Conference of Music Theory Midwest, Bloomington, Ind., May 1994), helped me sort out my thinking about Schenker's notion of Zug.

[19] *Musica et scolica enchiriadis*, ed. Hans Schmid (Munich: Bayerischen Akademie der Wissenschaften, 1981), 91. The diagram directly precedes an example in which the same tune is written out in three different registers.

Ex. 1.8

it rises, it has the effect of intensification, of development. One consequence of the ascending motion is an expectation for a complementary descent, thus a continuation of the content ("development" in this sense is a central concept in *Harmonielehre*). A rising Zug often has the effect, too, of regaining a tone and register previously abandoned, and a falling Zug often has the effect of leading to the inside of a sonority or texture. If the Zug passes between two voices in a sustained harmony, as in example 1.7, the effect of completion as it attains its goal is supported by the contextual consonance of both origin and goal, an effect that is even stronger if the goal is the harmonic root (or its octave), stronger yet if the Zug descends to rest on that tone, and strongest if the goal is timed to arrive on a referential timepoint (a metrical downbeat). By contrast, if the goal tone of the Zug is a passing tone in its own line, then that effect will color the completion of the Zug, commingling the effects of rest and motion.

Schenker's distinction between "authentic" and "apparent" Züge (*FS* 121/74) is based on consideration of the broader context in which the origin and goal tones can be placed. If either the origin or goal fails to be a tone in a line in the underlying counterpoint but is instead derived from such a line by some means (either by means of register transfer or what Westergaard calls "borrowing"), the Zug will only seem to pass between two voices (for one of the voices has no existence independent of the Zug). For an example see *FS* fig. 89-4, where the c³ that is the point of departure for the initial sixth-Zug has no successor in its register aside from a repetition. For another example, consider the first of Schumann's *Albumblätter* in which the g♯² that is the point of departure for the fifth-Zug in the middle section plays no role in a line in that register and so has to be conceived as a registral projection of an inner voice. When gauging the side-effects of a Zug, we will have to be careful to note just which types of voice are involved, whether, for example, one is an upper voice that spans an entire piece (the Urlinie), a voice that spans a formal section (as in the Schumann), or an isolated tone in the contextual triad.

Various effects result when the lowest voice of the configuration is set in motion against a Zug between two upper voices. The Zug in example 1.8*a* is, by itself, maximally closed. If the lower voice were to move in a neighboring motion around its tone, as in *b*, the closed effect of the Zug in itself would remain unaltered (though the synthesis of effects differs). But if the lower voice were to move to the third of the harmony just as the Zug reaches its goal, as in *c*, the resulting sixth would contribute its effect of mobility and thereby dampen the closural effect. A third possibility (and there are certainly others) is given in *d*, where the freer motion of the lower voice produces, in combination with the upper voice (and with a little interpretive imagination), a series of triadic effects; the ordering of triadic effects produces, in a sense to be explained below, the effect of progression around a circular path, in this case paralleling and therefore strengthening the Zug's closural effect.

The effect of a Zug also depends, as I said, upon the disposition of the voices in the broader interpretive context. While it is often the case that the starting and ending points of a Zug are absolutely consonant with one another, that each is contextually consonant, and that the interval spanned by the Zug belongs to the contextual harmony of the departure or the goal, none of these features is essential to being a Zug. As it happens, the compass of a Zug is usually a triadic interval. The explanation is fairly simple. The vocal principle limits the compass of a Zug to the interval of an octave or less, as any larger interval would have the effect of exceeding the compass of a single voice. Schenker accordingly interprets passing motions through intervals larger than an octave as involving a transfer of the origin or goal tone from the register of one voice into the register of another (a Zug passing through a tenth, for instance, would be interpreted in terms of a Zug through a third). The restriction of the Zug to intervals larger than a second but no greater than an octave leaves only one possible nontriadic span, the seventh. It is a separate question whether the origin and goal tones are contextually or absolutely consonant; it is also a separate question whether the interval spanned by the Zug belongs to either or both of the contextual triads to which the origin and goal are referred. At one end of the extreme, a Zug can pass between contextually consonant tones and through an absolutely consonant interval; at the other, a Zug can pass between contextually dissonant tones and through an absolutely dissonant interval. Examples 1.7 and 1.8 presented the first situation; the following series of examples progresses toward the most dissonant type of situation.

Example 1.9 shows a configuration in which a sixth, contextually dissonant with the sustained harmony, resolves downward to a fifth. The four-voice configuration shown in *a* has the potential, says Schenker, of admitting three Züge moving in parallel along the paths shown in *b*. Each Zug moves through an absolutely consonant interval, but only the upper two intervals are contextually consonant.[20]

The reverse situation, in which the interval between origin and goal is absolutely dissonant but contextually consonant, is also possible. This situation arises in cases where a dominant-seventh chord is the contextual harmony and where the configuration promotes the triadic intervals that the chordal seventh forms with the third and fifth of the triad. A similar situation may also arise when a diminished triad is the contextual harmony, in which case the chord's diminished fifth can be elaborated by a Zug. Schenker's allowance of the chordal seventh as a contextual consonance (making it what some have called an "essential dissonance") on the grounds

---

[20] Compare *Mw* 1: 102/55, where Schenker interprets a fourth-Zug starting from a neighboring tone (he also interprets this as an expansion of a third-Zug).

Ex. 1.9. Based on *FS* fig. 95-d1

Ex. 1.10. Brahms, Op. 24, Fugue, bars 7–8 (*FS* fig. 87-1a)

Ex. 1.11. Haydn, Sonata in E♭ major (Hob. XVI:52), I, dev. Based on *FS* fig. 62-1

of its sustaining triadic relations with members of the triad is clearly the object of his explanation of the seventh chord in *Harmonielehre* as the union of two triads (*Hl* 242–43/188–89). Example 1.10*a* presents two successive Züge moving down from an upper voice to an inner voice (see *FS* 124/76). The separating silence and the arrangement of the melodic line in groups of evenly paced sixteenth notes heading toward a longer eighth note might seem to suggest interpreting the melody in terms of sixth-Züge (mirrored after a fashion by inner Züge); in each case, the interval of the Zug would be consonant with the goal tone's harmony. Schenker, however, takes into consideration the action and pace of the lowest voice; in combination with the upper voices, it produces seventh chords changing every quarter note. The influence of the chordal effects, he claims, warrants interpreting the upper line in terms of Züge that pass through the absolutely dissonant but contextually conso-nant augmented fourths and diminished fifths shown in *b*. A similar situation is presented in example 1.11. Here there is an opportunity for the middle voice to pass to the upper voice, reaching the upper voice just as it passes through a dissonant seventh. Since the interval traversed is absolutely as well as contextually dissonant, the motion is said to be an apparent (*scheinbar*) rather than genuine (*wirklich*) Zug. Schenker draws attention to the rearticulations of the root in the lowest voice, which have the effect of dividing the seventh-Zug at root, third, and seventh; the

Ex. 1.12. Based on *FS* fig. 95-d2

triadic intervals of third and fifth that result from this division soften the dissonant effect of the larger span and support the Zug effect (*FS* 105/64).

Finally, an apparent Zug can even be created between tones that are dissonant in every respect. Example 1.12 shows a configuration of five voices. Two of the inner voices express the common suspension formation $^{6-5}_{4-3}$; the innermost voice executes a neighboring motion; and the outer voices sustain the harmonic root. Schenker describes a situation in which the upper and lower pairs of voices are converted into parallel Züge, as they were in example 1.9, and in which another Zug is created in the space between the dissonant fourth (f^1) and the neighboring note (b). The interior Zug, therefore, moves between two contextually dissonant tones that lie a diminished fifth apart, an interval dissonant in the absolute sense. The dissonant effect will be mitigated if, in the execution of the three Züge, the three lines make their final step in concert, thereby producing the triadic effects of VII–I (as in *c*). The triadic effect of VII is enough to make the span of the interior Zug (f^1–b) contextually consonant, at least temporarily. Moreover, because the dissonant Zug is executed in parallel with (hence in agreement with) a contextually and absolutely consonant Zug in the uppermost voice (c^2–e^1), it borrows the latter's consonant effect.[21]

IV

We are now in a position to consider a complex passing effect that Schenker "discovered" in the mid-1920s, an effect he regarded as the *sine qua non* of the musical artwork. Even if the universality Schenker claims for this basic effect is untenable in the face of much artful, engaging music composed in the centuries before and after, there can be no doubt that he makes a convincing case for hearing tonal works by composers of the eighteenth and nineteenth centuries in terms of this effect (the

---

[21] This is part of the sense to be made of Schenker's notion that the upper Zug in such a case "leads" or "guides" the inner and lower Züge; see *FS* 127–28/78. (Some rhythmic adjustments would be required to avoid consecutive fifths in the execution of *c*.)

basis and structure of the case is explored in chapter 2). Schenker posits this basic effect as one that should guide both the composition and interpretation of tonal artworks.

For Schenker, striving and fulfillment – *Spannung* and *Erfüllung* – constitute the aesthetic principle not only of music but of all the arts (*FS* 9/xxiv). The content of the *Urwirkung* is a synthesis of striving and fulfillment: striving manifested in motion toward a goal, fulfillment or closure in the stability of a single entity and in the attainment of the goal.[22] All the tonal material in a truly artistic work of music can be traced back to a basic tonal configuration that produces this complex effect, a configuration that he called the *Ursatz*, "basic contrapuntal setting."

Nearly all the effects we need to configure an Ursatz are in place.

(1) There must be an entity within which motion will occur.

A single major or minor triad will suffice to produce this effect.

(2) There must be a departure and a goal.

The single harmony will have to serve as both origin and goal of the movement if the configuration is to maintain the effect of being an entity; thus, a single harmony must form the content of the two events that sustain the effects of beginning and ending.[23]

(3) There must be a direct movement passing from beginning to end.

It must be direct, because only a direct motion produces the effect of sureness of purpose and goal, and stepwise, because only stepwise motion is unambiguously passing (leaps might signify detours). This effect can be produced by creating a Zug between two different tones of the harmony. Schenker termed this basic melodic line the *Urlinie* and often called it the *Urlinie-Zug*.[24] Believing that the tonal content of lower registers is naturally more restrained than that of higher registers, Schenker determined that the Zug's filling of tonal space is more appropriately placed in the higher register (in the highest register, actually, since that is where the ear's attention most naturally focuses) (*FS* 37/15).

---

[22] See *FS* 16–17/4 (on the effects of "movement," "striving toward a goal," and "completion of the path"), 31/11 (on the effect of "entity"), and 140/87 (on the effect of being a "closed formation").

[23] There is at least one musical artwork discussed by Schenker that, at its most basic level, does not begin and end with the same harmony: Chopin's Prelude in A minor, op. 28, no. 2, depicted in *FS* fig. 110-a3. The lack of an initial tonic intensifies the primary effect of striving. Significantly, the effect of beginning *in medias res* arises only from gauging the work's effect in terms of the Ursatz idea. For a slightly different case, compare Brahms' Intermezzo, op. 117, no. 2, depicted in an unpublished sketch (OC 34/106–10), reproduced in Allan Cadwallader, "Schenker's Unpublished Graphic Analysis of Brahms's Intermezzo Op. 117, No. 2: Tonal Structure and Concealed Motivic Repetition," *MTS* 6 (1984), 1–13.

[24] The distinction between the two terms is never rendered in the translation of *FS*, perhaps because the decision to render *Urlinie* as "fundamental line" would have led to the even more cumbersome locution "fundamental linear progression" for *Urlinie-Zug*.

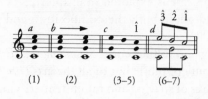

Ex. 1.13

(4) The Urlinie-Zug must come to complete rest.

The outermost voices must cooperate in producing this effect. The lowest voice must end on the root, since only this will produce a stable sonority, and the Urlinie-Zug must descend to the root (î) in the register of the upper voice, since only this will produce the effects of complete closure and agreement between the voices.

(5) The Urlinie-Zug must not traverse more than an octave.

By limiting the range of the Urlinie to the octave, Schenker restricted its point of departure to one of three possible consonant tones lying above the goal: 3̂, 5̂, or 8̂. Though he does not explicitly justify this limitation, Schenker might have reasoned that because the narrow range of the human voice is the measure of melodic compass, a line in excess of an octave would seem to join two registers rather than unfold as a single voice. If the initial tone were to lie beyond the octave, the line might appear to come to rest prematurely on 8̂ (there are ways this effect could be mitigated, but not without increasing the tonal content and at the same time exceeding the content of the basic effect); moreover, an Urlinie of more than eight tones would be exceedingly complex in its compositional execution and difficult to sustain as a perceptual strategy.

    Configurations satisfying these first five constraints are shown in example 1.13a–c. However, the configuration in c does not achieve the desired effect. The passing effect created in the upper line is counteracted by the unifying effect of the sustained tone in the lower voice; as a result, the configuration as a whole does not have the effect of passing, and the upper voice expresses only a single sustained tone, e^2 (FS 43/19). Only if the lower voice, too, is set in motion will it be possible to achieve the full effect of passing away from a point of departure and coming to rest at a destination. Hence,

(6) The lower voice must move in such a way as to promote and at the same time counteract the effect of the basic triad.

Only a movement from the root of the referential triad through its fifth and up to the octave will produce the desired effects. Schenker termed this move the *Baßbrechung*, "bass arpeggiation," and the tone that divides the octave at the fifth, the *Oberquintteiler*, "fifth-divider." Though the bass arpeggiation is seldom depicted by Schenker in its purely ascending form, it is only in terms of this form that the concept of the fifth-divider makes sense, namely, as the division of the octave space. In *Der freie Satz* he writes, "the lower voice, the bass arpeggiation through the fifth, avails itself of the ascending direction, which is the original direction of development and continues to serve the constant remembrance and presence of the natural sonority in the Ursatz" (30/10–11); also, "the fifth-division of the sonority" (66/37) and "in the fulfillment of the basic arpeggiation through the fifth of the sonority" (181/111). On one hand, the succession root–fifth–octave promotes the harmonic entity presented by the sustained tone in the lower line of example 1.13*c* by creating the very interval that unambiguously delineates the identity of that triad, while on the other hand, the conjunction of the fifth with the penultimate tone of the Urlinie (2̂) produces a fifth that delineates a different triad. Because the middle sonority is dissonant with respect to the primary triad, the Ursatz as a whole produces the succession consonance–dissonance–consonance and hence the desired effect of transition or passage.

Finally,

(7) The motion of the bass must reinforce the effects of striving and fulfillment.

The vocal principle that informed our interpretation of the difference in effect between a rising and a falling Zug is applicable here as well: the Baßbrechung must first rise to the fifth and then fall to the root. If the bass falls to the root at the same time as the Urlinie descends to 1̂, the two voices move in similar motion to the same tone (pitch class), thereby producing two effects of agreement in the achievement of closure.

These seven requirements fully determine the tonal configurations (what Schenker called the "forms of the Ursatz") that realize the basic effect. (Example 1.13*d* represents only one possible form.) These requirements do not, however, exhaust the effects produced by Ursatz configurations. In particular, they do not refer to one final effect that arises from the counterpoint of the Urlinie and the Baßbrechung: the effect of harmonic progression.

The movement of the lower voice upward and then downward by fifth is, as Schenker describes it in *Harmonielehre*, the quintessential mark of harmonic progression (*Stufengang*). Rising by fifths produces the effect of "development and procreation, an infinite forward motion," and falling by fifths, understood as an "inversion" of the developmental rising fifths, produces the effect of "devolution" and "returning" (*Hl* 44/31). The triadic succession of the Ursatz is the simplest form of a complete Stufengang.

The term *Stufe* (lit. "step" or "stair," hence "scale degree" or "scale step") refers the root of a triad to the diatonic scale of a key (this is reflected in the way Roman numerals assign Stufen to degrees of the scale). The nominal connection to the diatonic scale is misleading, however, since a Stufengang is not a stepwise motion of triads along that scale. Schenker never actually defines the conditions under which a triad has a Stufe effect, but it seems implicit in *Harmonielehre* that this effect arises when the triad sustains fifth relations (real or imagined) to other triads in the surrounding context.[25] A Stufengang is stairlike to the extent that the effect of a succession of triads can be gauged according to a flight of fifth-steps, either ascending or descending (see *Hl* 198/153 and 311–19/232–40).

A cycle of Stufen (*Stufenrund, Kadenzrund, Stufenkreis*) is a Stufengang that begins and ends on I, as in an Ursatz. A cycle of Stufen is not simply a passing motion, *per se*, but also a circular motion comprising the two phases of departure and return. The concept can be extended to circles that begin and end on other degrees, most commonly V, but II and IV are also possible (see, for example, the two "cycles" mentioned in *Tw* 8/9: 4: I–IV–V–I and V–I–IV–V). The effect of passing within the first phase of the basic Stufenrund can be activated either by arpeggiation (interpolating the third between root and fifth, thereby subdividing the basic fifth step into two stages) or by a step motion connecting the root and fifth. The harmonic results vary depending on how the tones of the Urlinie are arranged against the richer bass line.[26]

The path of a Stufengang is analogous to the logical path of a classical syllogism. Harmony "helps music deceive itself and the listener about its lack of a logic or causal connection. Harmony even behaves as if it bore in itself the compulsion of logic" (*EK* 144). In *Harmonielehre*, Schenker vacillates between describing harmonic logic as an interpretive disposition and as a property of the tonal material; he writes in one place of "the feeling of Stufen logic that is immanent in us" (252/192) and in another of "the natural logic of motion immanent in the Stufe" (203/158). The metaphor of *Stufenlogik* and *Stufenfolge* pervades *Harmonielehre*. The analogy is not strict, but seems to be this: the initial I is a hypothesis (see *Hl* 282/211–12), the mediating V the condition that would make I true, and the final I the affirmation of that truth. The traditional term for the close of a Stufenrund is, in fact, *Schluß*, a term that in logic indicates the "conclusion" of an argument.

Hearing two Stufen on the downward path of fifths (II–V), for example, warrants the expectation of such a conclusion (I). The effect of being in a key, he says, requires the "premises" and "conclusions" of a Stufengang (*Hl* 339/257). He also speaks of "the consequentiality of a normal modulation" (*Hl* 430/327) and describes a succession of triads that does not manifest the effect of a Stufengang as lacking compulsion and presenting instead the effect of "an *irrational* to and fro" (*Hl* 200/155; cp. 215/169, 217/172, and 219/173). The "logical" movement from premises to a conclusion is circular in that the content of the hypothesis and final affirmation are identical; it is not circular to the extent that the force of those statements differs.

Other terms used by Schenker that have logical associations are *Satz*, meaning

---

[25] See the section entitled "The Theory of Stufe Value" (*Hl* 332–37/251–55).

[26] See *FS* fig. 14. On the third-divider, see *Hl* 314/235 and *FS* 54–55/29. On step motion, see *FS* 55–56/29–31. The content of this bass Zug functions in Schenker's interpretation of configurations where the first or last passing tone is absent; in those cases, there is an additional effect of "leaping over" (*Überspringen*) the tone (Oster's rendering of this term as "omission" fails to convey the operative presence of the tone). (In *FS* fig. 14-4b, there should be a D passing between C and E.)

Ex. 1.14

"proposition" in logic and "phrase" in music, and *Vordersatz* and *Nachsatz*, meaning "antecedent" and "consequent" (as in a conditional statement). The associations are supported by Schenker's use of the term *Gedanke*, "thought," for what we might call the basic thematic units of a form. Often a Vordersatz and Nachsatz are the elements constituting a Gedanke.

The fundamental effect of striving and fulfillment, then, is cooperatively produced (a) by the Urlinie-Zug, which seeks its rest in î, (b) by the Baßbrechung, which underscores the primary harmony at the same time as it creates a triadic effect that is dissonant with the harmony (and so creates the effect of transition in its own fashion), and (c) by the Stufen, which progress from an initial premise toward a warranted conclusion.

V

The significance of the Ursatz principle for the creation of musical content is stated unequivocally in *Der freie Satz*: "All the content of music gets its start [*besteht*] only in arranging the indivisible Urlinie with the two-part Baßbrechung" (*FS* 37/15). The interpretation of content, too, gets its start with the basic effect realized by the Urlinie and Baßbrechung. It is the first norm in a process of interpretation (hence the prefix *Ur-*, indicating temporal priority), a process in which the individuality of a configuration is shown to arise, in large part, from the particular ways in which it deviates from the norm. Though the significance of this placement of the Ursatz will not fully emerge until chapter 2, we are already in a position to see how this interpretive process works and, more to my point in this chapter, to discover an entire family of effects that arises from such a process, namely, that of delay.

Each of the Stufen produced by the interaction of the Ursatz's two essential voices (the Urlinie and Baßbrechung) bears within itself a set of potential or imagined voices. These potential voices may be activated, as it were, by Züge that connect them to the Urlinie. Example 1.14*a* shows an Ursatz in C minor, with its essential voices in open noteheads and potential voices in filled-in noteheads; brackets indicate a selection of intervals from among the numerous possibilities, which are turned into Züge in *b*. The resulting concatenation of Züge is itself a line, but not one with the simple effect of setting out upon a path and reaching a destination. In this undulating line there is manifested, in addition, the effect of delay, a musical effect that was as essential to Schenker's experience of tonal music as passing.

The *goal*, the path, is the first thing; content comes only in the second place: without a goal there is no content.

On the way to the goal, in the art of music as in life, there are obstacles, reverses, disappointments, extensive paths, detours, extensions, interpolations – in short, delays of all kinds. Therein lies the seed of all the artistic delays with which a fortunate inventor can bring content into play that is continually new. In this sense we hear an almost dramatic course of events in the middleground and foreground. (*FS* 18/5)

The effect of "delay" (*Aufhaltung*) depends on the interpreter's ability to measure the timing of an event or stages of a process in terms of a model or norm.[27] Yet the temporal norms by which Schenker measured music are largely unstated. Consequently, few students of his theory have assimilated them and little attention has been paid to the "dramatic course of events."[28] After briefly stating the most important principles, I will present a series of examples showing how the principles inform the analysis of rhythmic effects.

Surely one of the most overlooked features of Schenker's interpretive practice is his habit of interpreting the rhythmic peculiarities of free compositions in terms of the rhythmic equilibrium of strict counterpoint. Simply stated, the principle for interpreting a tonal configuration that arises from a single transformation (for example, a passing motion, rearticulation, neighboring motion, or suspension) is a configuration that proceeds in equal note values. So far as I know, Schenker states this principle explicitly only with respect to suspensions:

Since free composition abandons the rhythmic paralysis of the cantus firmus, it succeeds on its own in using, instead of the half notes of the basic form ♩♩ ♩, any other durational values it pleases, even varied values. . . . But however these values are arranged, they can only be understood in an artistically correct manner, and at the same time correctly rendered (which is what it ultimately comes down to in free composition), if their deviation from the basic norm (of equal half notes) is assimilated into artistic consciousness. (*Kp1* 360–61/ 279–80)

This passage is, understandably, accorded a great deal of significance by William Rothstein in his exegesis of Schenker's rhythmic ideas. Rothstein produces examples from *Der freie Satz* in support of the claim that Schenker uses the same noncontextual rhythmic norm for passing motions: "There is nothing to suggest an equal-value rhythm for the passing motions [in the examples], other than the very

---

[27] An account of how musical experience is thick with, among other things, delayed and denied events is presented in J. K. Randall, "A Soundscroll," *PNM* 13 (2) (1975), 126–49.

[28] Notable exceptions are Carl Schachter and William Rothstein. For treatment of temporal principles, see the three installments of Schachter's "Rhythm and Linear Analysis," *MF* 4 (1976), 281–334, *MF* 5 (1979), 197–232, and *MF* 6 (1) (1987), 1–59, and Rothstein's "Rhythm and the Theory of Structural Levels," Ph.D. diss. (Yale University, 1981). Rhythmically sensitive analyses by these authors are numerous; see, for instance, Schachter's "The Triad as Place and Action," *MTS* 17 (2) (1995), 149–69.

existence of those motions. One can only conclude that Schenker believed the equal-value rhythm to be the norm for passing motions in general, *based solely on contrapuntal content.*"[29] The examples discussed below will show the interpretive consequences of holding to this norm.

A second principle, for which I will give but one example, complements the principle of rhythmic equilibrium: passages in free compositions that proceed in equal note values but arise from more than one operation (for example, a combination of suspension and passing motion) are frequently interpreted as an equalization of a rhythmically differentiated model.[30]

A third principle of cardinal importance concerns metrical stability and is based on the relation between the initiation of a tone, its duration, and the prevailing meter. Simply stated, a tone is metrically stable if its point of initiation is the strongest point (metrically speaking) within its duration.[31]

A fourth principle concerns metrical patterns: duple meter is the norm by which nonduple metrical patterns are interpreted (*FS* 192–94/118–19). This norm will figure in only one of the interpretations presented below.

The final type of rhythmic norm is contextual: the presented rhythm of a configuration is used to interpret other presentations of the same or similar content.[32]

I begin with a simple, preliminary example based on the paradigmatic passing motion. Imagine an upper neighboring motion followed by a descending third-Zug, D–E♭–D–C–B♭, proceeding in equal note values. The first step from D to E♭ has the effect of setting off, if not on a path toward a specific goal (Zug), then at least in a specific direction. When that step is retraced, E♭ to D, the E♭ in retrospect has the effect of neighboring, and the second D has the effect of postponing progress along the rising path. (This is the sense in which the neighboring note derives from the passing tone, as the abandonment of an intention to pass away; see *Kp1* 240–41/178–79.) Additionally, since the step-off to E♭ has already set the line in motion, the second D is also "passing" or "on the way." When the line steps down to C, the prospect of a return to the rising path becomes more remote, and when the line reaches B♭, the initial move to E♭ seems to have been a detour. Since the goal and the path (in this case, the third-Zug) are primary, Schenker hears the neighboring motion in retrospect as an addition, an interpolation, which both increases the melodic content of the descending Zug and postpones its completion (*FS* 74/42).

Brahms' *Variations on a Theme by Haydn*, op. 56, opens with a similarly expanded Zug, followed by a second third-Zug from e♭² to c² (ex. 1.15). Schenker describes the arrangement of the phrase as follows:

[29] "Rhythm and the Theory of Structural Levels," 46; the passage from *Kp1* is discussed on pp. 43 ff.

[30] The best discussion of this norm is Rothstein's "Rhythm and the Theory of Structural Levels," 28–34.

[31] This principle was first articulated by Arthur Komar in *Theory of Suspensions* (Princeton: Princeton University Press, 1971), 55 and 57.

[32] This type of norm is discussed at length in the latter part of Rothstein's "Rhythm and the Theory of Structural Levels"; see especially his sensitive treatment of the rhythmic problems inherent in interruption patterns (pp. 135–49). The contextual norm based on parallelism is a concept fundamental to his subtle and engaging interpretations in *Phrase Rhythm in Tonal Music* (New York: Schirmer Books, 1989).

Ex. 1.15. Brahms, *Variations on a Theme by Haydn*, op. 56, bars 1–5

The interpolation of a neighbor note into the first third-Zug leads to a 3-bar unit. Since the second third-Zug $e\flat^2$–d^2–c^2 retains its original 2-bar span, a 5-bar unit arises, clearly divided, however, into 3+2. A binary division is thus at work behind this 5-bar unit ... (*FS* 195/120)

Schenker's interpretation of bars 1–3 as an expanded two-bar unit would seem to rest on three factors: (1) the observation of a parallelism between the content of bars 1–3 and 4–5, namely, the third-Züge; (2) the observation of a contrast, both in length and in content (the neighboring motion in the first unit); and (3) a norm of duple metrical patterns.[33] This is not, however, the end of Schenker's interpretation of temporal effects in the theme, for the abnormal rhythm of the first three bars also defines a contextual norm by which to interpret the parallelism in bars 4–5:

... and the second third-Zug in bars 4–5 works [*wirkt*] only like an acceleration [*Beschleunigung*].

The slower, protracted Zug in bars 1–3, because it happens first, sets the pace for things to come; when the next third-Zug runs its course in bars 4–5 within a shorter span of time and without an upper neighbor to slow it down, it moves faster than the first and so seems to accelerate the pace of the piece. (Elaboration of $e\flat^2$ by a third-Zug from the inner voice c^2 briefly delays the appearance of $e\flat^2$ in bar 4.)

The effect of retardation (delay) can likewise be produced by interpreting the pace and content of one configuration in terms of an earlier one.[34] The melodic line in the right hand of Mozart's well-known variation theme (ex. 1.16) sets off on two

---

[33] See Rothstein, "Rhythm and the Theory of Structural Levels," 141–42.

[34] The best exegesis of Schenker's rhythmic theory is Rothstein's "Rhythm and the Theory of Structural Levels." The underlying principles receive their clearest statement in Peter Westergaard's *An Introduction to Tonal Theory.*

Ex. 1.16. Mozart, Piano Sonata (K. 331), I, bars 1–4

descending paths, from the third and fifth, respectively, of the A-major tonic harmony.[35] The theme begins, however, not with a simultaneous presentation of these
paths, but with an alternation between the two, producing an effect Schenker called
Ausfaltung "unfolding." A concomitant effect of the successive rather than simultaneous presentation is a delay, in this case a delay in the onset of tones in the upper
line from the downbeat to the upbeat of the bar (ex. 1.16*b*). The first two bars of the
theme set the pace for the unfoldings. (Another principle is to interpret patterns as
continuing to replicate.) A delay is effected when, in place of a third unfolding of the
inner and upper lines, the interval that separates the lines (that is, the interval pre-
dicted as the simplest continuation of bars 1–2; see *b*) is bridged by a Zug starting in
bar 3. What is crucial here is not, however, the Zug itself, which could have been
executed without disturbing the expected timing of events (see *c*); rather, it is the

[35] The interpretation in ex. 1.16 is based not on Schenker's analyses (to be discussed below), but on that of Peter
Westergaard (*An Introduction to Tonal Theory*, 37). Which of the tones to interpret as the start of the theme's basic
line has been the object of dispute among theorists. Arguments for choosing the third can be found in Fred
Lerdahl and Ray Jackendoff, *A Generative Theory of Tonal Music* (Cambridge, Mass.: MIT Press, 1983), 276–77;
on p. 341 n. 6 they acknowledge the greater weight Schenker assigned to parallelism in determining which
linear interpretation to prefer.

Ex. 1.17

Ex. 1.18. Mozart, Piano Sonata (K. 331), I, bars 1–8

fact that the three tones of the Zug occur at the same pace as the two-tone unfoldings in bars 1–2. The outcome of this equalization is a delaying of c♯² into the fourth bar (see *d*). (Other elaborations increase the content of bar 4, drawing c♯² further into the bar and postponing completion of the upper path until the very last eighth note.)

In this and the preceding example we have seen three different types of delay involving the timing of tones in a line:

• the *stretching* of a tone's time span and the consequent delay of the subsequent tone's onset,
• the delayed onset of a tone *within* its time span, and
• the delayed departure from a tone, extending it *beyond* its time span.

If delays of one sort rest upon a determinate sense of path, then the Ursatz – with its triple trajectories of Urlinie-Zug, Baßbrechung, and cycle of Stufen – ought to furnish the prospect of delays of the first order. For example, hearing the opening of Mozart's theme present 5̂ as the upper voice of an initial tonic harmony, we should expect the piece to run the course shown in example 1.17. But hardly does the theme reach the penultimate step in this path in bar 4 before it breaks off and presents a configuration initially like bars 1–2 (see ex. 1.18). The combined effect of reinitiation after breaking off before the final step is called *Unterbrechung*, "interrup-

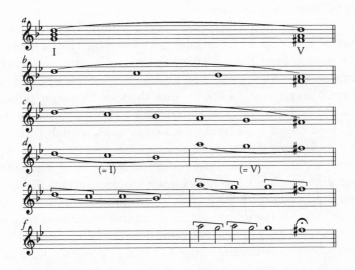

Ex. 1.19. Mozart, Symphony no. 40 (K. 550), I, bars 1–20 (based on *Mw* 2, suppl. VII)

tion": "At the first occurrence of $\hat{2}$, the voice leading undergoes an interruption; the interruption therefore creates not only more content but also, on the way to the ultimate goal $\hat{1}$, the effect of a delay, a retardation" (*FS* 66/37). After reinitiating the Zug from $\hat{5}$, Mozart's theme erases the delay of c♯² in bar 3 (cp. ex. 1.16c) and reaches the "ultimate goal" in bar 8.

The opening phrase of Mozart's Symphony in G minor manifests a combination of the rhythmic effects encountered in the variation themes by Brahms and Mozart. Example 1.19 depicts the stages in Schenker's interpretation.[36] The rhythmic notation used here is one frequently encountered in Schenker's graphs, in which whole notes represent relative rather than strict durational value, and not hierarchical status.[37] The relative rhythmic values are used to indicate the norms of rhythmic equilibrium and the postponing effect of linear transformations that interpolate new tonal content prior to reaching a particular goal. By expressing all the tones in whole notes, the example makes palpable both the lengthening of content and the holding-off of arrival at the goal. As Schenker writes,

On the way to the foreground as the ultimate goal, the transformations also signify a *deferral* (retardation); we are still far from the goal so long as striving [*Spannung*] and increase of content are held onto in the layers of transformation. Deferral accordingly counts among the most valuable compositional means. (*FS* 42/19)[38]

---

[36] See *Mw* 2: 118–20. The analysis presented here takes some liberties with Schenker's interpretation of bars 10–15. Additional aspects of Schenker's analysis are discussed in Rothstein, "Rhythm and the Theory of Structural Levels," 194–97.

[37] See, e.g., *LfS101* 44²52 fig. 38, *Mw* 2: 88 fig. 4, or *FS* fig. 138-1.

[38] Westergaard's line-writing rules are an excellent means for inculcating sensitivity to the interdependence between transformational expansion of content and deferral of closure (*An Introduction to Tonal Theory*, 55–59).

Completion of the immediate consecution shown in *a* is deferred by the execution of a Zug from the upper to the first inner voice of V (*b*) and deferred still further by the extension of that Zug into a second inner voice (*c*). That Schenker does not interpret the motion from the outset as a sixth-Zug requires an explanation: the passage forms an antecedent phrase, presenting the first attempt at completing a fifth-Zug from d^2 to g^1; were the line to reach that goal by passing through both a^1 and $f\sharp^2$, it would have the effect of approaching g^1 from two different paths and hence would have the effect of combining two paths in one line; that effect is here made explicit by showing the two paths as separate voices in *a*: $b\flat^1$–a^1 and g^1–$f\sharp^1$. The register transfer in *d* activates a new register and postpones completion of the Zug in the original register; both of these effects create a future in which the upper register is more fully utilized and in which closure is realized in the lower register. The register transfer also has the immediate effect, relative to the time span of this passage, of bisecting the sixth-Zug into two parallel halves, the first spanning an interval within I and the second an interval within V. The repetition in *e* of the middle tone in each half-span postpones the completion of each motion and at the same time creates the potential for a parallelism within each half-span (motivically realized in bars 1–9). Finally, there is the acceleration and repetition of a^2–g^2 in *f* and the fermata on the last tone that has the effect of postponing the onset of the consequent phrase.

The repertory of retarding effects, then, includes several that are a-metrical (or better, given Schenker's generative approach, "pre-metrical"). We might call these postponements to distinguish them from the measurable delays encountered in previous examples:

- postponement of a goal by means of interruption and reenactment, and
- postponement of a goal by means of transformations that interpolate or otherwise expand tonal content prior to the goal.

As the phrase in Mozart's symphony gets underway (ex. 1.20), the first three tones of the sixth-Zug are arranged as a pair of two-note motives: d^2–c^2, c^2–$b\flat^1$; each tone in this configuration lasts two bars, a duration that is reinforced by the pacing of the low bass tones starting in bar 1 and by the rhythm of the cycle of Stufen. The last of these tones, however, is cut short; the elision has the effect of hastening the progress of the sixth-Zug, an effect that is sustained when the Zug continues in bars 10–11 at double the previous pace; it is as if the force of prematurely abandoning $b\flat^1$ propelled the melody on its way more quickly and into a more intense octave. The repetition of the accelerated motive in bars 12–13 insists all the more upon proceeding at the quicker pace. The line of the Zug is subsequently taken over by the newly entering woodwinds in bars 14 ff. (after a fourth-Zug in bars 13–14 takes the violins into an inner voice). When the woodwinds take over, they also, in cooperation with the basses, return to the original pace. (The chromatic succession in the bass has the dual effect of a tone repetition and passing, commingling, as it were, the accelerated pace with the original; this commingling forms a transition between the

Ex. 1.20. Mozart, Symphony no. 40 (K. 550), I, bars 1–20

accelerated and original paces.) Coming after the acceleration of bars 10–13, the return to the original pace also has the effect of expansion (*Dehnung*), as the expected content of g^2–$f\sharp^2$ is "stretched" back into the original durations presented in the first half of the passage. The expansion delays the cadential dominant that would have been reached in bar 15 had the accelerated pace been maintained. The extended dominant harmony of bars 16–20 continues the process of deceleration begun in bar 14.

The arrival of V in bar 16 seems to realize the expected goal, while the subsequent bars seem to discharge the force of that arrival. That is, the effect of closure in one sense coincides with the downbeat of bar 16 and in another is distributed across the time span of bars 16 ff.[39] This suggests that the effect of closure does not neces-

---

[39] Ernst Oster beautifully describes the distribution of closure over the duration of a cadential harmony in his interpretation of Beethoven's Piano Sonata op. 27, no. 2; in "The *Fantaisie-Impromptu:* A Tribute to Beethoven," in *Aspects of Schenkerian Theory*, ed. David Beach (New Haven, Conn.: Yale University Press, 1983), 191: "the bass, having arrived at the dominant G♯, is sustained, and it is as if measures 9 to 14 represented one large fermata. To be sure it is not an ordinary fermata, the tones of which are struck only once. Instead it is prolonged and exquisitely elaborated, the motion of the preceding measures still vibrating within it. After the close of the

Ex. 1.21. Mozart, Piano Sonata (K. 545), I, bars 1–12

sarily rest exclusively on the arrival of the goal tones, but may also depend on the manner in which they are presented. Evidence that Schenker interpreted "closure" as an effect dependent upon multiple effects is provided by his analysis of Mozart's Piano Sonata in C major, K. 545, the opening phrase of which is provided in example 1.21. The basic line of the phrase is $\hat{3}$–$\hat{2}$. In a foreground depiction of the phrase (ex. 1.22), Schenker locates the onset of the line's goal at the downbeat of bar 9 (corresponding to the seventh bar notated in the example). By notating the fifth and sixth bars of the figure in half notes, Schenker draws attention both to the parallelism between bars 3–4 and bars 5–8 of the sonata and to the durational expansion of the second statement of this motive; this notation also helps draw out the contrapuntal inversion of the two lower voices within the motivic configuration.[40] In a more abstract representation of the phrase that places it in the context of the entire movement, Schenker shows the same goal tone but identifies the time of its onset as bar 12 (ex. 1.23). The best sense I can make of this is that Schenker interprets the effect of "closure on $\hat{2}$" to be delayed beyond the "onset of $\hat{2}$."[41] Obviously, the onset of the fifth divider, g, is delayed beyond bar 9 by the lower voice's f; this alone would

---

fermata, Beethoven carries on the initial idea with renewed and intensified vigor. The outward picture alone, the uniformity of the motivic material, indicates that the prolonged fermata was but an interruption, like someone standing still to catch a new breath."

[40] Jonas and Oster "corrected" the notation of bars 5–8 in *FS²* and in *Free Composition*, changing the half notes to whole notes.

[41] I am grateful to Stephen Peles, who, by asking me about the discrepancy between these two figures, prompted me to notice this bifurcation of closural effect. For another example, see Schenker's analysis in *Mw* 3 of Beethoven's Third Symphony, finale, bars 250–56, as presented in the *Urlinie-Tafel*, p. 29.

Ex. 1.22. *FS* fig. 124–5a

Ex. 1.23. *FS* fig. 47-1

account for the delay of closure until bar 11, as the upper voice "waits" for the lower to reach its goal so that together they might actualize the dominant harmony. If there is something in the presentation that warranted Schenker's interpretation of yet a further delay, it is probably the increase (rather than cessation) of rhythmic activity in bar 11, an activity that ceases only in the middle of bar 12 (the rhythm of bar 12 presents a rhythmic caesura).

I turn back to the analysis of the first phrase of Mozart's A-major theme, already discussed above, and look now at the analysis that Schenker presents in *Der freie Satz* under the rubric "the genesis and meaning of a rhythmic motion" (*FS* 198/122; see ex. 1.24). What motivates his analysis appears to be a desire to interpret the melodic content of the concluding bar as motivically parallel to the content of bars 1–3. The e^2 in the fourth bar (see ex. 1.18) is interpreted as a dissonant appoggiatura within a II Stufe, so the basic content of that bar is a three-tone passing motion, d^2–$c\sharp^2$– b^1. Schenker finds its parallel in the descent e^2–d^2–$c\sharp^2$ that spans from the start of the theme up to the concluding four-tone figure. At the same time, Schenker wants to interpret these two third-Züge as the articulation (*Gliederung*) of a fourth-Zug; Schenker does not indicate what rhythmic profile he attributes to the fourth-Zug, but it is reasonable to suppose that he would not have objected to the rhythmically neutral profile shown in example 1.24a. The tonal content of the third-Züge is produced, I infer, by repeating the two passing dissonances of the fourth-Zug, d^2– $c\sharp^2$, and thereby delaying the arrival of b^2 (*b*). That alone does not create the parallelism; what is needed is a differentiation such as that produced by the registral shift in the G-minor symphony. Here the differentiation is rhythmic: the concluding three tones of the six-tone passing motion are compressed into the time span of one tone

Ex. 1.24. Levels *a–c* by the author; levels *d–g* by Schenker, *FS* fig. 141

(*c*), producing the four durational units that will be the four bars of the phrase (compare Schenker's counterfactual possibilities in *d* and *e*). Subsequent transformations of *c* (*g*) mitigate the sharp contrast in rhythmic values between the first three-tone series and the second, in the course of which the onset of the second series is delayed.

As an example of how assimilating the basic principles of rhythmic equilibrium and metric stability can permit the emergence of rhythmic effects such as delay, consider the first prelude in J. S. Bach's *Well-Tempered Clavier* (bk. 1).[42] Though the evenly paced surface of the prelude seems at first glance to suggest hearing the composition as an animated first-species composition, the tied-over dissonances in bars 2, 6, 8, and so on, belie that interpretation and suggest thinking of the prelude in terms of a fourth-species model (see the outer-voice setting depicted in ex. 1.25*b*). This model can in turn be conceived as a deviation from a first-species configuration (ex. 1.25*a*), in which all but the first tone in the bass are delayed in relation to the tones of the upper voice. A few of the tones in the upper voice similarly deviate from the first-species rhythmic norm, with the result that some of the tones that are conceptually simultaneous in *a* are also simultaneous in *c*, though now at delayed timepoints (see bars 11, 13, 15, and 19). In bars 10 and 18, the lower voice borrows

---

[42] See *FUT* 36–37. Schenker's graph implies much, if not all, of the analysis represented here. In a letter to his student Felix Eberhard von Cube, Schenker depicts the parallel tenths in this opening span of the prelude in whole notes; the figure is reproduced, along with much valuable commentary, in William Drabkin, "A Lesson in Analysis from Heinrich Schenker," *MA* 4 (3) (1985), 244.

Ex. 1.25. Bach, Prelude in C major, *Well-Tempered Clavier* (bk. 1), bars 1–19

the root of the contextual triad, in each case producing an unambiguous harmonic effect (V–I) that reinforces the alignment of syncopated tones and at the same time divides the Zug of each voice into two spans. Because only the lower voice is thereby divided into spans that are contextually consonant (c¹–g–c in contrast to e²–b¹–e¹ in the upper voice), Schenker says that the lower Zug "leads" the upper. The first broad gesture of the prelude, then, unfolds as a pair of octave-Züge moving within the initial tonic Stufe. The Zug in the upper voice constitutes a detour from the course of the Urlinie and a delay in the consecution of e² to d². (Given that an octave produces a mixture of identity and difference, the effect of an octave-Zug is less that of passing between two independent vocal lines than it is passing a single tone from one vocal register to another. Schenker's term for the effects of transference are *Tieferlegung* and *Überlegung*, "lower placement" and "higher placement"; these terms are usually translated as "descending" and "ascending register transfer.")

An example especially rich in delaying effects appears in the exposition of the first movement of Beethoven's Third Symphony (ex. 1.26).[43] The third–Zug, g²–f²–eb², of the movement's Ursatz is presented in an interrupted configuration: 3̂–2̂ ‖ 3̂–2̂–1̂. After the exposition executes the first phase of this, the development extends 2̂⁄V and thereby further delays closure. This delaying effect is characteristic of the contrasting section of all rounded binary forms (*Hl* 12/11).[44] The first thematic group of the

---

[43] See Schenker's essay in *Mw* 3, esp. pp. 34–36.

[44] There is a misprint here in the English translation; the second line of the page should begin "a₁:a₂."

Ex. 1.26. Beethoven, Symphony no. 3, I, bars 83–91

exposition expands $\hat{3}$, after which a transition section leads quickly to $\hat{2}$ ($f^{3(2)}$), departs from it, slowly reattains that tone, and then concludes with a precipitous plunge through a fifth-Zug in bars 82–83. The brevity of the Zug, compared to the lengthy preparation, is heightened by the bare harmonic support of V–I (sounded forcibly by the brass). In effect, the Zug's point of departure is left in play (see discussion of ex. 1.13c), as if the descent to the root of the contextual harmony (B♭ major) could not discharge the force of the build-up without the cooperation of a more decisive bass progression.

It is in this context that the second thematic group begins. Knowing the path the Ursatz has set out upon and now knowing the failure of the transition to bring the first part of the interrupted configuration to a satisfying, if only temporary, conclusion, the beginning we should expect, being the simplest, is for the upper melodic line to resume f^2. Also operating at this juncture is the expectation that the line is obliged to return to the register on which it set out, which is why I say f^2 here rather than f^3.[45] But that is not what happens. In bar 83 the first clarinet quietly emerges from the bombastic cadence to lead the melodic line and the new theme. It begins, however, with d^2, and that immediately gives the effects of a delay, of an expectation disappointed, and of an obstacle encountered. The simplest solution would be for the melodic line to return to f^2, either directly or by means of a rising third-Zug (what Schenker terms an *Anstieg*, "initial ascent," to the first tone of a basic line). (See example 1.27.) But the theme, hardly even begun, takes a different turn. An inner voice of the tonic harmony pulls chromatically upward, leading to a 5–6 motion (f^1–g^1) above the bassoon's reiterated B♭. This upward surge seems as if it might help propel the upper line on its way up to eb^2. But the E♭ emphatically presented by the bassoon in bar 86 turns the clarinet's d^2 into a dissonant suspension, thereby placing it under the compulsion, as it were, to move, not upward as we expected, but downward, which it does at the end of bar 86. Schenker's figure in ex. 1.27b places the bassoon's E♭ in bar 85. This is not an error, but rather a prompting to hear the passage as a deviation from rhythmic equilibrium, as if the theme lingered too long in its opening sonority and had to rush through its first step.

[45] Schenker's first and oft-cited mention of the so-called law of obligatory register is *Tw* 1: 39.

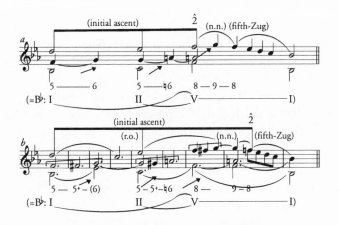

Ex. 1.27. *Mw* 3, suppl. fig. 10

No sooner does the suspension resolve than the first violins take over the melodic line with e♭² in bar 87. The leap from c² to e♭² has the effect of shifting the upper voice from the descending path of d²–c² onto a new, higher path (producing the effect Schenker termed *Übergreifen*, "reaching over"). As it effects a detour from the digressive descent (and thus potentially signals further delay), the shift to e♭² returns to the path that d² was originally expected to set out upon, namely, the climb to f². The reaching over, then, begins to reverse the deferring processes encountered in the opening bars of the theme. Bar 87 begins in parallel with bar 83, but this time the upward thrust of the melodic line is not delayed by turning its initial tone into a dissonant suspension; instead, the goal is delayed by completely different means, by surging beyond f² to the neighboring g² in bar 89. After all this preparation, with its multiple detours and reverses, and with the various tonal maneuvers that undid these effects in order finally to attain f² above the penultimate V harmony in bars 90–91 – after all that, this theme, like the transition before it had done twice, falls rapidly through a fifth–Zug, f²–b♭¹ (ob. 1, vln 1), again with only the bare harmonic support of V–I.

There is nothing in Schenker's theory that attaches an effect to the combination of a protracted preparation and hasty execution of a fifth–Zug, much less to the repetition of such a configuration. But that will not deter him from trying to pin down in words what that combination and its repetition "sound like." As we will see in chapter 3, Schenker interprets the content of this passage as a series of anticlimaxes in a dramatic plot.

VI

The third main category of effect in Schenker's interpretations of purely musical content is that of cohering as a single "unit" or "entity" (*Einheit*). This is an effect we have already observed in connection with the effects of Stufe, Zug, and motivic parallelism.

The effect of being an entity arises in two quite different ways. Either a configuration has the effect of being an entity in itself or that effect is conferred on it by repetition.

Repetition was a "purely musical principle" of cardinal importance to Schenker, one that he regarded as the hallmark distinguishing music from other arts.[46] The repetition of any configuration, regardless of whether it has the effect of being an entity in and of itself, confers that effect on the configuration. The most familiar entity of this type is the motive:

A motive is a tonal series that is repeated. Any series of tones can become a motive, but it is recognizable as such only if the repetition *immediately* follows. So long as immediate repetition is lacking, the series, even if it is subsequently raised to the rank of a motive somewhere else in the artwork, must be considered provisionally as just a component part of a higher whole.

Only repetition is able to raise the series of tones to something determinate, only it is able to clarify the identity of the series and what it wants. (*Hl* 4–5/4–5)[47]

But motives are not the only entities to arise from repetition. As Schenker's examples in §§4–5 of *Harmonielehre* demonstrate, repetition also defines the identity of phrases and even the largest "formal entities" of sonata form (*Hl* 5–19/5–12). It is also a "premise" of the temporal "units" by which the flow of musical time is measured (*FS* 192/118).

Some entities or units do not derive their identity from repetition. Among these are the individual tone and the triadic unit. Likewise the Stufe, the "proper role" of which is "to assemble, as it were, a larger series of counterpointing voices together into an entity" (*Hl* 183/141). "The Stufe preserves its higher character by means of embodying – ideally, as it were – its inner, unitary quality far above the individual phenomena" (*Hl* 181/139). As a harmonic entity, the Stufe is neither vertical nor horizontal; it encompasses tonal phenomena in both dimensions.[48]

Specifying what other kinds of multi-tone configuration produce the effect of an entity in and of itself is far more difficult. Schenker's primer on creating the effect of a self-contained melodic entity appears in the first book of *Kontrapunkt*. Though species counterpoint is traditionally understood as the study of how to set one or more newly composed musical lines against a given cantus firmus, Schenker begins with a lesson on how to create the cantus firmus itself. The rules given for writing a cantus firmus are aimed at producing the effect of a melodic line that, by itself, is a single entity with no discernible subentities other than its constituent tones. Schenker approaches the problem of constructing such a line by prohibiting various kinds

---

[46] See *EK* 138, *Kp1* 34–35/22, and *FS* 150–53/93–95.

[47] Borgese and Jonas leave out the word "provisionally" (*vorläufig*) and thereby create the impression that direct repetition is conceptually essential, whereas Schenker is talking only about the phenomenological emergence of a motivic concept.

[48] *EK* 143–44, *Hl* 176–77/133–34, *Kp1* 78/53–54.

of configurations that would produce a subentity, thus the prohibitions give us a glimpse of the effects that subserve the entity effect.[49] Those effects are: (1) that the line seem closed, (2) that no part of it "weigh" more than another, and (3) that it appear to be a single line. Each of these effects is secured by a set of rules or constraints on the composition of the cantus firmus.

(1a) The cantus firmus must always begin and end with the same tone (*Kp1* 51/33, 142/ 102).[50]

If the beginning and ending tones are identical, the unison relation between them produces the effect of agreement and identity. No other interval can secure that effect. It is obvious that if the relation between the two tones is dissonant, the entire line would seem to be part of a larger whole. Beginning on any tone other than that which is identical with the concluding tone will have the effect either of beginning in the middle of things (and therefore of pointing beyond the span of the line itself) or of starting before the beginning. Nevertheless, if the two tones are consonant, their harmonic unity would still encompass all the individual tones of the cantus firmus, and so support the effect of a single, closed, balanced line. Schenker allows that it is sometimes unavoidable for the cantus firmus as a whole to project a harmonic entity. As an example, he gives Fux's Dorian cantus firmus (see ex. 1.2): "the ear by itself follows first the third, F, and then adds to it the fifth, A, in order to obtain thus the impression of a triad, D–F–A, successively unfurled" (*Kp1* 79/54).

If the line is one of two or more lines in a contrapuntal setting, the responsibilities for closure are divided among lower, upper, and possibly inner voices. In Schenker's theory of cantus firmus design, however, he makes no distinction between the various roles the line might serve in a contrapuntal texture, consequently his design standards are underdetermined. The genius of Westergaard's adaptation of Schenker's contrapuntal theory is his realization that the closural design of the cantus firmus depends on whether that line serves as an upper, lower, or inner voice. The requirement of starting and ending with the tonic is essential only for the lower voice, for that is what guarantees a stable beginning and ending.

(1b) The penultimate tone of the cantus firmus must be either a step above or a step below the concluding tone (*Kp1* 142–43/102).

This is necessary "insofar as the effect of closure should be achieved in the most tranquil and most normal manner."

(1c) The antepenultimate tone must not leap more than a third to the penultimate tone and preferably moves by step (*Kp1* 143–45/103–4).

---

[49] My discussion of subentities within the cantus firmus is indebted to Dubiel, "'When You are a Beethoven'," 299–300, and to his insight that the purpose Schenker envisioned for the doctrine of strict counterpoint was to provide information about what configurations that doctrine rules out (298).

[50] Schenker actually requires that this be the tonic of the key, but that puts the cart before the effect; a line that begins and ends on the same tone and remains within a single diatonic system will project the effect of closing on a modal final, which is no less than the effect of closing on the "tonic."

Ex. 1.28

The end in view is "to reach the leading tone itself only in the most tranquil manner and to bring it that much more effectively into its closing function." Any leap larger than a third would "wrench open the effect of the conclusion," presumably because the penultimate tone would seem to be left hanging, in need of a melodic (i.e., stepwise) continuation; furthermore, it would also "claim for itself the expression of a particular mood," even though strict composition lacks the compositional resources to sustain and fulfill the demands of that sort of expression.

(2a) "All rhythmic variety must be avoided within the cantus firmus" (*Kp1* 27/18).

If one tone in the line were to have greater durational value than another, it would seem to protrude from its surroundings and thereby seem to take on an identity more conspicuous than its neighbors. At minimum, then, the tones of the line must be restricted to a "rhythmic equilibrium" in which no tone has more durational "weight" than another.

This rule is construed to include the initial and final tones, but that is not essential. Consider the two passing motions in example 1.28. The first has no variety "within" and gives rise to no discernible subentities. Not so the passing motion in *b*, where the "rhythmic variety" gives rise to the effect of two third-spans within the line and also the effect of an arpeggiation.[51]

(2b) No tone shall be presented twice in succession in the cantus firmus (*Kp1* 63/42).

Direct repetition of a tone would give that tone a duration of two bars, thus conflicting with the postulate of equilibrium. The cantus firmus must avoid "monotony" of any kind, be it direct repetition or even, by extension, reaching the same peak tone twice in succession (*Kp1* 140–41/100–101). Also, the concept of a text (viz., a polysyllabic word) is involuntarily associated with tone repetition, even though, again, strict composition lacks the compositional resources to sustain and fulfill the demands of that association. Joseph Kerman profoundly misunderstands the nature of this restriction when he cites it in his essay on Beethoven's Fifth Symphony, thinking that Schenker meant somehow to heap scorn upon anyone who would make such associations in free compositions.[52] What Schenker rejects is the idea that a specific content (for example, "fate knocking at the door") can be read off the tones (see *Tw* 1:30–31).

---

[51] For more on the complexity of the second configuration *vis-à-vis* the first, see Westergaard, *An Introduction to Tonal Theory*, 230.

[52] *Write All These Down: Essays on Music* (Berkeley: University of California Press, 1994), 208.

(2c) "A chromatic motion is prohibited in the cantus firmus" (*Kp1* 68/46).

If a line proceeds, for example, with the tones G–G♯–A, the chromatic succession is "in a certain sense a type of tone repetition" and for that reason is disallowed in the cantus firmus. In addition, it also has the "expression of a passing motion," which is an "effect that ties all three tones very clearly into an entity," though this entity effect is offset by the dissonance produced between G and A. Chromatic succession might also have the effect of mixture or modulation; strict composition is unable to realize fully the suggestion of these effects.

(2d) Avoid configurations that "circumscribe an individual tone by means of its neighbor note" (*Kp1* 28/19).

Any configuration that has a neighboring effect also has the effect of remaining in one location, since the neighbor has the effect of failing to pass away from that location. The static effect of a neighboring motion would attach at minimum, then, to a three-bar span, hence disrupting the rhythmic equilibrium of the line.[53]

(2e) "Avoid successions of tones that would be conspicuous as an arpeggiation or figuration of a single chord" (*Kp1* 28/19).

Since consonant leaps and their concomitant triadic effects are not prohibited, Schenker must have in mind the exclusion of triadic effects that span three or more tones of the cantus firmus (but something short of the entire line). This does not exclude simple passing motions through triadic intervals which span three or more tones in the cantus firmus, since the passing motion shows a mixture of dissonant and consonant effects, in which neither one is able to outweigh the other and thereby disrupt the equilibrium of the line.

(3a) "The cantus firmus must move only within the space of a tenth" (*Kp1* 61/41).

Schenker justifies this prohibition by appealing to the vocal foundation of all melody. To exceed the space of a tenth would be to exceed the comfortable range of a single voice and would therefore presumably have the effect of combining two voices into one line. (In fact, none of Schenker's examples exceeds the range of an octave.)

(3b) The closing successions $\hat{2}$–$\hat{7}$–$\hat{1}$ and $\hat{7}$–$\hat{2}$–$\hat{1}$ are prohibited (*Kp1* 144–45/103–4).[54]

The effect of closure, as noted above, must be secured by stepwise motion to the final tone. Either of the successions will, in retrospect, have the effect of employing both upper and lower leading tones in the approach to the final tone and hence the effect of departing from one path and assuming another. This mixture of two paths in one melody undercuts the desired effect of unity in the cantus firmus.

---

[53] A tone repetition, as Westergaard explains, is conceptually prior to neighboring motion (*An Introduction to Tonal Theory*, 35).

[54] This effect, of combining two paths to the goal in one line, is the basis for Schenker's analysis in *LfS101* 28–29²19 (fig. 10).

(3c) The cantus firmus must avoid several leaps in different directions (*Kp1* 131/92).

"The ear wants to and must understand the leaps only as detours for a shorter and more direct path that, in any event, was possible; the path in fact results of its own accord when we see the place where the subsequent leap reaches its end." Going off on a tangent is tantamount to combining the effect of two different paths in one melody. Schenker gives as an example the succession d^1–a^1–e^1 and describes the effect as follows: "our ear must conjecture, once the second leap a^1–e^1 has led to a conclusion on e^1, that the path from d^1 to e^1 was obviously the path originally intended and therefore also the simpler path" (*Kp1* 131/92).

(3d) The cantus firmus must avoid several leaps in the same direction (*Kp1* 132/93, 77–78/ 53).

Successive leaps in one direction may lead outside the limited range of the cantus firmus, and so seem to unite two vocal registers in one melody, or they may produce the entity of a triad or seventh chord, and hence come into conflict with the requirement of equilibrium.

(3e) The cantus firmus must avoid all dissonant leaps, either directly or as the sum of a succession of tones (*Kp1* 75–78/52–53).

Schenker again resorts to the vocal basis of music to justify this prohibition. Dissonant leaps, he states, are more difficult to sing and are consequently more complex intervals than the consonances and the seconds. Furthermore, they have expressive consequences which strict composition lacks the resources to sustain. As Schenker points out in several examples, a compound line is one of the effects dissonant leaps may produce in free composition (*Kp1* 81/55).

What configurations, then, produce the effect of "an entity-in-itself?" The lessons of cantus-firmus construction point to four kinds of self-contained entities. A *tone* that protrudes from its surroundings, whether because of repetition, durational "weight," or tonicization, is an entity. A *motion* that begins and ends, whether it is neighboring or passing, a Zug or a cycle of Stufen, is an entity. A *triad*, whether presented vertically as an unembellished simultaneity or horizontally as an arpeggiation, whether figured with neighboring or passing motions in one voice or unfolded simultaneously in several voices, is an entity. A *line*, whether it is the straight line of a Zug or the closed, singular, balanced line of the cantus firmus, is an entity. And the entity *par excellence*, because it manifests and unites each of these four kinds of entity, is the Ursatz.

VII

In music it is quite important, very important in fact, to observe every phenomenon, even the smallest, and to hear in every individual detail, even the most trifling, the cause that belongs to it. For hearing in this way does the most justice not only to the artist but also to the music itself. Music's uniqueness obtains in the very fact that it permits several laws to work at the same time, regardless of whether one is stronger than another, so that the strongest law which most intrudes into our consciousness in no way mutes those laws which keep the smaller and more restricted groups of tones in order. (*Hl* 103/82)

If there is a lesson to be learned from the preceding overview of the effects Schenker included in his interpretive constructions of purely musical content, it is that attentiveness to the whole need not be achieved at the expense of the detail, just as attentiveness to one effect need not be achieved at the expense of another: "the more manifold the effects that lie about the tones, the better; not only do they not suffocate the main effect, rather, they promote it!" (*Kp1* 83/56).

Even in configurations of only four or five tones, we saw that the set of effects produced by the tones is more than a simple disjunction of effects. Effects manifest different orders of complexity. Some effects, such as consonance and dissonance when they are produced independently of any other effects, are of a first order of complexity. The simplest passing effects are second-order effects, for they rest on an arrangement of the simpler effects of consonance and dissonance. The second-species passing configurations in example 1.5 also produced a second-order effect of consonance or dissonance that depended on the sum of the two boundary sonorities; a third-order effect of closure (whether strong, weak, or absent) rested on this second-order effect and on the first-order effects of (in)stability which attached independently to the two consonant sonorities.

As the quotation above suggests, effects have relative degrees of prominence and interact with one another, either cooperatively or antagonistically. Schenker expressed these two features in 1895: "Every prescription and proscription, fundamentally relative, supports a certain musical appeal [*Reiz*] – nothing more and nothing less – and so it upholds that appeal so long as the more intense interest of another is not in play. The less intense interest of the one then yields to the more intense interest of the other. The sum of all these interests forms the piece" (*EK* 142). Though this passage is primarily about compositional desires – the appeal of musical ideas and an interested, purposive involvement in realizing them (see chapter 2) – we can infer that the resulting content is also a "sum" of effects desired and realized. It is a sum that includes the relative degrees and synthetic interactions of effects.

The degree of an effect is, in many cases, affected by the presence of other effects. Take, for example, a situation in which two voices move in similar motion to an octave, producing the effect of two voices temporarily relinquishing their independence in favor of a common goal. This effect is undesirable in strict composition for two voices, since the unmitigated effect of agreement contradicts the requirement that the two voices retain their independence and manifest agreement only with respect to origin and goal. If a third voice were at the same time to move in contrary motion against these two voices, however, and thereby produce with respect to each of them the effects of excluding agreement and affirming independence, then the effect of similar motion would be counterbalanced by the effect of contrary motion. In the three-voice configuration, the effect of similar motion is made to recede in prominence.

Ex. 1.29. From Schubert, "Der Kreuzzug" (based on *Kp1* figs. 260–62)

Although the interaction of effects is a part of what Schenker meant to include in content, there are no hard and fast categories of interaction other than the distinction between cooperative and counteractive relations; beyond this one can only distinguish different degrees within each category on a case-by-case basis. Schenker uses a range of metaphors in the first book of *Counterpoint* to describe the conflicting or mutually supportive interests of effects. One effect "paralyzes" or "stifles" another; sometimes an effect is "ruptured and destroyed" by another (xxiv/xxv–xxvi; 197–98/142–43; 117/83–84). Good effects can "compensate for" a poor effect or "render" it "innocuous" (157–58/114; 196/142). Or, using a more explicit battle metaphor, the good effects may be "counterforces . . . engaged against" a bad effect, so that the bad effect is "smitten" (197–98/142–43). On other occasions, Schenker uses a metaphor drawn from competition among stage players, saying that one effect "pushes" another "into the background" or that a good effect "steps in front of" (upstages) a poor effect (194/141, 197–98/142–43; 196/142).

Furthermore, the effect produced by a tone in one context may be incompatible with the effect it produces in another context.[55] Schenker presents a dizzying display of flip-flopping effects in example 1.29.[56] The f$\sharp^1$ in the context of span *a* has the effect of resolving the suspended g$\sharp^1$; relative to span *b*, however, the same f$\sharp^1$ (the second eighth note) has the effect of anticipating a resolution of g$\sharp^1$ on the third eighth. Relative to span *c*, g$\sharp^1$ seems as if it might have the effect of passing (upward to a^1?), but relative to span *d* it has the effect of a portamento anticipation of the appoggiatura g$\sharp^1$ on the fifth eighth. The effects of the sixth eighth in spans *e* and *f* parallel the effects of the second eighth in spans *a* and *b*.

A piece also contains effects that are suggested but never fully realized, as when a

---

[55] In "Contradictory Criteria in a Work of Brahms," first presented at the Fifth Annual Meeting of the Society for Music Theory, Ann Arbor, Michigan, 1982 and subsequently published in *Brahms Studies*, vol. 1, ed. David Brodbeck (Lincoln: University of Nebraska Press, 1994), 81–110, Joseph Dubiel shows how one might hold incompatible interpretations by carefully differentiating the contexts (spans) that are the perceptual objects of interpretation while at the same time noting the extent to which the contexts share content. Similar themes are followed up by David Lewin in "Music Theory, Phenomenology, and Modes of Perception," *MP* 3 (4) (1986), 327–92.

[56] Based on *Kp1* figs. 260–62 and Schenker's discussion on pp. 252–53/188–89.

Ex. 1.30. Beethoven, Piano Sonata op. 110, I, bars 20–25

segment of a configuration seems as if it will produce an effect but then fails to do so. The phrase "seems as if it will produce" implies a person who hypothetically imagines that the tonal configuration will continue in a way that it will not. The definition of content, then, as noted in discussing delaying effects, must include reference to a listener who attributes effects to tonal configurations. Consider, for example, the imaginary cadential effect that a listener could expect in bar 24 of the first movement of Beethoven's Piano Sonata, op. 110 (ex. 1.30). Schenker provides a rhythmically simplified picture of bars 20–24 (ex. 1.31*a*), from which we may gather that the motive bracketed in *a* and displayed in *b* "stems directly from the preceding seconds which were moving along in quarter-note values." To this he adds an assertion that the motive "essentially forms a syncope in honor, as it were, of the half close, I–V, which is intended to follow" (*LfS110* 34²24). The prospected half cadence shown in *c*, then, is regarded as part of the content, even though the requisite root-position dominant Stufe does not materialize in bar 24.

Further effects are observed in his advice to performers. "On the second quarter of bar 23, one should take care not to deliver the sixteenths simply in the strictly metronomic sense; rather, one should be mindful of the fact that here they are an amplification [*Ausgestaltung*] of just a single tone (g²), which vibrates, as it were, in sixteenths, and therefore one should apply a small acceleration in the sixteenths figure." The content of the configuration can be made more or less manifest by how a performer renders it. This relationship between the quarter-note pace underlying the sixteenth-note motive and the identical pace of the preceding content, incidentally, does not disturb another motivic effect that attaches to them *qua* sixteenths: "the amplification [*Ausgestaltung*] into sixteenths, in another respect, must be traced back in return to the suspension formations in bars 22–23" (*LfS110* 36²30; see ex.

Ex. 1.31. From *LfS110*: (*a*) fig. 10 (²11); (*b*) fig. 11 (²12); (*c*) by the author (*d*) fig. 12 (²13)

1.31*d*). These two relationships (quarter-note pace and sixteenth-note suspensions), then, are part of the work's content. But that is not all. Schenker goes on to ascribe two more effects to the sixteenth-note motives in bars 23 and 24: "The neighbor notes in both cases should not only fulfill the simple vocation of neighbor notes in general but should, beyond that, also announce the V and II Stufen in advance, as it were, Stufen which then only actually appear on the second quarters of bars 24 and 25" (*LfS110* 34²25).[57]

Finally, consider the explanation that Schenker offers for why Beethoven indicated that a crescendo should begin on the third quarter of bar 23:

The *cresc.* on the third quarter of bar 23 has the following significance: since the construction seems to lead toward a half close here, we would probably, if left to our own devices, be inclined to apply a *diminuendo* on that quarter, with the effect, as it were, of a comma; the *cresc.* marking, however, gives us a warning, by way of exception, not to yield to the norm

---

[57] The interpretation given here of the dual effect of the neighboring sixteenth harmonies (i.e., neighboring and announcing the next Stufe) is reaffirmed by Schenker a decade later in *Mw* 1: 183–84.

[*Norm*] in this case (the norm to which Beethoven, too, would otherwise yield), for a different task awaits us instead, that of surmounting the impending half close by keeping in mind later events that are still to come. In the third quarter of bar 24, the situation is more favorable from the outset, for here the neighbor-note harmony that alludes to a $II^{\natural3}$ Stufe does not, in and of itself, give rise in us to the feeling of a half close. The *cresc.* marking therefore does no violence to this passage, since it proceeds instead in parallel with the harmonic causality that lies in the neighbor-note harmony. (*LfS110* 36^229)

These remarks again point to the prospective moment in Schenker's idea of musical content, namely, that a given arrangement of tones ("the construction") can create in us expectations for a future course of events; in this case it is the Stufen, as bearers of "harmonic causality," that are primarily responsible for determining our prospects for the future course of events.[58]

---

[58] One of the most amazing descriptions of harmonic causality at work is found in Schenker's essay on the Prelude in E♭ minor from book I of Bach's *Well-Tempered Clavier*. Schenker lavishes an entire paragraph on an apparent V_3^4 chord which seems "logical" when it arrives but proves to be without consequence for what follows (*Tw* 1: 42). For discussion of this passage, see my "Zen and the Way of Soundscroll," *PNM* 30 (1) (1992), 228–31.

2

INTENTIONS

> Here, in the study of counterpoint, the apprentice can obtain the foundation for the first insight and conviction that there actually is a connection between the artist's intention with regard to the tones and their effect, a marvelous connection of which the lay-world has no inkling, and that in the best of cases – these are precisely the geniuses, and they alone! – intention (i.e., prediction of effect) and effect completely coincide, while in by far the greatest number of cases the tones, acting of their own accord, as it were, and behind the backs of the authors, bring about an entirely different effect than they perhaps intended. (*Kp1* 22/14–15)

At the end of 1891, two years after withdrawing from the Conservatory of Music and the Performing Arts in Vienna, Schenker slowly began a career as a writer with a few reviews for Ernst Wilhelm Fritzsch's "new music" journal in Leipzig, the *Musikalisches Wochenblatt*.[1] But looking back in 1922, Schenker attributed his real start to the Berlin publisher Maximilian Harden, who had had the courage, he said, to publish his first attempts as a writer in *Die Zukunft*, a new journal started by Harden in 1892 (*NTB* 11). For over six years, from the fall of 1891 to the spring of 1898, Schenker earned part of his income writing essays and concert reviews, on and off for Fritzsch and Harden, and more regularly for two Vienna weeklies, *Neue Revue* and *Die Zeit*. Among the hundred or so texts written in these early years is a handful of essays in which he articulated ideas that would become the basis for a series of books and essays published after the turn of the century: ideas about musical creativity, the purpose and content of music theory, and the relation of harmony and counterpoint to free composition.[2]

Schenker had already begun to work on this project as early as 1895. In an essay

[1] When Schenker's father died in 1887, Schenker assumed financial responsibility for his mother, as well as his sister, younger brother, and a niece (*NTB* 4–5, 11). He continued his studies, but in November 1889, shortly before receiving his law degree from the University, he withdrew from the Conservatory (*NTB* 6). Ernst Ludwig, Schenker's piano teacher at the Conservatory, made some of the contacts that brought Schenker income in these early years, introducing him to Julius Epstein, who provided occasional subventions for compositions, and to Irene Graedener, whose son became one of his many piano students (*NTB* 7).

[2] The essays are: "The Music of Today (New Variations on an Old Theme)" (1894; *EK* 62–64), "Hearing in Music" (1894; *EK* 96–103), "The *Geist* of Musical Technique" (1895; *EK* 135–54), "Toward Musical Education" (1895; *EK* 154–66), and "Impersonal Music" (1897; *EK* 216–21). For insightful discussion of Schenker's early views, see Allan Keiler, "The Origins of Schenker's Thought: How Man is Musical," *JMT* 33 (2) (1989), 273–98.

published that year by Fritzsch after being delivered as a lecture to the Philosophical Society at the University of Vienna, Schenker refers to a "detailed text" in which he undertakes "to elucidate harmonic and contrapuntal pre- and proscriptions" and "to bring what is called 'the school of harmony and counterpoint' into the vicinity of free creativity" (*EK* 142). This is no less than a précis of the magnum opus whose writing occupied him till his death some forty years later, the three-volume *Neue musikalische Theorien und Phantasien*.

The title of the essay and the topic of the subsequent treatise is "The *Geist* of Musical Technique." Schenker's project was to offer a rational reconstruction of the effects composers must have desired, given the way they configured tones, beginning with the effect that must not be sacrificed, the striving and fulfillment of a complete and unified tonal motion. Not, of course, that Schenker ever pretended to explain what composers consciously thought they were doing or to explain the actual genesis of a composition.

In sections I and II, I present the content and general historical roots of Schenker's early conception of what constitutes musical unity, and I illustrate how he used that conception to argue for the unity of a particularly problematical work, the third movement of Beethoven's Piano Sonata, op. 110. I then turn, in sections III and IV, to consider the same issue from the point of view of Schenker's late theory, first digressing to trace some of the specifically Hegelian themes that inform the structure of that theory and then returning to the main thread of the chapter to examine Schenker's first demonstration of a work's triadic unity, found in his remarkable essay on Beethoven's Piano Sonata op. 101. In the course of that demonstration I explore the intentions that shape the generative structure of Schenker's interpretations, namely, the intentions to elaborate and transform. Section V rounds out a theme of the chapter by showing how the several senses of *Geist* – mind, spirit, and ghost – are woven into Schenker's theory of the musical mind.[3] Section VI rounds out another theme by showing how intentions function in Schenker's notion of compositional "necessity" and specifying another of the general intentions that inform Schenker's generative accounts, the intention to diminute.

During the turbulent years between 1915 and 1921 when the commentaries on op. 110 and op. 101 were published, Schenker worked steadily on the second book of *Kontrapunkt*, the text of *Der freie Satz*, his complete performing edition of the Beethoven piano sonatas, and perhaps some of the essays that would later appear in the "literature supplement" of *Der Tonwille*. This period of five or six years, during which no publications appeared, marks a divide in Schenker's interpretive practice between what may be called, superficially, his early "foreground" interpretations and

---

[3] It is not at all coincidental that Schenker first planned to issue the second volume of his magnum opus under the title *Psychologie des Kontrapunktes* (*Hl* vii/xxvi) and that "psychology" is a frequent topic in the pre-war writings. "Psyche," after all, is the Greek equivalent of "Geist." The infrequent appearance of the term "Psychologie" in Schenker's later writings may be attributable to the emergence of his preference for Germanic words and a desire to distance himself from the psychological theories of Carl Stumpf and Ernst Kurth. The shift does not, as this chapter will amply demonstrate, signify an abandonment of the psychological point of view.

his later "background" interpretations.[4] I say "superficially," because this way of characterizing the two periods (one that Schenker himself sometimes encouraged; see *FS* 50–51/26) suggests that the idea of the background was newly invented during the years when the great political unity of the Habsburg Empire dissolved. I will show in the course of this chapter that there is in fact a deep continuity in Schenker's outlook spanning the four decades between the 1895 essay and the final volume of his magnum opus.

I

In the opening paragraphs of the 1895 essay, Schenker speculatively recounts the creation of the musical art as the gradual appearance of three reasons for making music (*EK* 135–36). Music's origin lay in nonlinguistic vocalizations that spontaneously express psychical or physical pleasure, a state we might call primitive song but not art (see *Hl* 68/53). This pleasure principle is music's original, direct motivation (*Ursache*). Music was gradually loosened from this direct motivation as people began to fashion sounds on the basis of a "play-impulse" peculiar to music alone (see also *Hl* 209/163). This play-impulse is an intrinsically musical motivation. Later, people thought to fashion sounds in response to "ideas or images of objects and feelings." This associative principle is an external motivation. It may seem surprising that one who so championed "absolute" music and so carefully charted the domain of the "purely musical" should nevertheless include in "content" anything like a musical response to "ideas or images of objects and feelings." By the end of this book, however, we will have a better idea of what this meant to Schenker in later years.

"The content of the musical work" usually rests "on the interaction" of all three motivations, none of which "is so egoistic that it wants to refuse the cooperation of the others." But music is art only if it arises and unfolds out of its peculiar play-impulse. This artfulness, which consists of the skillful exercise of technique, is the focus of Schenker's essay.[5] Only when this "formal creative principle" governs the fashioning of sounds does music rise to the level of art and sustain its own "refined, absolute practice [*Kultus*]." It is the realm of this "purely musical principle," sketched for the first time in this essay, that Schenker elucidates in the more sustained treatments of his theoretical writings.

Though the scope of Schenker's interpretive practice is narrow and nostalgic, it would be mistaken to take this as a simple form of blindness, willful or otherwise. Certainly ignorance of other music cannot be called upon to account for the fact that in his later writings he wrote approvingly only of the so-called masters of musical technique, those music-historical individuals who fully manifested the *Geist* of musical technique. For the essays and reviews Schenker wrote in the 1890s fre-

---

[4] For a penetrating analysis of the changes in Schenker's thought during this period, see Leslie David Blasius, *Schenker's Argument and the Situation of Music Theory* (Cambridge: Cambridge University Press, 1996).

[5] *Kunst*, "art," always carries with it this connotation of skill, as does the Greek root of "technique."

quently concerned new music (reviews of concerts, opera productions, and even a couple of reviews of newly published compositions by Johannes Brahms and Hermann Grädener) and it is said that he knew well all the symphonies by his teacher Anton Bruckner. By the same token, there is no substance to Joseph Kerman's insinuation that Schenker drew the objects of his study "from the stable of symphony orchestra war horses and from the piano teacher's rabbit hutch" because of a "tacit acceptance of received opinion as to the canon of music's masterpieces."[6] Rather, Schenker's choices rested upon a positive and substantive ground: it was the trio of music-making impulses laid out in the 1895 essay.

He clearly recognized that much of what does and ought to count as "musical" lies outside the reach of his theory; even certain questions about the genesis of the acts and artifacts that do lie within the domain of his theory nevertheless remain outside its purview. A charitable explanation for Schenker's narrow interpretive focus would be this: that he designed his theory for a limited class of musical artifacts and the motivated behavior that produced them. Complicating matters is the undeniable fact that Schenker valued what lay within the domain of his theory more highly than and to the exclusion of anything that lay without in the wider musical domain; his theory is at once a theory of the musically possible and a statement of the musically desirable. In the past, some Schenkerians attempted to defuse objections to Schenker's bias by claiming that the domain of the theory extends far beyond Schenker's narrow field of inquiry. One upshot of this was the tacit attribution of similar underlying desires and intentions to composers in widely different historical contexts, as different as those in which we find Anton von Webern and Japanese koto music.[7] Schenker, by contrast, recognized a variety of different motivations that might lead to music-making, among which there was one that he regarded as the most valuable and essential to any music that would be Art. That motivation, briefly put, is the creation of an artifact or event that is musically sufficient in itself.[8]

The historical emergence of musically self-sufficient art began with music's emancipation from the word. We find this view articulated in the opening pages of "The *Geist* of Musical Technique," the opening pages of *Harmonielehre*, of the first book of *Kontrapunkt*, and recapitulated late in *Der freie Satz* (§251), in short, we find it expressed in the précis and in each volume of *Neue musikalische Theorien und Phantasien*. It would be wrong to infer from Schenker's assertions about music's emancipation from the word that he thought texted music was essentially less artful

[6] *Write All These Down*, 17–18.

[7] See Roy Travis's contribution to the "Analysis Symposium: Webern, *Orchestral Pieces* (1913): Movement I ('Bewegt')," *JMT* 18 (1974), 6–12, and David Loeb "An Analytic Study of Japanese Koto Music," *MF* 4 (1976), 335–93. Felix Salzer, who studied with Schenker in the early 1930s, was the first to attempt such extensions, in his dissertation *Sinn und Wesen der abendländerischen Mehrstimmigkeit* (Vienna: Saturn-Verlag, 1935), and later in his pedagogical adaptation of Schenker's ideas, *Structural Hearing* (New York: Charles Boni, 1952).

[8] Saul Novack recognizes this bias in Schenker's theory and uses it to great advantage in tracing the development of tonality in "Foreground, Middleground, and Background: Their Significance in the History of Tonality," in *Schenker Studies*, ed. Hedi Siegel (Cambridge: Cambridge University Press, 1990), 60–71.

than nontexted music. There are enough analyses of songs among his writings to belie that interpretation. Rather, what he meant was that to the extent that the organization of the tones could not be understood independently of the verbal structure of the text, the artwork was not a genuinely musical artwork. As Schenker saw it, the history of musical technique progressed toward the development of a musical art in which arrangements of tones could be interpreted independently of a text or an idea or image or objects and feelings. The first sign of that independence and of the purely musical play-impulse was repetition; but repetition in itself was not the mark of a fully attained independence.

From the point of view of musical technique – Schenker's point of view – the creation of an autonomous musical work is a higher and far more difficult achievement than the creation of a musical work whose tonal arrangements must be interpreted with reference to nonmusical factors. From this point of view, the essentially heterogeneous artwork is a lesser species of music, though it may well be a valuable artwork.[9] When Schenker does turn his attention to the song or the programmatic work, it is only to those whose tonal content can be interpreted independently as well as in light of the text or program.

If repetition marked the beginning of the emergence of genuinely musical artworks, the culmination of that historical evolution was marked, for Schenker, by a tradition of improvising and composing works whose tonal content could be interpreted as generating from a single triad. Judging by the interpretive practice he developed in response to that tradition, Schenker believed that the basic intention of composers in that tradition was the intention to project dynamic unity through a diverse manifold of tones by purely musical means. That intention is the initial premise in his rational reconstructions of composed works from the tradition. He drew support for both the content and placement of this premise from statements made by what are generally regarded as the tradition's leading composers. In his introductory comments on musical form in *Der freie Satz*, for example, he quotes from C. P. E. Bach, Haydn, Mozart, Beethoven, and Brahms, to the effect that each regarded an intention to produce a whole as essential to their art. "One must have a vision of the whole piece," wrote C. P. E. Bach, and Beethoven is reputed to have said, "Even in my instrumental music I always have the whole in view" (*FS* 207–8/ 128–29).

There is nothing particularly astonishing in Schenker's holding the view that realizing an intention to produce a whole is an essential condition of the musically sufficient, for it is an artistic ideal with a long and distinguished history. In his grand compendium of the eighteenth century's aesthetic lore and theory, J. G. Sulzer defines the purposive artwork as the artist's realization of an intended "plan":

In that the maker of such a work has before his eyes its ultimate purpose [*Endzweck*], the effect that it should make, he deliberates by what means the purpose shall be maintained.

---

[9] I think it is likely that Schenker would have regarded some categories of art – most notably opera – as inescapably heterogeneous.

When he has discovered the means, he seeks also the best arrangement according to which one thing must follow another. Through this deliberation he defines the principal parts of his work according to their material qualities and the order in which they must follow one another. This is called the *plan of the work*.[10]

The artist's "arrangement" of materials is guided by both the specific purpose and the general intention to produce an observable and "indissoluble whole" from the individual "parts":

That a whole work, according to the nature of the intention, presents the imaginative faculty [*Einbildungskraft*] in the most advantageous manner; that it appears as an indissoluble whole [*Ganzes*] in which there is neither lack nor superfluity; that every part, through the place where it stands, makes the best effect; that one surveys the whole with satisfaction and in the idea of the same takes careful note of each principal part, or in the observation of each individual part is led to the idea of the whole; these are effects of good arrangement.[11]

Schenker's concept of musical unity is consistent with (and more determinate than) the cultural expectations for musical artworks; furthermore, he believed that his concept of musical unity articulately expressed what was intuitively known by the composers of such works.

Schenker would eventually contribute to the tradition by defining in a highly determinate manner the conditions under which tonal arrangements could realize the ideal articulated by Sulzer. But in his early writings, up to the time of the First World War, he worked with a looser determination of what kind of tonal arrangements produce the effect of the whole. He first articulated the musical conditions of that effect in "The *Geist* of Musical Technique." There he divided musical technique into three domains: repetition, polyphony, and harmony. At its simplest, making music "consists of producing melodies individually." The artificial principles of repetition and polyphony allow composers to proliferate melody, successively and simultaneously, and hence to proliferate tonal content. Repetition increases melodic content by simple multiplication. Polyphony produces new content by the addition of new lines in counterpoint to the melody, each new line casting a particular light on the melody. Schenker is quick to point out that the fruits of these observations are meant to serve the composer as he chooses to arrange tones for some purpose: "The phantasy sees how infinitely many aspects there are to fashioning a given melody, learns to examine how one change of aspect carries with it a change in expression, and, what is most important, through such a rich schooling eventually becomes capable of selecting, from the infinitely many arrangements which it sees, that one which best suits the artist's character at a certain time." But the artifices of polyphony and repetition do not, of themselves, produce the "feeling of a whole."

[10] Johann Georg Sulzer, *Allgemeine Theorie der schönen Künste*, 2nd edn (Leipzig, 1792; reprint, Hildesheim: Georg Olms, 1970), s.v. "Plan." A translation by Thomas Christensen appears in *Aesthetics and the Art of Musical Composition in the German Enlightenment: Selected Writings of Johann Georg Sulzer and Heinrich Christoph Koch*, ed. Nancy Kovaleff Baker and Thomas Christensen (Cambridge: Cambridge University Press, 1995), 69–74.

[11] S.v. "Anordnung"; see Baker and Christensen, *Aesthetics and the Art of Musical Composition*, 74–76.

That feeling is something projected by an individual melody whose manifold of tones can be gathered under the natural concept of a single triad. In 1895 he recognized what would take him a lifetime to elucidate, namely, that this natural triadic principle can encompass "the tonal succession of the whole," despite the appearance within that whole of diverse melodies in diverse keys (hence in different triads). From the very beginning of his career, then, Schenker realized that it was the conceptual entity of the triad that was the mark of musical unity. But in his early years, the content of that determination was simply that musical unity depends on unity of key. And several elements essential to genuine art had yet to be incorporated into his conception of the ideal musical intention.

II

One of his most extraordinary arguments for the intended unity of a musical artwork dating from the first period of his writing career is the one he provides for the third movement of Beethoven's Piano Sonata op. 110, a movement that by all appearances is a heterogeneous mixture of adagio, recitative, arioso, and fugue, of vocal and instrumental styles, of genres, and of forms.

Schenker's argument begins with the observation of something minor and inaudible: Beethoven's unusual notation of the "Arioso dolente" in six flats, and not the seven appropriate to its key of A♭ minor. That the notation is in Beethoven's hand – and thus arguably intended – is crucial to Schenker's argument, for that is an essential link in the chain of inference that leads to his imputing to Beethoven an intention to project "the feeling of a whole." The argumentation from the unusual key signature to the realization of an intention to produce the effect of a whole, however, is by no means straightforward. In order to demonstrate Schenker's move from observable evidence to the inference of that intention, I have distilled his complex and sometimes bizarre argument into a series of syllogisms. Reconstructing his argument in this way will also allow me to formulate a point of connection with his later theory of the background.

Schenker begins by considering three possible arguments for the unusual key signature, taking it as given that the Arioso is in the key of A♭ minor and that Beethoven knew the proper signature for that key. All three arguments are valid, but the first two have at least one false premise. The falseness of the premise is in each case ridiculously obvious and I doubt Schenker would have wasted a word on them had not the second argument been put forward by Hugo Riemann.[12]

(A)   1. Notating more than six flats is bothersome or inconvenient.
  2. Beethoven avoided the bothersome or inconvenient.
∴   3. Beethoven notated only six flats.

---

[12] In a footnote to his edition (Berlin: N. Simrock), Riemann asserts the content of proposition 6.

Evidence for the truth of the assumption that Beethoven knew the proper key signature of A♭ minor is also evidence for the falsity of this conclusion: in his manuscript for the "Marcia funebre" in the Piano Sonata op. 26 he repeatedly wrote seven flats in the key signature; it too is in the key of A♭ minor. As for premise 2, what could be more inconvenient, from the composer's point of view, than to use a signature that required writing a flat sign before nearly every F?

(B)   4. In the haste of composing, Beethoven would occasionally forget to write down one or another of the more mechanical notations.
      5. Beethoven wrote six and not the required seven flats.
∴   6. Beethoven forgot the seventh flat.

Schenker shows that premise 4 does not apply in the case of op. 110. On one hand, there is the fact that Beethoven wrote the six-flat signature not once but several times; moreover, the six-flat signature is used in two separate autograph versions of the movement. If that is not enough to convince you that Beethoven did not simply forget, then Schenker asks you to consider the fact that Beethoven wrote numerous flats before F in the Arioso, and thereby demonstrated that he was fully aware he had omitted a flat from the signature; had it been only a matter of forgetting, would he not have simply added a flat to the signature instead of continuing to add flats to the F's? Finally, Schenker notes that Beethoven also jotted a note in the margin of one of the autographs asking, in reference to the placement of a flat before one of the F's, "[I wonder] whether in Berlin?" (i.e., whether the correction had been entered into the Berlin edition).

    This leaves but one other possible argument, namely, that the signature was intentional. The question now is, what is the intention realized by the unusual notation. Schenker advances a hypothesis which, conjoined with another premise, yields the desired conclusion:

(C)   7. Beethoven intended to promote visually the idea that the Arioso is not an independent piece.
      8. Using a "neutral" key signature would accomplish that intention.
∴   9. Beethoven used the neutral signature of six flats for the Arioso.

To explain the added premise, Schenker makes reference to the practice of writing recitatives:

(D) 10. The content of a recitative typically involves frequent changes of key.
     11. Frequent changes of key signature are inconvenient (distracting, disorienting).
∴   12. Recitatives use a signature that remains neutral with respect to the content (i.e., does not indicate the particular key of the content).

Having now established the visual impression of the signature, Schenker begins his move toward establishing the effect of unity projected by the movement as a whole.

(E)   13. The Arioso is preceded by a passage appropriately designated "Recitativo."
      14. The signature of the Recitativo is neutral.
      15. The signature of the Arioso is also neutral.
∴   16. The "character" of the Recitativo is extended to the Arioso.

Argument E is supported by the fact that the Recitativo and the Arioso are in the same key; while evidence to the contrary is the fact that the form of the Arioso is more definite than that of the Recitativo (the Arioso has well-marked phrases and cadences). Note also that premise 13, if true, is evidence in support of inferring that Beethoven was familiar with the practice described in argument D.

(F)   17. If the Arioso shares key and character with the Recitativo, it is not an independent piece.
      18. The Arioso shares key and character with the Recitativo.
∴   19. The Arioso is not an independent piece.

There is more.

(G)   20. Both the Recitativo and the Arioso have a declamatory character; they are based upon a "vocal substrate."
      21. The second movement does not have a declamatory character; it is absolute music.
      22. A drastic contrast between absolute music and music based on the idea of the declamation of words would be indecorous.
      23. Beethoven observed decorum when it came to the conjunction of absolute and declamatory types of music.
∴   24. Beethoven mediated the contrast between the two movements by providing the Recitativo with an introduction that does not have a declamatory character.[13]

Evidence for the plausibility of this argument is found in the final movement of the Ninth Symphony, where, after three movements of absolute music, Beethoven composed an instrumental "antecedent" as preparation for the entry of voices and text (see *NS* 253–58/231–35).

(H)   25. Recitatives often have introductions.
      26. The content of such an introduction typically consists of preparatory cadences or modulations.
      27. The passage preceding the Recitativo consists of a series of modulations and cadences: B♭ minor → C♭ major → A♭ minor.
∴   28. That passage constitutes an introduction.

By connecting an introductory passage to the Recitativo–Arioso pair, argument H lends further support for the conclusion of argument F.

---

[13] Ian Bent (personal communication) amplified Schenker's point by pointing out that the double-dotted pattern

And now to the series of arguments that constitutes Schenker's argument for Beethoven's primary compositional intention:

(I) 29. The third movement has four parts: (1) Adagio/Arioso, (2) Fugue, (3) Arioso, and (4) Fugue.

  30. The four parts manifest only two distinct characters: "adagio" and "fugal."

∴ 31. The movement represents an amalgamation of two parts.

In what follows I will refer to these four parts as A_1, F_1, A_2, and F_2. These designations will help avoid confusing the first adagio part with the few bars of that part that are headed by the indication "Adagio."

(J) 32. If a piece begins and ends in the same key, it will have the effect of a whole.

  33. The key of A_2 is not the same as that of A_1.

∴ 34. The conjunction of A_1–A_2 is not an independent whole.

Thus the Arioso, the larger formal entity of the Adagio–Recitativo–Arioso, and the conjunction of A_1–A_2 are all dependent, incomplete entities.

(K) 32. If a piece begins and ends in the same key, it will have the effect of a whole.

  35. The first fugal part (F_1) begins in the same key as ends the second fugal part (F_2); the fugue projects that key by an exposition in F_1 and a reprise in F_2 and separates them with a modulating section (i.e., in the customary manner of fugues).

∴ 36. The conjunction of F_1–F_2 constitutes an independent and complete whole.

(L) 37. The first adagio part (A_1) prepares the key of the fugue's exposition.

  38. The key of the second adagio part (A_2) fits into the modulatory scheme of the fugue's modulating section.

∴ 39. "The two Arioso parts [A_1 and A_2] are completely adapted to the tonal requirements of the fugue."

(M) 40. The four parts are based on two (A_1–A_2 and F_1–F_2). (I)

  39. A_1 and A_2 are adapted to the tonal requirements of the fugue. (J, L)

  36. The fugue is an independent whole. (K)

∴ 41. Amidst diversity, the third movement projects the effect of unity in the fugue.

The last four arguments show how the proposition that a musical artwork is unified in virtue of its determination of a single harmonic concept functions in Schenker's theory: it is a major premise.

---

of the first beat of the introduction alludes to the French operatic overture and hence to instrumental music in the broader context of music with words.

III

If Schenker's basic argument for the unity of a musical artwork is this,

(N)   42. If a tonal arrangement can be brought under the concept of a single triad, it has the effect of a whole.

43. Tonal arrangement A can be brought under the concept of triad T.

∴   44. A has the effect of a whole.

then his later theoretical work can be construed in part as establishing the general conditions under which it is possible to affirm the antecedent of premise 42 and his analytical work can be construed in part as demonstrating the truth of premise 43 in individual cases. Establishing the truth of premise 43 does not by itself prove that the work is a genuinely musical artwork, for in addition to unity, Schenker would want evidence that warranted inferring other basic intentions, not the least of which are the intentions to produce variety within repetition, to produce a dynamic motion that reaches closure, and to elaborate the basic tonal setting (Ursatz) in such a way as to produce diminutions.

The "theory of organic connection" presented in *Der freie Satz* is Schenker's fullest statement of the truth conditions for premise 42. "Organic" tonal content is generated from a single triadic entity, in a process that Schenker understood in Hegelian terms. In this section I digress from the topic of intention in order to pick up several Hegelian themes that inform Schenker's organic theory; in the next section I will return to the topic of intention and look more closely at Schenker's declarations about the manifestation of *Geist* in musical artworks.[14]

The clearest evidence for the Hegelian roots of the theory of organic connection is found in the very first sentence of the first part of *Der freie Satz*:

The origin of every Life in a nation, a race, and in the individual, is at the same time its Destiny. Hegel conceives Destiny as ". . . the manifestation [*Erscheinung*] of that which specific Individuality is in itself, as an inner, original qualitative determinacy."

The inner law of Origin then accompanies all later Development [*Entwicklung*] and is ultimately in every Present. (*FS* 13/3)[15]

---

[14] The only case made for a direct association with Hegel's dialectic is Michael Cherlin's brief but suggestive essay "Hauptmann and Schenker: Two Adaptations of Hegelian Dialectics," *TP* 13 (1988), 115–31. I am grateful to Stephen Peles for remarking to me on several occasions that the structure of Schenker's later theory is indebted to Hegel and for pointing me to *The Philosophy of History* as the most likely source. Several authors have noted commonalities between Schenker's theory and Goethe's morphological theory. While these commonalities are suggestive, I think the analysis herein will show that the Hegelian themes run deeper, which is not to say that the connections with Goethe's thought are thereby laid aside, since the influence of Goethe on Hegel is well known. See William Pastille, "Music and Morphology: Goethe's Influence on Schenker's Thought," in *Schenker Studies*, ed. Hedi Siegel (Cambridge: Cambridge University Press, 1990), 29–44. References to other literature on Goethe and Schenker can be found in Pastille's article (29 n. 4); see also Gary W. Don, "Goethe and Schenker," *ITO* 10 (8) (1988), 1–14.

[15] For this translation of "Bestimmtheit" as "determinacy," see Michael Inwood, *A Hegel Dictionary* (Oxford: Blackwell, 1992), 77–78. The quotation is written on a scrap of paper (OC 23/2) and includes a cryptic bibliographical reference that I am as yet unable to decipher. Nor have I been able to locate the source of the quotation in any of Hegel's texts; it is possible that Schenker is (mis)quoting from memory. The language is

As far as I can tell, the relevant context is Hegel's presentation of the philosophical method of history, in the Introduction to *The Philosophy of History*.[16] I will limit myself to sketching parallels with four key aspects of Hegel's Introduction: (1) history as the manifestation of Reason, (2) the dialectical development of Spirit (*Geist*) in history, (3) the means by which Spirit is realized in history, and (4) the ultimate form of that realization, the State. I will attempt to bring out the parallelisms by juxtaposing quotations from Hegel's Introduction and descriptions of similar ideas in Schenker's theory. Later I will introduce passages from Schenker's texts that reflect the Hegelian themes, but for now I think it best to avoid the complications of such passages, since they are always inextricably involved in serving other purposes.

(1) Hegel begins his Introduction with a survey of the basic forms of history: original, reflective, and philosophical history. Original history consists in a representational, narrative report of what has been seen and remembered; its scope is limited. Within reflective history Hegel distinguishes four types: universal history, which, because of its larger scope (for example, the history of an entire nation or country), has to rely on the abbreviating power of abstractions of memory; pragmatic history, which tells stories about the past in the service of a present moral purpose; critical history, which is a history of historical narratives (i.e., historiography); and, finally, fragmentary history, which, as the history of an idea (for example, art, law, religion), is only a partial story of the larger whole which is the history of Spirit. The latter is the domain of philosophical history.

Both Hegel's philosophical account of world history and Schenker's theoretical account of music are rational reconstructions. Both presume that rationality is inherent in the object:

The sole thought which philosophy brings with it [*to the treatment of history*] *is the simple thought of Reason:* that Reason rules the world, and that world history has therefore been rational in its course. This conviction and insight is a *presupposition* in regard to history as such. (20/11)

Both Hegel and Schenker arrived at this thought on the basis of empirical observation which they regarded as faithful apprehension of their objects:

Only the observation of world history itself can show that history is rational in itself, that it has been the rational, necessary course of the World Spirit, the Spirit whose nature is indeed always one and the same but exposes its one nature in world existence. (22/12)

strongly reminiscent of §§341–52 of Hegel's *Elements of the Philosophy of Right*, a text to which Hegel refers at the outset of the Introduction to *Lectures on the Philosophy of History*. It is highly likely, though again unsubstantiated, that Schenker would have encountered Hegel's legal treatise at some point during his four years studying law at the University of Vienna (1884–88). To my knowledge, all that is known of the contents of Schenker's personal library is preserved in a bookseller's catalogue drawn up shortly after his death; this catalogue, however, is undoubtedly partial in that it lists only books having to do with music and drama (two copies of the catalogue are preserved in the JC 35 f.2).

[16] References are given to the version of Hegel's text printed in vol. 12 of the Suhrkamp edition of his works (1970) and to *Reason in History: A General Introduction to the Philosophy of History*, trans. Robert S. Hartman (Indianapolis, Ind.: Bobbs-Merrill, 1953), with English pagination following the German separated by a slash. All translations from Hegel are my own. An extremely useful resource for understanding Hegel, and one I have frequently consulted in working on Schenker's language, is Inwood's *A Hegel Dictionary*.

In history it is the Reason of God that is put into operation; in the musical artwork it is the Reason of Genius:

The question of what the *determination* of Reason is in itself, insofar as Reason is taken in its relation to the world, coincides with the question of the *ultimate purpose* [*Endzweck*] *of the world*. This expression implies that the ultimate purpose is to be realized or actualized. Two things, then, must be pondered: the content of this ultimate purpose (the determination itself, as such), and its actualization. (29/19)

The very determination of Music (*qua* Art) coincides with the question of its ultimate purpose, namely, the manifestation of the dynamic whole, its counterpart to Reason's manifestation as the moral whole, the State.

(2) Hegel begins his introduction to the philosophical method of history as follows:

It must be observed at the outset that our object, *world history*, goes on in the realm of Spirit. …Spirit and the course [*Verlauf*] of its development [*Entwicklung*] is the substance of history. (29/19)

Schenker recognized but did not pursue a philosophical history of music *per se*, though the few passages he devotes to the topic suggest that he held a teleological view similar to Hegel's.[17] Far more significant, from the standpoint of his interpretive practice, is his adaptation of Hegel's agenda to the task of elucidating the presented artwork in itself:

The particular form of Spirit not only passes away naturally in time but is sublated in the self-acting, self-conscious activity of self-consciousness. Because this sublation is the activity of thought, it is both preservation and transfiguration. While on one hand Spirit sublates reality, the subsistence of what it is, it also obtains the essence, the thought, the universal of what it *only was* [i.e., of its transient condition]. (102/94)

The particular form of Spirit in classically tonal music is the Idea of the Triad.[18] In itself, as a concept, the Triad is a system of relations. It becomes a for-itself only when its inner potentiality is unfolded into the explicit actuality of tones. The Ursatz is its first realization, its first concrete embodiment, and its first transfigura-

---

[17] See, for example, *Hl* 75–76/58–59, where Schenker characterizes the church modes as "an indispensable stage of development in the history of music" and states that "it is no offense against the Spirit of History" if one views them as experiments which, on the whole, proved beneficial for the "Development of our Art." See also *Mw* 1: 99/111 and *FS* 52–53/27. Novack's "Foreground, Middleground, and Background: Their Significance in the History of Tonality" is an exemplary implementation of Schenker's historical view.

[18] The Idea for Hegel is a "fully actualized concept"; see Inwood, *A Hegel Dictionary*, 124. In the opening of the second half of *Harmonielehre* (§115), Schenker states that "in the practical art the point is generally that of realizing [*realisieren*] the concept [*Begriff*] of the harmonies ([the concept] of a triad or seventh chord) by means of a living content," giving as an example the "abstract concept of a triad B–D–F♯" and its actualization in the opening of Chopin's B-minor Prélude (*Hl* 281/211; see also §§76, 78 and 81–82). Cherlin ("Hauptmann and Schenker," 131) makes a brief but compelling case for rejecting William Pastille's claim that Schenker's "idea" in *FS* is Neoplatonic (see Pastille's "Ursatz: The Musical Philosophy of Heinrich Schenker," Ph.D. diss., Cornell Unviersity, 1985).

tion; it is the initial stage in the course of a historical development; a development
that ends with the present, the presented artwork.

The manifestation of the triadic Idea in the Urlinie unfolds the triad through a
dialectical process. Take the potential Urlinie series F–E–D as the manifestation of a
D-minor triad. The effects of this succession of tones were discussed in chapter 1 in
the context of Fux's cantus firmus (bars 2–4 of ex. 1.2). Recall that, given the F, the
effect of the E is a negation of the F's presumed consonance, and the D is a reinstate-
ment of F's consonance.[19] But F's presence during the time of D is ideal; it is
sublated, both present and absent. Note, too, that the logical form of the second tone
is dependent, bound by its relation to the first:

> The nature of Spirit . . . Freedom is the sole truth of Spirit. . . . Matter has its substance
> outside itself; Spirit is *being-by-itself-alone*. And this, precisely, is Freedom, for when I am
> dependent, I relate myself to another, something that I am not; I cannot be without the
> other. I am free when I am by myself alone. (30/22–23)

As long as the triad remains in itself, as a concept independent of any particular
tones, it is indeterminate. It becomes determinate when it is actualized by a particular triadic configuration of tones that negates all other triads at the same time as it
determines one particular triad. The triadic configuration of tones in itself is also
indeterminate *qua* material entity. It becomes determinate only when set in contrast
to other things, namely, to tones which are not of that triad. Negation produces
determinacy. The process leads to an individuality whose identity is the process of its
determination. The contrapuntal conjunction of the Urlinie and bass arpeggiation
actualizes one triad and at the same time brings into being a series of three triads,
each of which can become the thesis of a new dialectical process. This is the life of
the musical Idea: its process of becoming for itself in the process of assertion, negation, and sublation.[20]

And now we are at the point most closely connected with Schenker's quotation
from Hegel, the manifestation of Spirit in history:

> An individual traverses various stages of formation as *one* and remains the same individual;
> so also a nation . . . .
> . . . The principles of the national spirits [progressing] in a necessary series of stages are
> themselves only moments of the one universal Spirit which in history elevates and closes
> itself through them into a self-comprehending *totality*.

Thus, in that we are dealing only with the Idea of Spirit and considering everything in
world history as nothing but its manifestation [*Erscheinung*], we are dealing, when we

---

[19] Westergaard's formulation of the effects of linear consecutions foregrounds these conceptual relations. If the
second of two tones is a step away from the first, it explicitly denies the conceptual status of the first tone. If the
second repeats the pitch of the first, it confirms the conceptual status of the first; and if the second is a skip away
from the first, it leaves the conceptual status of the first pitch in doubt. Westergaard, *An Introduction to Tonal
Theory*, 30.

[20] Hegel writes in the *Science of Logic*: "something is for itself in so far as it transcends otherness, its connection and
community with other, has repelled them and made abstraction from them. . . . [B]eing-for-self consists in
having so transcended limitation, its otherness, that it is, as this negation, the infinite *return* into itself" (158).

traverse the past (no matter how extensive it might be), only with something *present*. All is not lost to it in the past, for the Idea is ever present, the Spirit immortal. That is, Spirit is not past nor is it not yet now; rather, it is essentially now. This implies that the present form of Spirit comprehends all previous stages within itself. These, to be sure, have unfolded themselves independently and successively, but Spirit is what it has always been in itself, the distinction [among its stages] is only the development of this in–itself. The life of the present Spirit is a cycle of stages that subsist beside one another and only appear to be past from another point of view. The moments which Spirit seems to have left behind it, it still possesses in the depth of its present. (104–5/94–95)

This passage sheds light on what some have seen as a problematic aspect of temporality in Schenker's theory of organic connection: the tension between the chronological unfolding of the artwork's presentation and the conceptual chronology from the earlier background to the later foreground (there is also the real historical chronology of the work's genesis, but that is a matter that falls outside Schenker's theory).

The continuing presence of a past event – whether it be the consonant point of departure for a passing motion or the Ursatz's realization of the conceptually prior triadic concept – is absolutely central to Schenker's conception of music. The Hegelian dialectic of historical development models both the conceptual and the phenomenological chronologies of the musical artwork: background to foreground, beginning to end. Schenkerians have tended to erase the historical, conceptual development from background to foreground by replacing Schenker's "earlier" and "later" with the spatial terms "higher" and "lower." In an engaging study that is unusual for its close attention to Schenker's language, Kevin Korsyn argues for a strong Kantian influence on Schenker, with the express intent of revealing and restoring "the role of temporality in Schenker's thought." Likening the Ursatz to an atemporal Kantian ego, however, he necessarily concludes that the temporality of the Ursatz as origin cannot be accommodated within Kantian epistemology.[21] If, as I suggest, the Ursatz is viewed as the first stage in an artwork's conceptual history, the temporality Schenker attributes to it can be preserved. Korsyn also argues compellingly for an intimate connection between "synthesis" and time-consciousness, yet his Kantian account reveals little of the internal dynamics of that phenomenological synthesis. A Hegelian account fills that gap by showing that the "manifold" is the synthesis of a manifestly temporal succession in which the consonant point of departure is negated by the passing event and subsequently sublated in the consonant point of arrival.

(3) The means by which Spirit realizes itself in history is the individual, whom Hegel describes as follows:

The *first* [moment] is this: . . . what we have called principle, ultimate purpose, destiny, or the nature and concept of Spirit, is only something general, abstract. A principle, as well as a rule or law, is something internal which, as such – however true in itself – is not completely

---

[21] Kevin Korsyn, "Schenker and Kantian Epistemology," *Theoria* 3 (1988), 1–58; see p. 41 in particular.

actual. Purposes, rules, and so forth are in our thoughts, initially in our inner intentions but not yet to be found in actuality. What is in itself is a possibility, a potentiality, not yet emerged from within into existence. A *second* moment must be added for [i.e., in order to produce] actuality, and this is activation, realization; and its principle is the will, the activity of man in general. It is only through this activity that that concept as well as the determinations within it are realized or actualized. (36/27–28)

Responsibility for the actualization of the musical Idea rests with the individual artist, whose purposive will determines the manner of its actualization. Just as actualization of the Idea is assumed to be rational, so too it is assumed to be purposive and intentional.

(4) The ultimate form of Spirit's realization is the State. At first glance it will seem as if Schenker has to part company with Hegel when it comes to both the specific means and the ultimate form of Spirit's realization. For it is men and women, above all the world-historical individuals, who actualize Spirit in history and enter into the manifold forms of life that Hegel comprehended under the term "State." The world-historical individuals who actualize Spirit in music are master composers, but the individuals that enter into musical forms of life are mere tones. As Ian Bent writes, "Schenker's primary analytical voice . . . is one in which tones have functional obligations that they fulfill, tones that move in certain prototypical formations and fashion contrapuntal frameworks, are confronted with alternative possibilities the choices among which are determined by surrounding conditions, have constraints imposed on their motion, are threatened with dangers that they must avoid, and give rise sometimes, as they live out their lives, to new possibilities hitherto unforeseen. These tones, and their formations, are in a very real sense the 'characters' of Schenker's narrative."[22] The tone is an individual with rights and obligations, governed by law, moved by freedom, motivated to act, acting both rationally and rightly. When Schenker presents the "basis of the tonal system" in *Harmonielehre*, he does so in terms of drives and desires: the drive to procreate, to maintain a position of authority over the heads of one's descendant families, to enter into other relations, and to invest oneself in them with as much vitality as possible.[23] These basic drives and volitions, as well as many others (see Bent's list), are the means by which the artistic Spirit realizes itself in tones.

The Hegelian State is a synthesis of individual agents, whose forms of public intercourse are embodied in a constitution. Essential to a proper constitution is

the inner development of the rational (i.e., the political condition), the setting free of the successive moments of the concept; that the particular powers differentiate themselves, that each one complete itself, but at the same time freely cooperate for one purpose and be held together by it, i.e., that they form an organic whole. (65–66/60)

[22] Ian Bent, "History of Music Theory: Margin or Center?" *Theoria* 6 (1992), 13–14.
[23] These "biological moments" of tonal life are summarized in *Hl* 106–7/84–85. For Hegel's specific comments on the individual, the family, the family's representation through its head, the patriarchal condition and the subordination of individual interests to the interest of the whole, and so forth, see 60/55–56; for his comments on the constitutionally bound unity of institutions, see 61–62/57–58.

For Schenker, the general constitution of artistic music presented in his theoretical writings indeed sets free the moments of its concept: the particular powers of repetition, voice leading, and harmony are differentiated, each complete in itself and also cooperative in the formation of the whole. Schenker also recognized that such a constitution could assume a variety of specific forms and that these forms could change over time: the constitution of a minuet has provisions that one will not find in the constitution of a fugue; even the constitution of an individual artwork may have its own unique laws.[24]

IV

Having suggested several points that Schenker's interpretive practice has in common with the dialectical model of rational history developed by Hegel, I now want to return to the central theme of this chapter: the intention to produce an organic whole. In this section I will look at declarations Schenker made about a correlation between the structure of his interpretations and the composer's mind, beginning with one of his clearest statements about what constitutes the "organic" in tonal music:

The concept of sonata form, as theory has taught it until now, lacks exactly the essential characteristic, that of the organic, as only that characteristic is caused [bedingt] by the invention [Erfindung] of the parts out of the unity of the primary triad, that is, by the compositional execution [Auskomponierung] of the Urlinie and the bass arpeggiation. The capacity for such a perception [Durchempfindung] of the principal triad is a prerogative of genius that is enjoyed from Nature; the geniuses dissolve the principal triad into the melodic motion of the Urlinie and simultaneously into a few individual triads which they divide again and again. (Mw 2: 45–46)

The logically necessary condition or cause[25] of the organic is the invention of parts out of a single triadic entity, and the first realizations of that invention are the Urlinie and the bass arpeggiation. One wonders whether there was a connection in Schenker's mind between his neologism "Ursatz" and the common word "Vorsatz," meaning intention, design, project, or plan. Both have prefixes that indicate temporal priority. In chapter 1, I suggested that "Ursatz" borrows from the logician's use of "Satz" as "proposition" or "premise." The Ursatz, then, is both the "first" or "principal" premise (Grundsatz) in an argument for musical unity and the triadic realization that, for composers and noncomposers alike, is the point of departure for interpreting musical artworks.

---

[24] Dubiel (" 'When You are a Beethoven'," 306) draws attention to such a case in Schenker's essay on fugue in Mw 2, where Schenker mentions that Bach's C-minor fugue (WTC I) has a law that requires each statement of the principal subject to be followed by a descending scale in sixteenths. Schenker goes overboard (or, as Dubiel puts it, his thought "slips its mooring") here when he also identifies the fugue itself as the source of the law and not Bach: "the fugue itself gave birth to this law, not Bach – with the strength of a genius, he only recognized it and submitted to it" (Mw 2: 66; the translation is Dubiel's).

[25] Schenker's "bedingt" is ambiguous between logical and causal senses.

Schenker claims that the composer of genius both perceives the Idea and invents in accordance with it. "Auskomponierung" has the sense of realizing an entity by dissolving it into its components, as if it were an abbreviation for a longer expression on the order of "die Ausführung einer Idee (oder Einheit) aus seiner Komponenten" (execution of an Idea [or unit] from its components). ("Ausführung" is the term Schenker most often used for the notated score, the symbolic object that represents the "realization" in tones of all the effects intended by the composer.) To preserve the Hegelian flavor and at the same time the overtly musical sense of "composition," I will render "Auskomponierung" as "compositional execution." If "Erfindung" suggests a conscious design and the execution of that design, its etymological mate "Durchempfindung" suggests that the composer's "sense" of the Idea may be less than fully conscious, as if the composer dimly perceives the unifying force of the primary triad "through" (*Durch-*) the plethora of tones. This knife-edged poise between assigning compositional will to the conscious and to the unconscious is essential to Schenker's position. Schenker understood his "analyses of content" as demonstrations of the logical form of musical invention, cognitively operative but not necessarily open to consciousness.

I will have more to say later about Schenker's views on musical consciousness, but first I want to establish beyond doubt that Schenker did in fact view his method of representation as coincident with the structure of the composer's mind.

The view is spelled out unequivocally in the first yearbook of *Das Meisterwerk in der Musik*: "What matters to the composer is the compositional execution of a triadic sonority; this concern guides him from a background Ursatz, across the prolongations and diminutions, to a foreground setting. ... It is incumbent upon the reader or player, by contrast, to retrace [the composer's path], from foreground to background" (*Mw* 1: 188/104–5). In the examples that follow this remark, Schenker provisionally indulges the reader by representing content "with the contemplator and not the composer in mind, hence in the exceptional direction of foreground to background" (*Mw* 1: 188–89/105).[26] Later in the same essay he addresses the question of why, elsewhere in his writings, he proceeds from background to foreground. Doing so, he says, accords more with "modeling how it actually develops" ("den wirklichen Vorgang abbilden") even when doing so may not "underscore the demonstrative force" of his theory. I take this to mean that Schenker believed his interpretations would be more convincing if he offered them in a form that began with presented tonal configurations and deduced from them the most general features, but he believed this procedure would misrepresent the Spirit of musical technique, which must begin with the Idea of the triad and the whole. He explicitly states that what motivated his decision was the desire to "pull the paths of the phantasy striding through the transformations back into the light," presumably out

---

[26] Despite the spatial reorientation, the letter names that identify the layers in these examples still start with the most background layer and move toward the foreground. The contrast between Schenker's spatial reorientation and a truly reductive interpretation is explored by Allan Keiler in "On Some Properties of Schenker's Pitch Derivations," *MP* 1 (2) (1983–84), 201–5.

of the obscurity into which the editors and theorists of his day had plunged them (*Mw* 1: 192/107).[27]

The object of Schenker's representations, then, is not the material substance of the artwork but rather its intellectual property, the working of the productive musical mind (*Geist*), whose purest and richest manifestations are the Germanic geniuses.

The interconnection of generative representation, inference of composerly actions and intentions, and a Hegelian view of the artwork as the rational realization of an Idea is made explicit for the first time in his commentary on Beethoven's Piano Sonata op. 101. It is no coincidence, I suggest, that this is also the text in which Schenker first introduced the idea of the Urlinie and gave his first and most explicit defense of this new feature of his interpretive practice:

A god and yet also a servant of the tones – Beethoven metes out to each individual tone the measure of justice to which it is due. He places them all in the service of one Idea [*Idee*], creates the higher and lower orders necessary for its realization [*Ausführung*] . . . and so achieves the euphony of an organic whole [*Ganzen*]. (*LfS101* 59²85–86)

Here is the rational agent of the sonata's historical development, Beethoven, ordering the activities of a just state of rational subjects.

Despite announcing the idea of the Urlinie in his introductory remarks, Schenker interprets none of the sonata's three movements in terms of such a line. The term appears in the main body of the text only in connection with a depiction of the first eight bars of the second movement. From the fact that he addresses the possible objection that all Urlinien look alike and thus fail to capture the individuality of the musical artwork, and from the paucity of Urlinien in this text, I surmise that he had already worked out some of the analyses that would start to appear a few months later in *Der Tonwille* and that his remarks were aimed at forestalling objections that were sure to arise.

The longest span in op. 101 that Schenker interprets in terms of a fluid melodic line (i.e., a line moving stepwise with a balance of rising and falling motions) is the Adagio, which, together with a quotation of the first movement's opening phrase, forms the introductory section of the third movement. This is also the first time he presents a multi-layered derivation of tonal content and effects. And while it is true that the Adagio is not fully independent in the sense of generating from a closed Ursatz formation, Schenker nevertheless manages to interpret it as the compositional execution of a single triad, namely, a preparatory dominant. The argumenta-

---

[27] Schenker's views on lightness and darkness and the culpability of editors are articulated earlier in the yearbook, p. 43/20 (see also *FS* 7/158). Schenker actually claims that it makes no difference which way the graphs are presented, but in view of the fact that the presented configuration of tones typically underdetermines his interpretation (this fact being one source of well-formed alternative readings of the same piece), his choice of direction is best suited to the analytical process: choose a background and see how it can be diminuted and transformed into the presented configuration.

tion he provides for this interpretation deserves closer examination, for it is more or less tacitly assumed in all later interpretations of this type, including those based upon an Ursatz configuration.

Though the illustration of the Adagio's content is a striking and important development in Schenker's thought, it would be misleading to say that somehow Schenker invented the multi-layer representation *ex nihilo* sometime between the publication of the commentary on op. 111 in 1915 and that on op. 101 in 1921. Even in the first decade of the century Schenker occasionally represented passages in terms of simpler arrangements (often fundamental bass lines in the earliest writings); the first three commentaries on Beethoven's last sonatas (published in 1913, 1914, and 1915) have similar illustrations, covering progressively longer spans. Even in his commentary on op. 101, there is as yet no such depiction covering the span of an entire movement. The first such representations are found later that year in the first volume of *Der Tonwille*. And as I have pointed out on several occasions now, the commitment to a view of the whole, if not a means for representing it and thereby demonstrating it, was present from the outset.[28] The particular content of the Ur-Ideen – Urlinie and Ursatz – changed as Schenker gradually purged them of lingering traits of individuality. What remained constant in the Urlinie was that the content of the idea is the simplest upper voice in terms of which Schenker interprets the entirety of a span. At first, these lines reflected the individual content of the musical artwork; from the start the Urlinie was constituted primarily, if not exclusively, of stepwise motion, for the step is the hallmark of the melodic, "the quality of fluent song" (*Kp1* 116/83 and 133–38/94–99). The ebb and flow of the individual work was reflected in the rising and falling Züge of the Urlinie (*LfS101* 22²8). By the time the second yearbook of *Das Meisterwerk in der Musik* appeared in 1926, the Urlinie was a single descending Zug. It is safe to say, I think, that what began as an attempt to represent the most basic feature (Zug) of the individual artwork ended up as a representation of the most basic feature (Urlinie-Zug) of classical tonality. There has been some movement in recent years to restore individualizing features to the Ursatz. The attempts seem to me to arise from a desire to capture the basic trait of a subset of classically tonal works, a desire that is at odds with both Schenker's first and final formulations of the concept. Obviously, there are classes of work that share a particular deep structure, but I can see no compelling reason why the individuation of such a class need be theorized as a special class of background structures rather than, say, a class of first middlegrounds. This is not to say that I regard Schenker's later formulation as superior to his first attempts at interpreting overarching lines and counterpoints; many of his Ursatz descriptions from the early 1920s portray vividly in one layer representations (particularly parallelisms) that would be distributed

---

[28] A cursory history of the background idea, told from the standpoint of "melodic fluency," can be found in William Pastille, "The Development of the *Ursatz* in Schenker's Published Works," in *Trends in Schenkerian Research*, ed. Allen Cadwallader (New York: Schirmer Books, 1990), 71–85.

across several layers of interpretation in later analyses (for example, the Stufenrund motive in the Ursatz for Chopin's Etude in E♭ minor, op. 10, no. 6, in *Mw* 1: 148/82 fig. 1).[29]

The picture of the Adagio (see ex. 2.4 below) is said to represent "the paths taken by Beethoven's imagination" (*LfS101* 43²52). Schenker was well aware that his claim to have represented the musical mind of a master such as Beethoven would not go unchallenged. How could anyone know what Beethoven intended? Schenker replies to this hypothetical objection by appealing to the common practice of interpreting human action as intentional. So immediately after presenting a figure showing "the paths taken by Beethoven's phantasy," and before giving a detailed interpretation of the figure, Schenker addresses the question: did Beethoven "know" about the paths represented in the figure? The hypothetical question is framed in terms of articulated knowledge (*Wissen*) and Schenker's answer comes in terms of intuitive know-how:

Yes. As darkness and brightness are opposites of one another, so also the bright and the dull man. While the dull man does not also have the knowledge [*Wissen*] that belongs only to the bright man, and is therefore not enlightened in the same measure as he, what use is it to him to want to force entry into this puzzle's solution through the portal of a common word and concept like this word "knowledge?" If the dull person is going to speak of "knowledge," then a new word must be coined for the bright person just in order to differentiate him; that's how little the word "knowledge" is common to the two. But I suppose the dull person could get a rough idea of the other's knowledge if he examines his own experience in areas in which he himself is also bright. And so let him ask himself just what would happen in himself if he were to speak or write: does he or does he not always have a "knowledge" of the words that he puts together into sentences? Surely – for how could it be otherwise – the words bore in themselves the conscious purpose and showed this or that form? And he must likewise admit that the knowledge of the spoken or written words is constantly present in him, as difficult as it might be for him to conceive how logic readies that knowledge to keep step with the running words. And now let him transfer this experience to the knowledge of tones in a genius like Beethoven and he will at least sense that which, [because] condemned to dullness in this very area, he will obviously never quite grasp. (*LfS101* 44²53)

Schenker's interpretation is, in part, an exercise in making that very transfer, as he explicates the logic of musical language that allows one to "keep step" with the tones and with Beethoven's mind. Examining the analysis in detail will bring out several important connections between the structure of language and tonal music and give a fuller picture of what Schenker claimed for the rationality of his cognitive theory.

Beethoven's Idea for the Adagio is a repetition of the motivic idea that he used to initiate the first movement: a "compositional execution of the dominant." The form which that execution takes is a pair of motions between tones of the dominant: one

---

[29] See David Neumeyer, "The Three-Part *Ursatz*," *ITO* 10 (1/2) (1987), 3–29; and John Benoit, "The Composite Fundamental Structure and its Manifestation in Three Songs by Schubert" (paper presented at the annual meeting of Music Theory Midwest, Iowa City, Iowa, April 1995).

rising, the other falling. In the first movement, only the first of these is traversed as a Zug, while in the Adagio both intervals are crossed by step. What we learned about the Zug in chapter 1 can be adapted to include the composing artist: the Zug is the embodiment of an intention to reach a determinate goal in the most direct manner possible. Here is Schenker's description of the Adagio's actualization of the Idea:

> . . . the picture of the prime series of tones (*Ton-Urreihe*); it is the principal motive changed into the minor mode, rising from g$\sharp^1$ to d^2 and falling from d^2 to b^1. From the very beginning (*Urbeginn*) it stands before the master's imagination, tone by tone, mysteriously beheld. But long – oh, how long! – it takes for one tone to reach another! A virtual image of longing. (*LfS101* 44^{2}53)

The precise derivation of the motivic configuration is slightly different in the two movements: given Schenker's interpretation of the first movement's principal motive (see ex. 2.1), the initial Zug arises as an unfolding that, in effect, concatenates two Züge, one from g$\sharp^1$ to b^1 and the other from b^1 to d^2. In the Adagio, by contrast, the fifth-Zug could be generated in a single operation (see ex. 2.4). In both cases, I think, the d^2 would arise in an antecedent configuration as a passing tone coming from e^2; notice that e^2 is expressed (sublated) as an appoggiatura in bar 2 of the first movement and is similarly introduced in level *b* of Schenker's fig. 38.

Before going further into the details of Schenker's interpretation of the Adagio, it will be helpful to have, for the sake of comparison, a reconstruction of his interpretation of the first movement's opening bars and a brief discussion of common ways in which Schenker abbreviated his representations. The content of the first movement's principal motives are given in examples 2.1 and 2.2 as they are presented in bars 1–4, along with Schenker's interpretive illustrations. Example 2.3 spells out the details of Schenker's interpretive claims. In the first level I have shown the disposition of the dominant sonority that is the object of elaboration; Schenker indicates this both with the word "Dominante" in his text and with the indication "V——"

Ex. 2.1.   (*a*) Beethoven, Piano Sonata op. 101, I, bars 1–2; (*b*) *LfS101* fig. 1

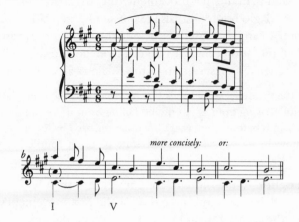

Ex. 2.2. (*a*) Beethoven, Piano Sonata op. 101, I, bars 3–4; (*b*) *LfS101* fig. 2

Ex. 2.3

Ex. 2.3. *continued*

beneath fig. 1 (see ex. 2.1). The next stage of the idea's development should be represented, I think, as a descending fourth-Zug within the sustained dominant. I take Schenker's placement of "7" beneath bar 2 in fig. 1 to indicate the onset of that scale degree; this inference is also in agreement with Schenker's claim that the seventh arises either in passing or as a suspension (*FS* 104–5/63). The continuation from the seventh through c♯² and b¹ in dotted halves is explicitly stated by Schenker in fig. 2 (see ex. 2.2); likewise, the outer voices of the third level in my example are explicit in Schenker's figs. 1 and 2. The two parallel third-Züge arise as passing motions within a second-species setting. Schenker is silent about the effect of the e² in bar 3, whether perhaps it should be understood as a manifestation of an implicit tone in the contextual harmony or as a substitute for the e² elided from the beginning of the fourth-Zug. The bass line of bars 3–4 arises, I surmise, as a Zug between the fifth and octave of the dominant harmony. In *d*, I infer from the fact that Schenker places an a¹ in parentheses beneath a² in his fig. 2, that a² arises as a transfer of a tone from an inner voice, a connection that is made palpable by the portamento-type connection from the last eighth of bar 2 (see g). The outer voices in e are taken from Schenker's figs. 1 and 2. The brackets are my own addition, meant to indicate that the faster motion arises from an unfolding and concatenation of the two third-Züge shown in c; a fourth-Zug connects a^2 and e^2.

The connections between e and the actual presentation are all of my own invention. In f I add passing motions in an inner voice that accompany the upper line first in thirds and then in tenths; I also add the Zug in contrary motion in a lower inner voice. Between f and g I have omitted a stage in which the e^2 of bar 3 is suspended through the fourth eighth note of bar 4; notice that the tenor's $c\sharp^1$, derived in f as a follower of the upper voice, adheres to that rhythmic formation. The multiple delays in bars 3–4 that have now postponed the arrival of b^2 to the very last eighth note are given further support by the silence that delays the onset of $c\sharp$ in the exposed tenor voice. The upper line is further elaborated by the parallel insertion of appoggiaturas on the downbeats of bars 2 and 4; the delaying effect of the appoggiatura in bar 2 is supported by a suspension in the alto voice. Finally, the activation of the inner voice by means of arpeggiations and rearticulations in h produces a steady eighth–note pulse that is interrupted only at the articulation between the two segments in bar 2.

This is a virtually exhaustive reconstruction of how Schenker would derive the tonal content of bars 1–4. And despite the number of derivational stages, I still employed several abbreviations. In addition to the gap already mentioned between f and g, for example, there should be a stage intervening between a and b that shows the unfolding of the tonal space filled by the fourth-Zug. In keeping with Schenker's preference for rhythmically balanced lines, the two tones of that unfolded interval should be represented as two dotted whole notes; the fallout of that interpretation is an even more remarkably complex delay of b^2 from the downbeat of bar 3 all the way to the end of bar 3.

Schenker employs a number of standard abbreviations in his interpretive practice. He typically omits the unfolding of an interval if the next stage is the execution of a passing motion through that interval (though other considerations, such as parallelisms, may induce him to represent the unfolding as such). Similarly, he routinely omits rearticulations when they are followed by the insertion of a neighboring tone.[30] Another type of abbreviation arises when a subsidiary line is derived at the interval of a fifth or octave, thereby producing consecutive fifths and octaves; Schenker tends to avoid representing the fifths or octaves without at the same time representing the intervals that mitigate the effect of the consecutives; this is especially true of cases where a series of consecutive fifths or octaves is at issue. Yet another type of abbreviation one encounters in his writings is associated with common figured-bass patterns.[31] These often involve the conflation of several deriva-

---

[30] On the conceptual dependency of neighboring on rearticulation, see Westergaard, *An Introduction to Tonal Theory*, 35–36.

[31] I am grateful to Stephen Peles for drawing my attention to this type of abbreviation.

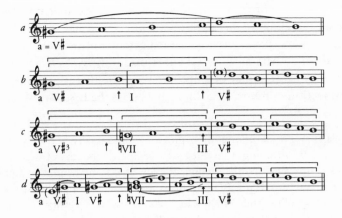

Ex. 2.4. *LfS101* fig. 38, *a–d*

tional stages into one. One such figure frequently used by Schenker is the neighboring 3–4–4–3, sometimes accompanied by 5–6–7–8. A conceptual reconstruction of the neighboring figure would involve the rearticulation of a single 3 into two tones of equal duration, followed by the insertion of a neighboring 4 within the time span of the first, and then, finally, the suspension of the neighboring 4 into the time span of the second 3.

The reason for adopting such abbreviations is quite simply stated: economy. The most detailed reconstruction among Schenker's interpretations is that provided for the subject of Bach's Fugue in C minor (*WTC* I); this reconstruction consists of a six-layer figure and two pages of copious commentary and yet still makes use of numerous abbreviations (*Mw* 2: 60–63).[32] If Schenker were to reconstruct the conceptual derivation of an entire symphony with anything like the same rigor, no publisher would accept the manuscript and no reader would indulge the author. Economization also purchased the opportunity to focus on individualized traits of the derivation; for Schenker, this usually meant focusing on parallelisms that arise in the course of development, both within and between stages. Nevertheless, economy of representation should not mask the fact that it is the full content of the conceptual reconstruction that Schenker attributes to the working of the composer's mind.

The relation between conceptual reconstruction and the composer's mind is, as I said, an explicit theme in his interpretation of op. 101's Adagio, so it is to that account that I now return. The first part of Schenker's illustration is reproduced in example 2.4. The transformation from *a* to *b* is similar to one we encountered in Mozart's G-minor Symphony in chapter 1, where the tonal content of a Zug was increased through repetition of one or more passing tones. The effect is similar to

---

[32] This interpretation is significant for the fact that Schenker implicitly acknowledges the underdetermination of such analysis by providing two equally plausible possibilities for the first two stages he depicts. The details of the analysis are discussed by Maury Yeston in *The Stratification of Musical Rhythm* (New Haven, Conn.: Yale University Press, 1976), 59–64.

that of an appositional phrase in a sentence; such a phrase adds no new functional content, instead shedding further light on a content that has already been put into play, while at the same time delaying the expected continuation of the sentence's content. This is surely part of what Schenker meant in *Der freie Satz* when he said that "there is but one grammar of Züge, the very one that is presented here in the theory of connection in music" (*FS* 22/160). Here is the first part of his description of level *b*:

The master's clairvoyance of diminution begins the work initially (see *b*) by dividing up the tones of the rising direction into two three-tone segments, the first of which has to supply the tone b^1 as its last event, and the second, c^2. Now if, on one hand, this division effects a deferral of the arrival of c^2 – precisely in this is expressed strikingly what I wanted to say above with the image of longing – then it logically necessitates [*bedingt*], on the other hand, a similar division for the falling direction as well, lest the weight be shifted in favor of the rising direction. (Whoever is familiar with the art of language will recognize such a balancing technique as an essentially related trait [*Zug*].) (*LfS101* 44²53–54)

He goes on to state that, because of the smaller number of tones in the descending third-Zug, the operation of division leads to a repetition rather than an expansion of the Zug; the e^2 is interpolated.

In the description of the next stage, Schenker attributes to Beethoven the ability to sense the implications of a formulation and to fashion a more elaborate setting that makes those implications explicit:

Now the harmonic feeling [of Beethoven] stood before the task of averting the monotony of the chords (Stufen) as they are compositionally realized in the first two segments as if automatically. Now if, as here, b^1 one time precedes c^2, then that quite obviously suggests using the occasion of this succession as a leading tone step and interpreting c^2 in the sense of the C chord, as a III Stufe of the main key. Of course, this chord then presupposes that the earlier $g\sharp^1$ will somehow be displaced by a g^1. Now if, as is to be seen in *c*, this happens by means of interpolating g^1 before a^1, then by that means is also obtained a more forceful fourth-progression g^1–c^2, and in the sense of VII–III besides, [two] things that together promote the expression of the tonality. (*LfS101* 44²54)

In describing the next stage, Schenker imputes to Beethoven the desire to avoid exact repetition by the admixture of contrast, achieved here through the use of synonymy: for the series of tones that would realize VII and exactly parallel a prior elaboration, namely, g^1–a^1–b^1, Beethoven substitutes a series that elaborates another interval in the same harmony in the same way, namely, b^1–c^2–d^2:

The [master's] diminution is able to increase the material obtained in this way even more richly if it keeps on refracting as before. The result is shown in *d*, where one now also sees how much farther apart the endpoints of the first and second segments, b^1 and c^2, are thereby pulled from one another than in *c*. If e^1 is inserted [by Beethoven] at the beginning, then it happens in order to achieve a three-tone quality, and if diminuting in exactly the same manner as in the first segment is avoided in the second – [fig. 39] – and if in place of that a series of tones lying a third higher is given, then only an exact repetition of the same series of tones shall be avoided. (*LfS101* 44–45²54)

In describing the next stage of the Adagio's development, Schenker draws upon a parallel with rhetorical rhythms:

Yet one more step and the phantasy is already at the point of conversion into actuality, which in art obviously never ceases to remain a mirror-image of that primal world of tone [*Ur-Tonwelt*]: the phantasy of the master now binds itself voluntarily – and this, too, is again a trait [*Zug*] familiar to the connoisseurs of language – to the fetter of introducing every one of the initial subsegments e¹–a¹, b¹–d², and e²–b¹ in a more protracted rhythm than the second ones, thus the first step as pensive and the second as more active, the preparation more hesitating, as it were, and the completion more pressing. This mysterious rhythm of events is now genuinely the decisive pulse of our piece. (*LfS101* 45²54–55)

After this point, the analogy with language drops away as Schenker describes in more detail the derivations that lead from *d* to the presented configuration of tones.

In *Der freie Satz*, Schenker again tackles the question of whether composers knew what he imputes to them, and again he begins by attributing to the artist a particular form of intuitive know-how, the content of which is described by his theory of organic connection:

With their compositions the masters have shown a know-how [*Können*] that attests, operating in the work as a fore- and after-knowledge [*Wissen*], to a clear overall knowledge of the laws of art which relieved them of [having to provide] any self-commentary: for isn't an artistic deed, like any deed whatsoever, given with a preview of its internal connections?! From this it follows that whenever and wherever the reader of this text finds himself having to confess that there is an agreement between a composition and what I have said about it, he is then consequently obliged to assume [that there was] also in the masters the keenest knowledge [*Wissen*] of the given connections! (*FS* 2–3/xxii)

He also draws on the analogy with knowing a language:

Any sort of connection in the foreground is concealed, as it were, behind the tones, as it is in language behind the words. (*FS* 21/6)

And he presents his theory as an articulation of that intuited grammar:

My theory for the first time offers an actual *theory of tone-language,* similar to the theory of language taught in the schools. (*FS* 28/9)

And later in the same work he fills in the outlines of this analogy by comparing the composer's musical disposition to the language-user's intuitive knowledge of semantics and syntax:

The voice-leading compulsion [*Zwang*] is what brings into music the same flow as language shows in the constant readiness for thoughts and words. In language the flow rests on the fact that the speaker from the outset knows and fashions what he has to say, for were he to think only while speaking, only stammering would result. In music, however, there are also well-gifted men, creative as well as re-creative, who are still far from a similar readiness. An actual musical flow like that found in language is found only in the work of the genius.

What contributes all tone-readiness is solely and exclusively the Ursatz and its later transformations.

. . . Tone-readiness presupposes the whole. (*FS* 63–64/35)

At the same time, Schenker also draws a clear limit to what his theory is able to say about the psychology of composition:

[The picture of the Ursatz forms] in no way raises the issue of expressing anything definite about the chronology of creation; it presents only the *strictly logical determinacy in the connection* of simpler and more complicated series of tones, namely, the connection not only in the direction of simple to complex but also in the inverted direction of complex back to simple. It is an inviolable law that everything complex or differentiated comes from something simple that is anchored in consciousness or intuition [*Ahnung*]. . . . Only in this alone, in the layers of transformation ever present in the intuition, present in being directed thither toward the foreground and vice versa, only in this lies the secret of balance in music: this intuition always accompanies the composer, otherwise every foreground would degenerate into chaos.

If creation may set off from anywhere, from this or that layer of voice leading, from this or that series of tones – conception remains, thank God, a miracle inaccessible to metaphysics – yet all growth, every continuation, deviation, improvement, is consummated always under the total control of the Ursatz and its transformations, through the constant rapport of back-, middle- and foreground. The Ursatz is always present in creation in this way; it accompanies all the transformations in the middle- and foreground, as a guardian angel accompanies children.

What eludes the graphic representation of the logical connections from back- to foreground and vice versa, simply because it is withheld from any graphic representation whatsoever, is therefore this:

The Ursatz remains ever creative; it is always and everywhere present and active. The simultaneity in the intuition of the artist, however, is certainly no greater miracle than, say, the miracle of experiencing a moment that permits, despite its being the smallest space of time, acquiring a similar feeling of past, present, and future. (*FS* 41–42/18)

V

Schenker's view of compositional psychology is indebted not only to Hegel's Idea of rational Spirit in history but also to a musical source, C. P. E. Bach's *Versuch über die wahre Art das Clavier zu spielen*.[33] Like Bach, Schenker hoped that by recording and articulating the spiritual content of a tradition, he might preserve a dying practice of music-making (see *FS* 2/xxii).[34] Schenker's writings can be viewed as manifesta-

---

[33] Facsimile reprint of the first edition, ed. Lothar Hoffmann-Erbrecht (Leipzig: Breitkopf and Härtel, 1957). Translated as *Essay on the True Art of Playing Keyboard Instruments*, trans. and ed. William J. Mitchell (New York: Norton, 1949). In subsequent references English pagination follows German, separated by a slash.

[34] On this aspect of Schenker's rhetoric, see chapter 4 and my "Schenker's Senses of Concealment," *Theoria* 6 (1992), 97–133.

tions of a survival instinct: preserve your thought-ways and the thought-ways imputed to those you revere (whom you feel are necessary to your survival) by giving others the means and the incentive to cultivate the same thought-ways. Among Schenker's failings was the fact that he often provided a disincentive by making readers feel as if they were not worthy of or able to cultivate those thought-ways. As his 1895 sketch of motivations for music-making suggests, Schenker's intention was nothing less than to probe the compositional mind of eighteenth- and nineteenth-century Germanic composers who, to his way of thinking, composed the most complex absolute musical artworks ever encountered. A decade later, in *Harmonielehre*, he would describe his work as an attempt "to interpret the instinct of artists" (*Hl* 33/21). He would strive, in other words, to bring the working knowledge of composers and performers to the light of reflective knowledge. Doing so would be the chief means for achieving his ultimate goal of reforming the poor artistic instincts of his contemporaries.

The relevant part of Bach's view of composition is expressed in the culmination of the treatise, in the concluding chapter on the "free fantasia," a chapter to which Schenker devoted an exegetical essay in the first yearbook of *Das Meisterwerk*, under the title "Die Kunst der Improvisation" ("The Art of Improvisation," 11–40/2–19). We have already uncovered several of the ideas Schenker adopted from Bach. One is that the principal idea of musical invention is the execution of a plan. In the final section of his chapter, Bach provides an illustration: the score of a free fantasia and a figured-bass representation of it. The latter he calls its "skeleton" (*Gerippe*); the score is its "realization" (*Ausführung*) (340/441–42). It is essential to the fantasia, says Bach, that it begin and end in the same key and that it dwell for some time in that key at the beginning and at the end so that "the main key will be well-imprinted upon the [listener's] memory" (327/431). In between it may wander from key to key; the longer the fantasia, the more far-flung the modulations can be. The basic intent, then, is clear: actualize a plan through diminution of a triad.

In §§1–2 Bach writes that whereas many can learn recipes for constructing a free, unmeasured fantasia, a "knowledge of the compass of composition" is required for the "writing of a measured piece or extemporaneous invention" (325–26/430). Schenker, likewise, thought the pinnacle of development for the compositional mind was the achievement of an "improvisatory phantasy" or "extempore imagination" (*Stegreif-Fantasie*). The mindset that would allow one to do that without reflective deliberation must be a working knowledge of tonal laws (what effects tones must produce) so thoroughly assimilated as to be virtually instinctual.[35] Schenker points to this kind of unconscious know-how with an analogy: "Bach's knowledge [*Wissen*] is comparable, to cite an example from daily life, to the knowledge of a man who in every situation hits upon what is correct without spending hours in soliloquy examining the philosophical argumentation of a Spinoza or Kant, or even the

[35] For a thorough study of this idea as it relates to improvisatory compositions, see John Rink, "Schenker and Improvisation," *JMT* 37 (1) (1993), 1–13.

stipulations of the penal code in its application to the given case" (*Mw* 2: 92). The laws and principles captured in the words and concepts of his theory are at work, as Schenker says of Beethoven, "behind his consciousness" (*Hl* 77/60).

Schenker celebrates the instinctual, extemporaneous nature of the musical mind principally in the essay "Vom Organischen der Sonatenform" ("Of the Organic in Sonata Form"), where his programmatic statement – "The whole must be invented extemporaneously" – incorporates a direct quotation from §1 of Bach's chapter on the free fantasia. Schenker introduces this statement after a passage I quoted in part at the start of section IV; the passage is worth quoting in its entirety because of the way it weaves together the themes of extemporaneous improvisation and the specific arrangement that produces the effect of a whole and of unity:

The concept of sonata form, as theory has taught it until now, lacks exactly the essential characteristic, that of the organic, as only that characteristic is caused by the invention of the parts out of the unity of the primary triad, that is, by the compositional execution of the Urlinie and the bass arpeggiation. The capacity for such a perception of the principal triad is a prerogative of genius that is enjoyed from Nature; the geniuses dissolve the principal triad into the melodic motion of the Urlinie and simultaneously into a few individual triads which they divide again and again. Such a perception cannot be cultivated in an artificial way, which is to say that only extemporaneous invention vouchsafes the unity of compositional execution. So, then, in order to express the general more correctly, [something] must still be added to the concept of sonata form: *the whole must be invented extempore*, if it is not to be just a blurring of individual parts and motives in the sense of a schema. (*Mw* 2: 45–46)[36]

In the same essay Schenker states that Haydn

knew no formal theory as we know it; the new life that he begets, he creates from the life of his mind [*Geistes*]. The Urlinie and bass arpeggiation ruled him with the power of a natural drive and from them he also drew his ingenious tensive power [*Spannkraft*] for getting mastery of the whole as a unity. (*Mw* 2: 46–47)

He writes, too, that we can imagine "the picture of a mind of genius [*Genie-Geist*] ... mysteriously creating out of the background of an Ursatz" (*Mw* 2: 52).

In these accounts Schenker suggests that the genius was not in full control of his compositional faculty but, rather, was possessed or "ruled" by Spirit. And that calls to mind the fact that the term "genius" has its origin in ancient Roman folklore, where it referred to the spirit of a particular place or locale. On several occasions Schenker writes of Beethoven as if he were possessed by such a genius. The first occasion is in *Harmonielehre*, where Schenker describes Beethoven's intention to write the "Heiliger Dankgesang" of the String Quartet op. 132 in the Lydian mode:

It is often peculiar to great talents and genius that they go the right way, like sleepwalkers, even when they are prevented from hearkening to their instinct by one thing or another, or, here, even by fully intending something false. It is as if composing mysteriously behind their

---

[36] Hans Wolf recorded similar statements from his lessons with Schenker; see "Schenkers Persönlichkeit in Unterricht," *Der Dreiklang* 7 (1937), 176–84 (reprint, Hildesheim: Georg Olms, 1989).

consciousness and in their names there is the far higher power of a Truth, a Nature for whom it matters not at all whether the fortunate artist himself desired the right thing or not. For if it were to go entirely in accordance with the consciousness of the artist and his intention, how often would his works turn out poorly – if by good fortune that mysterious power did not order everything itself for the best...

... [Beethoven] had no inkling how, behind his back, precisely that higher force of Nature led his pen, so that, while he himself believed he was writing in the Lydian mode, and indeed even simply because he so desired, the piece nevertheless went on in F major on its own. Is that not wondrously strange? And yet it is so. (*Hl* 76–77/60–61)

As Ruth Solie suggests, Jean Paul Richter's *Vorschule der Aesthetik* (1804) is a likely source of Schenker's idea that the genius is not quite in control of itself.[37] Solie quotes the following passage from Jean Paul: "The genius is in more than one sense a sleepwalker; in his clear dream he is capable of more than when he is awake, and in darkness he climbs every height of reality; but when the dreamy world robs him, he tumbles into the real world" (my translation). This passage, incidentally, is from a footnote appended to Jean Paul's discussion of the penultimate level of artist, which he describes as "the feminine, conceiving, or *passive genius*, as it were the spirits who write in poetic prose." In "The *Geist* of Musical Technique" Schenker speaks of the composer's imagination in feminine terms, as that which gives birth (*hervorbringen*) to melody and motive, and here it is the passive Beethoven who allows his pen to be guided by a higher force.[38]

A few years later, when writing of Beethoven's Piano Sonata op. 110, Schenker furnishes an illustration showing a "hidden line" that "expresses, as it were, the ultimate sense of the content" of bars 3–7 of the third movement's introduction and Recitativo. Having traced the line through these apparently erratic bars, he voices his wonder and pauses with an unanswered question:

How delicate the threads on which the master's inspiration glides, and yet what miraculous certainty of path! Did the Creator's blessing rule over him when, like a sleepwalker, he strode upon such paths as were perhaps hidden even from him, or did he know this path? (*LfS110* 51²62)

That Schenker is not now forthcoming with an answer may perhaps portend a shift away from belief in a hypernatural power toward the decisive affirmation of Beethoven's knowledge given in his commentary on Beethoven's op. 101: if in 1906 he is certain that Beethoven was not fully aware of all that he did, in 1915 he is unsure, and in 1921 he is certain that Beethoven did, in one sense, know what he was doing. But we should not too hastily accept this conclusion, for in the very same essay of 1915 he affirms Beethoven's knowledge of a hidden path, and in 1926, in the essay on sonata form, he seems to fall back into his original position. Moreover, the original speculation in *Harmonielehre* is introduced in the subjunctive ("as if"),

---

[37] "The Living Work: Organicism and Musical Analysis," *NCM* 4 (1980), 155.

[38] For a brief and informative treatment of Jean Paul's distinctions, see Gisela Wilkending, *Jean Pauls Sprachauffassung in ihrem Verhältnis zu seiner Aesthetik* (Marpurg: N. G. Elwert, 1968), 44–47.

causing me to doubt further whether Schenker actually believed his speculation about the "mysterious power" of Nature. In fact, I think it likely that what he indicated in such ways of speaking was his belief that there was no imaginable way to cultivate the skill of a composer like Beethoven. These passages cast more light on Schenker's personal psychology than on Beethoven's, for it is plausible, I think, to read them as Schenker's way of coping, on one hand, with the belief that he, like no other before him, had probed the *Geist* of genius and, on the other, with a realization that even he could not turn that reflective knowledge into the intuitive know-how required for artful composing.

Schenker's vacillation may also be his way of pointing to the ultimate undecidability of whether his rational reconstructions coincide with the actual intentions of the composers. At best they are useful fictions. An artwork is interpretable as an artifact contrived to fulfill a host of sophisticated intentions. Interpretation rests on imputation of intent. But the maker may well have had no such intentions. As Daniel Dennett points out, there is nothing terribly unusual in this: "Is there anything self-contradictory in the reflection that a certain move one has just made . . . is actually cleverer than one at first realized?" "We often do discover what we think and what we mean by reflecting on what we find ourselves saying – and not correcting. So we are, at least on those occasions, in the same boat as our external critics and interpreters, encountering a bit of text and putting the best reading on it that we can find."[39]

VI

When Schenker proclaimed the primacy of content and announced his plan to elucidate the content of Beethoven's Ninth Symphony in all its individuality, he set out to prove a sweeping claim about that content, namely, that the symphony had to have this content and no other:

Analysis of the *content* gave me the desired opportunity to exhibit those tonal necessities that have remained hidden until now, necessities that caused the tonal content to arise in just this way and not otherwise. As evidence [for this claim], it was thus necessary to prove not only the individuality of that content as specifically that of the Ninth Symphony but also, to a still higher degree, the primary character of such content in general.

In the beginning was content! (*NS* vi–vii/4)

The principal target of this declaration, as I said in the Introduction, was Wagner. Schenker wanted to counter Wagner's proposed revisions of the Ninth's tonal content, revisions that were premised on the claim that Beethoven frequently did not fully accomplish what he set out to do, in short, that realization sometimes fell short of intention. Schenker prefers to err on the side of charity: if you sense a discrepancy between intention and realization in an artwork by a master of Beethoven's rank,

---

[39] Daniel Dennett, *Consciousness Explained* (Boston: Little, Brown, 1991), 245.

you should assume that there has been a mistake in your inference of intention and not in Beethoven's realization. Wagner's hubris was to put the tonal content into question rather than acknowledge its "primary character" in matters of interpretation, including the interpretation of what Beethoven intended. Schenker reached his judgment, it seems, by making the following assumptions. First, it was an article of faith (and a charitable proposition) that "intention and effect completely coincide in the masters" (*Kp1* 22/14–15; see also *Hl* 396/299). In other words, he assumed that what is effected was intended (even by Schenker's lights this assumption is hypothetical). Second, he believed that the indications of the notated score (the composer's autograph, above all) "merely express the desire for a specific effect" (*Mw* 1:44/21).[40] Thus the notated score is a reliable indicator of intention. Consequently, Schenker counters every example of Wagner's revisions by inventing a set of intentions that would explain why the content of the passage took the form it did and not that proposed by Wagner.

As I see it, there are three problems with Schenker's assertions that it was *necessary* for composers to intend and achieve as they did and not otherwise. The first is that he typically provides no arguments that would persuade us of the truth of such assertions. This problem can be remedied. Schenker's talk of necessity also conveys the impression that composers sometimes have no choice in what they do. This problem can be partially remedied. The third problem, however, is intractable. Schenker assumes that the content of his interpretation is the way it must be, and offers no defense (or even, in most cases, an acknowledgment) of his interpretation *vis-à-vis* competing alternatives.[41] In order to see what can be salvaged from Schenker's assertions of necessity, I will construct arguments in defense of a particular case and in the process attempt to explain further the basis of such assertions.

The case is Schenker's essay on the Largo of J. S. Bach's Sonata no. 3 for Solo Violin (BWV 1005), published in the first yearbook of *Das Meisterwerk in der Musik*. I selected this essay for two reasons. First, at nearly every level of interpretation Schenker mentions necessities that impinged upon Bach's composition of the opening bars, making it convenient to discuss a number of different assertions without having to reconstruct a great deal of musical content. Second, the extreme attenuation of his rational reconstruction of the passage, together with his tacit assumption of other premises, gives me the opportunity to clarify one of the meanings "diminution" had in his interpretive practice.

---

[40] Schenker extends the bond between notation and desired effect to include his notated examples as well, a move that is in accord with his claim to have represented compositional intentions and the means by which those intentions are realized; he writes in *FS*, "The notated examples presented here are not to be taken only as a practical aid; rather, they are of the same power and conviction as the printed form of the foreground. Or, to put it differently: the example must come into consideration not as a pedagogical expedient but rather [in the same way] as the actual composition" (5–6/xxiii).

[41] Schenker states this position clearly with respect to the Ursatz in material drafted for *FS* (in the 1920s?), where he writes that while it may be difficult to decide whether the first tone is the octave, fifth, or third, "there is no doubt at all that *only one solution* is the correct one" (OC 38/215). See Keiler, "On Some Properties," 207–8, on Schenker's reluctance to pursue the topic of alternative Ursatz interpretations.

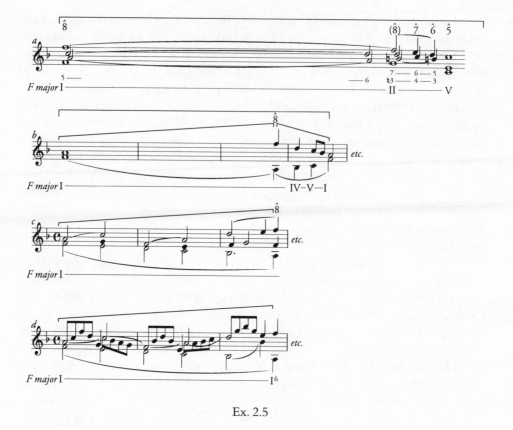

Ex. 2.5

Schenker begins the essay in a way that had become standard practice for him: a declaration of the particular Ursatz configuration, followed by derivations of formal units from articulations or transformations of the Ursatz. Early in the process of derivation, an intended effect has undesirable side-effects that the composer is obliged to remove. That obligation is the first necessity mentioned by Schenker. The context under consideration is that represented in example 2.5*a*.

Not only do consecutive fifths have to be relieved in the succession of the first two roots I–II⁴³ (as in any step of a second), but also, too, the evil of a succession of two major thirds. (*Kp1* 202; *Mw* 1: 63/31)

While it may not be readily apparent from this sentence just who it is that is under the pressure of these obligations, whether the interpreter or the composer, Schenker makes the subject explicit in the next sentence:

Bach checks the first [effect] through a 5–6 exchange, but was able to counter the second only through a considerably greater development of the diminution [see ex. 2.5*b*]. (*Mw* 1: 63/31)

Schenker presents the problem, imputes an intention to solve it, and looks to the piece itself for evidence of the specific means the composer selected to realize that intention. That consecutions of perfect fifths and major thirds pose a problem "for Bach" may be explained, I suggest, by analogy with chess. While it is certainly possible, say, to move a knight diagonally forward one square, it would not be playing by the rules to do so directly. The execution of such a move (a Zug!) requires a minimum of two moves. Just as a direct diagonal step would not be "chess-rational," Schenker seems to say that a direct consecution of fifths or major thirds would not be "music-rational." As such, the rationality of a move is relative to the particular game being played; conceivably there is a game (we could invent one) where such direct consecutions are permitted by the rules. But classically tonal music is not such a game. Operating with the presumption of rationality and outfitted with a contrapuntal rule book that models the forms of rationality (the sort of book, recall, that Bach does not have to consult every time such-and-such a situation arises), Schenker prefers, if possible, to conclude that Bach will hit upon one or another way of making two or more moves in place of these direct consecutions.

One of Schenker's faults is his refusal to grant value to musics whose rules of rationality depart from those of classical tonality, Schoenberg's music being the most obvious case. Schenker's pupil Hans Wolf reports the following statement, in which Schenker makes himself out to be pro-life and Schoenberg out to be pro-machine, as if tonality were the only viable form of music:

The great proof against Schoenberg is the people; they have never gone along with him and never will. There are not two summits in an art. Schoenberg has already experienced the one, a second, like the one now being cultivated, cannot blossom. Schoenberg produces a homunculus in music; it is a machine. Machines are supposed to be a substitute for human strength, a surrogate. Now there are of course surrogates, such as the one for traveling, the automobile, but never can there be a surrogate for the soul. Such a complicated operation is not intelligible for it. All that wastes away of its own accord, like dust. One need not even write against it, it will dispose of itself, as it were. Many writers want to fire off a shot; now they shoot it out among themselves. The product of Schoenberg's machine shall not be used.[42]

This is the substance behind Schenker's remark in *Der freie Satz* that "the quest for a new form of music would be the quest for a homunculus" (*FS* 27/9).

The analogy with games oversimplifies Schenker's view of rules and the rationality of free composition. The rules in question here are those of strict composition, where the play of compositional desire is abnormally restricted. In free composition, it is entirely possible that a composer might, for one reason or another, choose to write consecutive major thirds. What could make the composition of such a consecution rational would be an intention to produce a musical effect that could be realized by that means. An example of such is found in bars 40–43 of Beethoven's String Quartet op. 59, no. 3, first movement.[43] According to Schenker, Beethoven's primary intention in the passage was "to indulge in a strong longing for conclusion,"

---

[42] "Schenkers Persönlichkeit," 179.
[43] Schenker discusses this passage in *Kp1* 73–75/50–51.

which he realizes by abbreviating the motive that is in play and thereby hastening the onset of the harmonic conclusion. Furthermore, says Schenker, in order to reinforce the effect of that abbreviation and the compression of its content, Beethoven arranges for the abbreviation to include consecutive major thirds, thirds which by the rules of strict counterpoint would have to be achieved by at least two moves. Only on the basis of a prior imputation of that intention is Schenker able to talk about the necessity of a harmonization for the motive that not only presents the consecutive major thirds but also a consecution of Stufen that appears to elide a middle term (thus having the effect of a harmonic abbreviation).[44]

If interpretation is to allow for the possibility of breaking the rules of strict counterpoint in free composition (so long as a musical purpose is served), there shall have to be a more flexible interpretive rule, on the order of: assume from the outset that the rules of strict composition will be adhered to, and if observation of the tonal content cannot sustain that assumption in a given instance, look for a musical effect that could be served by the infraction.

A premise of Schenker's argument for the necessity of relieving the consecutions of perfect fifths and major thirds in Bach's Largo is that the Ursatz is the one Schenker describes. Typically, and this case is no exception, that premise is left begging for an explanation. Constructing a plausible argument for this premise is difficult, in part because the process of constructing an Ursatz interpretation is a topic about which Schenker has virtually nothing to say, and in part because doing so means reading a great deal into the text.

The stages by which Bach allegedly realized the concept of the Triad are presented in example 2.6. I have reconstructed these stages from the order of the terms in Schenker's initial description of the Ursatz. No English translation can capture the precision with which Schenker articulates these stages, the first several in particular, so I present here the text in German, with superscript letters corresponding to the levels of example 2.6 prefixed to the appropriate words and phrases: "Die [a]den Dur-Klang [b]F hier auskomponierende, das heißt horizontalisierende [d]Urlinie-[c]Oktave . . ." – note that in a compound construction the first word modifies the second and therefore the second word is conceptually prior (i.e., the space is prior to the line) – "[e]gliedert sich deutlich in 8̂–5̂ und 5̂–1̂. Danach ist die Form zweiteilig, T. 1–8 und T. 8–18. . . . [f]Das Bild bei a) führt den Ursatz vor bei der Stufenbewegung I–II$_{♮3}^{7}$–V im ersten, V–I im zweiten Teil und I–IV–V–I in der Koda" (*Mw* 1: 63/31). Each stage represents an intended effect, and the order of the stages is a rational reconstruction of the progressive determination of the Idea: to write a tonal piece,

---

[44] Rothgeb and Thym's translation makes it seem as if the specific choices of how to configure tones were incumbent upon Beethoven, but in the original German Schenker's talk of obligation and necessity applies only to the guiding intention and the need to realize it in some appropriate fashion. Dubiel, who discusses this example in "'When You are a Beethoven'" (295–98), notes that Schenker is not clear about the sense in which Beethoven is obliged to use the chromatic succession and suggests that Schenker ascribes a function to the progression and then invokes that function to explain the progression. My account differs only in making it explicit that the ascribed function is, for Schenker, the content of Beethoven's intention.

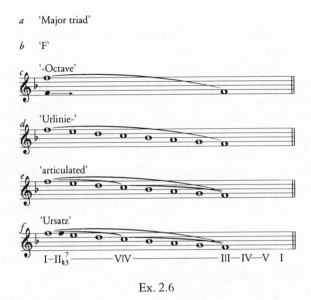

Ex. 2.6

in a major key (not minor), in F (and not any other key), unfolded as an octave space (and not a fifth or third), and so forth. Now, presumably, each stage is somehow verified by looking at what Bach did (as recorded in the score); this verificational procedure is another part of what I take Schenker to have meant by the "primary character of content" and the biblical pronouncement "Am Anfang war das Inhalt!" The sequence of interpretive questions is easy enough to reconstruct: is this a tonal piece? What is the key note? What is the mode? What is the basic tone-space? And so forth.[45] What is unclear is how one is to read the answers off the presented configuration, even given the limited possibilities. A rule of thumb might be this: advance a hypothesis, perhaps taking into account some salient feature of the piece (such as a prominent melodic cadence on 5̂ roughly a third of the way into the piece) and take it as a hypothetical premise. If you can rationally derive the presented configuration from that premise, it is thereby proven (which is not to say that it is the only provable premise). Allan Keiler aptly characterizes the rough and tumble of interpretive heuristics. Schenker's method, he writes, consists of "various informal practices of eliminating surface detail in order to arrive at a workable hypothesis about background levels. But it is just as acceptable to start with a plausible or just merely hypothetical form of an Urlinie for any piece, and then to see how various kinds of detail would be derived from such a hypothesis."[46]

Schenker implicitly asks us to accept the hypothesis of the octave Urlinie, taking the remainder of his commentary as demonstration of its truth. What, then, is the

---

[45] Note that the heuristics of interpretation does not strictly parallel the represented sequence of compositional decisions.

[46] "On Some Properties," 210.

next stage? The articulation of the Urlinie into two segments, and a coda extending the final tone, each marked in like fashion with a formulaic cadence (trill and antici- pation). The next question seems to be this: what harmonic progression could counterpoint the Urlinie in such a way as to produce the effect of that articulation? If $\hat{5}$ is somehow to appear as a terminus, a harmonic conclusion is required. We can tell from looking at the piece that $\hat{5}$ is supported by V and not I (those being the simplest if not sole candidates). The effect of harmonic conclusion requires a V–I effect, in this case transferred to V; the Stufe succession that would produce that effect is $II^{\natural 3}$–V. Thus the simplest Stufen counterpoint for $\hat{8}$–$\hat{5}$ that would produce the desired (hypothesized) segmentation of the Urlinie is I– $II^{\natural 3}$–V. From looking at the piece, we can see that the execution of II, which starts in bar 6, involves a seventh; given the separate contents of the Urlinie and the hypothesized Stufen counter- point, the two must be arranged such that the $\hat{8}$ of the Urlinie is retained over $II^{\natural 3}$ (hence $II_{\natural 3}^{7}$), unless, that is, something prevents us from maintaining this hypothesis. If we are correct, then the fall through $\hat{7}$ and $\hat{6}$ also takes place over II, since V and $\hat{5}$ are the intended (hypothesized and verified) goals.

Now all of this argument – absolutely all of it – is, speaking charitably, assumed by Schenker. You will not find a word of it in his text. Because his penchant for abbre- viation is frequently taken to such an extreme, his texts are difficult to understand, often misunderstood, and often unpersuasive. After all, an abbreviation such as this suspends the demonstrative force of argument. And that, coupled with a penchant for casting hypothesized and subsequently verified interpretations in the indicative mood and for making them premises in arguments for the necessity of this or that move, makes Schenker's interpretations all the more difficult to entertain. I hope my attempt here to fill in the immense gaps in his argument goes some way toward redeeming his declarations about the necessities Bach faced in executing the first segment of the Urlinie.

The next mention of a necessity arises in connection with the second stage of Schenker's depiction (see ex. 2.5b), which he describes as showing "the first paths of the diminution, the motives of the first order." The content of this stage originates from the transformation of vertical intervals (in level a) into horizontal intervals, some of which subsequently undergo other transformations:

In bars 1–4, a sixth is unfolded in the upper voice, upward and downward; likewise in the lower voice, but in reverse order. In the fourth quarter of bar 3, at the apex, f^2 merges into the Urlinie. This explains why the first striving [*Spannung*] of the upper voice had to be only this particular sixth and no other. (*Mw* 1: 64/31)

As before, the argument is entirely lacking and the premises are never expressed. Briefly stated, the required argument is this:

    45. The first Urlinie tone f^2 must be actualized.

    46. The first tone presented is a^1.

∴   47. The first melodic span must be a^1–f^2.

Ex. 2.7

It is assumed that, of all the possibilities, the first Urlinie tone is most simply actualized right at the outset, and if not then, at least within the time span of the initial tonic Stufe. Schenker would appear to prefer an interpretation that sustains the simplest possible hypothesis for as long as possible. If premise 46 is true (see the score of bars 1–4 in ex. 2.7), Schenker will have to interpret a delay of f^2 from the downbeat of bar 1 (ex. 2.5a) to a later timepoint. Rather than taking the f^2 in bar 1 as the actualization of the expected Urlinie tone (for reasons given later in the essay), Schenker interprets the actualization of f^2 as delayed until bar 3.

Before continuing, I want to make three minor points about the rhetoric of the passage just quoted, focusing on the expressions "is unfolded," "merges into," and "striving." As I mentioned earlier in the chapter, Schenker frequently deletes mention of the composing agent in order to concentrate on the intended effect or the resultant configurations that actualize that effect. The passive construction "is unfolded" is just such a case, keeping the explanatory strategy in play, as it were, behind the scenes. In the published translation, by contrast, Rothgeb chooses to render the sentence in the active voice. Rather than make the composing agent explicit, he displaces it and makes the upper voice ("treble") the grammatical agent responsible for executing the unfolding. While it is true that Schenker often turns tonal entities into grammatical subjects (a topic I will take up in chapter 3), here that transformation has the effect of suppressing the intentional content, a content that is essential to the explanation offered in the next sentence. In a passage where Bach is not mentioned at all, I think Schenker's construction is preferable to Rothgeb's.

The implicit presence of the first Urlinie tone, as the interpretive measure of melodic activity in the opening span, is expressed by the verb of the second sentence – "merges into" – which has the sense of flowing into something already in existence, as a river empties into a sea or a street into a plaza. The implicit presence of the f^2 is what is meant by Schenker's alignment of this tone in ex. 2.5a with the downbeat of bar 1. As Schenker states later in the volume, the Urlinie is an imagined ("gedacht") voice; the actual upper voice "passes through tones of the Urlinie, among others" (Mw 1: 188/105). Only if this tone is fixed in one's mind does it make sense to refer to the path from a^1 to f^2 as not just a "span" but a "striving." "Spannung" combines these senses: it is the tension of incompletion, the span of time during which the tension is experienced, and the striving to find completion.[47] To Schenker's way of thinking, there could be no striving that was not determinately fixed upon some goal as the object of its completion; that presence as the object of an intention, as the not-now and not-yet-achieved, is just what it means for f^2 to be, as I said above, the interpretive measure of melodic activity in the opening span.

The next stage in Schenker's account of the Largo's actualization is this:

The illustration in c of [ex. 2.5] shows the *diminution motives of the second order*:

The first sixth in bars 1–3 is fashioned into three smaller arpeggiations, each spanning a third. (*Mw* 1: 65/33)

Notice that the agency of the composer is once again concealed within the passive construction; Rothgeb, as before, substitutes an active construction whose verb does not support the inference of a composing agent ("The first sixth, in bars 1–3, comprises three smaller arpeggiations, each spanning a third"). One result of the transformation of the sixth a^1–f^2 is a new motive: an ascending third. Schenker's statement of the transformation is quite matter of fact, and yet the derivation of the three thirds – a^1–c^2, f^1–a^1, and d^2–f^2 – is by no means straightforward. The following explanation of their derivation will bring to light an important rhythmic principle of Schenker's interpretive practice.

The adjective "smaller" in Schenker's statement refers not to the size of the new intervals relative to the sixth, but rather to the durations of those thirds relative to that of the sixth: pairs of half notes relative to the longer but apparently indeterminate values in level b. This is the sense in which the content of level c is a "diminution" with respect to level b. What is less clear is the sense in which the new content is a diminution "of" the content in b, much less of "the sixth," for there is no standard transformation (for example, unfolding, Zug, arpeggiation) that could lead directly from what is given as the content of b to the series of thirds in c. A rational reconstruction is not impossible, but it requires several steps. The basic thrust of the reconstruction provided in example 2.8 is twofold: first, that the series of thirds is, strictly speaking, a diminution of the entire content of the initial event of level a (and not of the sixth as Schenker seems to say); and, second, that a hypothesized intention to sublate the sixth in this diminution is required to explain why the diminution takes just this form and not another (which is the reason, I suggest, why Schenker asserts the sixth at the level intervening between a and c). Three desires motivate the way I will formulate the reconstruction: (1) I want to show that it is possible to adopt a strict rhythmic interpretation of "diminution" as the relation between some adjacent levels in his interpretation. (2) I want to elucidate further

---

[47] Schenker makes a similar pun on "Spannung" later in the essay (*Mw* 1: 68/35). The tension of incompletion is illustrated in *Hl* (45/31–32) in the sphere of language.

Ex. 2.8

Schenker's assertion that the process of developing content begins with transformation of a vertical situation into a horizontal one. (3) I want the reconstruction to support Schenker's hypothesis (which he states elsewhere to be a "law") that the *Genie-Geist* characteristically chooses diminutions that manifest repetition.[48]

The Stufen in ex. 2.5*a* are represented as proceeding at an even pace. Elaboration of the Stufen produces an imbalance, stretching out the time of the initial tonic and refracting it into smaller units. The first of the units shown in ex. 2.5*b* lasts three bars. In order to understand *c* as a diminution of *b*, it is necessary to attribute a three-bar duration to the initial sonority (see ex. 2.8). In the original configuration (ex. 2.8*a*), the only interval instantiated more than once is that of a third; both instances of the third involve a^1, the first tone of the intended melodic span. If f^2 is to be involved in a diminution that parallels the diminutions involving a^1, then it, too, must enter into the relation of a third; thus the fifth must be set in motion to the upper neighbor d^2 (ex. 2.8*b*).[49] Given the hypothesized intention to execute the sixth a^1 to f^2, and the necessity of preserving that relation in the diminution, the two lower thirds bracketed in *b* must be placed before the higher third; there are two possibilities (ex. 2.8*c*), one of which produces a simpler contour than the other. If these thirds are to be unfolded and still preserve the effect of the sixth, the first unfolding must start with a^1 and the third must end with f^2; the inner third can be unfolded in either direction. Of the possibilities for sublating the sixth while also unfolding the thirds (two are shown in ex. 2.8*d*), only one consists of parallel unfoldings (the second option in *d*). Assuming intentions to sublate the sixth and at the same time to create parallelisms,

---

[48] This hypothesis amounts to a rule for interpretation: prefer reconstructions that manifest parallelisms to a greater degree. This is why Schenker frequently cites the production of parallelism in support of his interpretation. Richard Cohn ("The Autonomy of Motives in Schenkerian Accounts of Tonal Music," *MTS* 14 [2] [1992], 150–70) is mistaken, I believe, when he claims that "it is not unreasonable to infer, from Schenker's insistence that identification of motives depends on an understanding of their relation to the whole piece, that an image of the whole be congealed *before* the motivic details can be understood with any degree of certainty" and proposes that it is a tenet of Schenker's practice that "recognition of motivic relations results from analysis, but does not influence the analytic process" (p. 155, emphasis mine). Cohn offers no evidence from Schenker's writings to justify his inference, and by his own admission (p. 156), the interpretive practice of Schenker and a host of Schenkerian writers fails to follow the dictates of that inference. In short, the weight of Cohn's own evidence is against the inference. Also flawed is his proposition that "the Ursatz alone is the source of motivic unity" (p. 150); the passages cited from Schenker do not support this proposition, though they might be adduced in support of the weaker claim that the tonal contents of motives must originate in the Ursatz; this weaker claim was suggested by Joseph Dubiel in the discussion period following a paper premised on Cohn's article, delivered at the conference "Critical Perspectives on Schenker" (Notre Dame, Ind., March 1994.)

[49] Given Schenker's description in ex. 2.5*a*, the neighbor must return to the fifth in bar 3; c^2 succeeds to d^2 irrevocably only later, in bar 5.

the diminution of a had to assume this form and no other. This form of diminution has the added virtue of supporting the rising effect of the sixth by unfolding each third upward.

To appreciate what Schenker meant by "diminution" in its strictly rhythmic sense, we need to have in hand a principle for assessing the effects of dividing a larger span into smaller ones. Westergaard formulates a principle for gauging the stability or instability of a rhythmic diminution: a binary segmentation will be stable if the duration of the first segment is equal to or greater than that of the second.[50] It is relatively simple to add to this principle a means for discriminating degrees of stability by attending to the proportions between the two segments: if the two are equal, the segmentation is maximally stable. We can now formulate a rule of interpretation to cover diminutional relations: gauge the effect of less stable or unstable segmentations in terms of how they deviate from a maximally stable segmentation (i.e., from a state of rhythmic equilibrium). In his effort to economize and abbreviate, Schenker's illustrations often do not include a simple picture of such equilibrium, but the general principle is evident in the progression from half notes in example 2.5c to eighth notes in d and finally to sixteenths in the score (ex. 2.7). The stages of transformation mediating these shifts are depicted in the left-hand side of example 2.9. As we saw in connection with example 2.8, Schenker does not specify the exact content that is subject to diminution (compare ex. 2.9a and b with ex. 2.5c). The lines in example 2.9b show the path of the unfolding that results in the eighth-note diminution of Schenker's next level (shown to the right in ex. 2.9). Schenker's account is further complicated by the fact that there is no simple way to move from his eighth-note level of diminution to the level of sixteenths in the score. Here is the reason: the rhythmic transformations that alter the equilibrium – the appoggiatura g^2, the suspension of d^2 into the third quarter, and the delay and consequent compression of the Zug from c^2 to f^1 – are best understood as transformations of the model shown in b and not Schenker's realization of that model in eighth notes. Schenker does not depict the rhythmic transformations that alter the equilibrium of the model and instead skips directly to the configuration presented in the score, where further elaborations (see e) restore the semblance of rhythmic equilibrium, now in sixteenths.

---

[50] *An Introduction to Tonal Theory*, 227–35. Westergaard's formulation is more precise and is also extended to cover diminutions that subdivide a span into more than two segments. Westergaard's formulation differs in an important respect from Schenker's practice. Take the transformation described in example 2.3a and b that produces a fourth-Zug in the upper voice. By either theorist's account, there is an intervening interpretive stage showing the intention to execute a Zug between e^2 and b^1. According to Westergaard's theory of interpretation, that stage includes both the setting of the goal and a determination of when that goal will be reached (in effect dividing the phrase span into two subspans, the first containing the departure tone and the second containing the goal); in the next stage, the first subspan is subdivided into three segments for the departure tone and the two passing tones. In Schenker's practice, by contrast, only the tonal content of the goal is set between stages a and b; Schenker handles the interpretation of pacing in the next stage: the execution of the Zug produces a tonal content of four tones, which is then paced in equal durations using metrically stable spans (Westergaard's segmentation rule recognizes that not all tonal contents permit distribution of all tones in equal durational segments).

Ex. 2.9

Schenker prefaces his portrayal of the penultimate stage of diminution with general remarks about its content and about the process that has led to it:

An even more advanced state of diminution, [comprising] *the motives of the third order,* is shown in the Urlinie-Tafel [ex. 2.5*d*]. Finally we look down to where the phantasy of the composer conjures up the foreground and begets motives whose intrinsic corporeality compellingly commends itself to the short-hearing ear as [that of] so-called melodies. But whence these melodies come has been shown to us by the course of the voice leading, from the Ursatz on; that their development happens in this way and not otherwise is not at all the whim of a phantasy aiming for melody but rather is a necessity of a voice leading anchored in an Ursatz. (*Mw* 1: 67/35)

Speaking of the "corporeality" possessed by the third-order motives is Schenker's way of acknowledging that there is only a slight difference between this stage and the presentation of the score, for "the final realization [i.e., the last stage of the content's development] animates the eighth-note figures of the Urlinie-Tafel with sixteenths" (*Mw* 1: 68/35). That the course of the development from level to level is a "necessity" is less easily explained. Part of what Schenker means is that the set of transformational possibilities inherent in a given configuration (assuming the forms of rationality Schenker describes) constrains the composition of melodies. But Schenker did not believe that specific choices among those possibilities were determined in advance. Like Hegel, for whom "the essence of Spirit is Freedom" (30/22), Schenker did not desire to deny freedom altogether. In fact, he lays great stress on the "freedom of the transformations" when he introduces the idea of transformational development in the first chapter on the middleground in *Der freie Satz*:

It is not that a specific form of the Ursatz demands only specific transformations – otherwise all forms of the Ursatz would have to lead to the same forms of transformation – but rather the choice of transformations is fundamentally free, if only the indivisibility and binding of all connections is preserved.

What is critical in the choice of transformations, then, in a more restricted sense, is rapport with the Ursatz in question. ... This rapport is the content of the depiction of back-, middle-, and foreground. (*FS* 49/25–26)

Schenker's rational reconstruction of the artwork can be viewed as the presentation of a series of choices. Once made, a choice has the force of necessity: its content must be preserved. The choice, then, becomes an intention that must be realized. This is the path from freedom to necessity. Constraints upon choice are always general: diminute coherently in a way that can be traced back to an Ursatz, preserve the simple in the complex, prefer repetitions.

Now, then, to the content of the penultimate stage of diminution presented in the Urlinie-Tafel (ex. 2.5d):

In bars 1–3 we see figures that describe arcs of a sixth. The implicit danger of taking the peak of the new motive, f^2 in the third eighth of bar 1, as the decisive pitch is escaped only through a feel for the genuine motive of the arpeggiated third (see [ex. 2.5c]), which knows nothing at all of f^2. One sees how important it is to get at the basis of the diminutions. (*Mw* 1: 67–68/35)

If there is something in danger here, perhaps it is Schenker's reconstruction of Bach's choices and intentions, which specifies that the decisive pitch in the first half of bar 1 is a^1. To take f^2 as the interpretive measure ("the basis") of that span would be tantamount to a rejection of the path by which Schenker led us here.[51] On the other hand, perhaps the danger lies in that assuming the f^2 in bar 1 as the decisive pitch could not lead to a rational reconstruction of the Largo – Schenker does not say. In the absence of a demonstration to that effect, we have but Schenker's word to take. On the first account, Schenker betrays his personal investment in the interpretation, on the second, he strains credulity.

---

[51] If f^2 in bar 1 is not the decisive pitch and not the first tone of the Urlinie, its origin lies elsewhere, as the actualization of an implicit Stufe tone.

3

SYNTHESIS

I

What is the effect of a diminished fourth? Such a low-order effect ought to be easy to interpret: since its constituent tones cannot both belong to the same triad or even the same diatonic system, it is dissonant and has a transient effect. That much is taught by strict counterpoint. But now give the interval a place in the unfolding of a piece, in the company of a musical entity whose tones had hitherto formed a consonance. What, now, is the effect of this diminished fourth, now that it provokes a change of harmony within its companion entity?

Imagine the finale of Mozart's Symphony in G minor, which opens with the series of tones shown in example 3.1a. Within moments this series of tones is repeated, albeit within a different harmonic context (ex. 3.1b), and thereby becomes a motivic entity. For nearly two hundred bars and over thirty appearances, this motive appears only in configurations that project a single harmony in each of its two bars.[1] But then, in bar 191 and only moments before it will be recapitulated in its original forms, Mozart alters it (ex. 3.2). The motive in play at this point extends the original by two bars with a step motion leading from the appoggiatura in the second bar to a pair of angular leaps, each of which spans a diminished fourth (see the brackets in ex. 3.2; some of the fourths are compounded or inverted). Imitation between the outer voices brings the dissonant leaps of the extension into play against the arpeggiated portion of the motive, which is now altered so that it meets each tone of the diminished fourths with a consonance; this alteration produces a change of contextual harmony within the arpeggiation. Schenker conveys the effect of this motivic response to the "fiercely beautiful and shocking diminished fourths" as follows:

[Mozart] now for the first time reshapes [abwandelt] this very motive, namely, to two different harmonies in one and the same bar, and by that means, in a most frenzied mental state

[1] Schenker describes the entire two-bar motive as "fashioned out of a *single* triad or seventh chord" and identifies the single harmonic concept of the motive's first two instances (ex. 3.1) as "G³" and "D⁷" respectively (*Kp1* 99/70 fig. 73). These interpretations, if understood at the same level of abstraction, are contradicted by his later analysis (*Mw* 2: 151 fig. 16), where the first motive elaborates bb^2–a^2 above I–V and the second elaborates eb^3–d^3 above V (eb^3 and the c in the bass voice are interpreted as appoggiaturas). Since the basic content of the motive is the step of a second (preceded by an arpeggiation), the harmonic content of the motive must be bifurcated. Note, however, that in the sequential passage starting in bar 135 each statement of the motive (in a variant of its second form) is supported by a single harmony.

Ex. 3.1. Mozart, Symphony no. 40 (K. 550), IV: (*a*) bars 1–2; (*b*) bars 5–6 (cp. *Kp1* fig. 73)

Ex. 3.2 Mozart, Symphony no. 40 (K. 550), IV, bars 191–202 (*Kp1* fig. 72)

[*Stimmung*], as it were, he rends the original entity – with enormous vehemence, as it were – in twain. (*Kp1* 99/69–70)[2]

The image of an abnormal mental state conveys the drastic conflict of effects: unity, conveyed by repetition and a history of harmonic unity, and now within that unity the most extreme disunity, produced by the most extreme, nondiatonic dissonance. A fragmented sentence, complete but syntactically rent, also conveys this conflict. The constituent effects – motive, triads, intervals – can be analyzed, but their synthesis and their placement at just this point in the unfolding of this movement falls under no law of cause and effect in Schenker's theory.

   Schenker indicates in a footnote that this remark on Mozart's symphony was elicited by a performance he had recently heard. The conductor, Richard Strauss, "failed to empathize with the experience of the principal motive." As a result, or perhaps as a cause, Strauss failed to distinguish between the effects of consonance

---

[2] The verb "abwandelt" is most closely associated with linguistics, where it means "inflect," in the sense of the changes undergone by a word in its conjugations or declensions.

and dissonance, that is, between the consonant quality of the motive's earlier appearances and these wrenching dissonances (*Kp1* 99 n. 1/349 n. 18). This indictment of Strauss for lack of empathy invests the motive with subjectivity. And that draws us into an interpretive vein Schenker articulated in *Harmonielehre*, for it is as if the motive whose experience eluded Strauss were a character in a drama. In *Harmonielehre* Schenker states that what is paramount to composing forms like the sonata and the symphony is "the task of representing the destiny, an actual life destiny, of this or that motive," as in a drama (*Hl* 19–20/12–13). Though calculated to induce certain compositional desires (for example, the desire to provide contrasts in repetition), this analogy also promotes certain considerations when interpreting the effects of motivic repetition, first and foremost the impact of context upon interpretation. Accurate chronicling of a motive's "life" in the musical artwork will have to take into account the appearance of the motive in a variety of "situations," in which various "qualities" of the motive's "character" are "proven"; indeed, "what is character but simply the synthesis of these qualities as they are confirmed by the successive situations?" Even a single tone can be such a character. When Schenker writes of this same Mozart symphony in the second yearbook of *Das Meisterwerk*, he represents the whole of the first movement as unfolding the story of $\hat{5}$:

The $\hat{5}$, which at first stands in the interval of the fifth [above the bass], tests itself successively with the first arpeggiation of the bass also as a third and fifth [*recte:* octave] before returning to the position of fifth; only after this confirmation does it finally proceed along with the second [bass] arpeggiation to $\hat{1}$. The change of intervals signifies self-experienced contrasts, as it were, for the $\hat{5}$, an "I must persevere through this" for the original [intervallic] position, the regaining of which gives the signal for uncoiling the Urlinie's fifth-Zug. (*Mw* 2: 109)[3]

Schenker's appeal to drama is intended to make vivid the continuity and development of motivic identity, but he does not hesitate to use other analogies to bring out other features. For example, to underscore the phenomenological emergence of the motive – that is, the notion that a series of tones is not recognizable as a motive in its first statement but only after repetition – Schenker uses a cognitive analogy: just as the concept of a biological species is predicated upon the observation of many individuals with like features, so too the concept of a motive (*Hl* 6/6). And in later years Schenker uses an agricultural analogy to underscore the phenomenological emergence of the motive and its place in compositional intention: as a seed sown is unobservable until it has germinated, so too the motive; moreover, just as the purpose of sowing seed is to produce fruit for harvest, so too a purpose of presenting a series of tones is to produce fruit for the harvest of repetition (*Tw* 4: 22).[4]

Just as the metaphor of sprouting and growth is embedded within a context of human action (sowing and reaping), so too the dramatic plight of the diminished

---

[3] This picture of the Urlinie differs dramatically from the description in *FS* 70/40, where Schenker claims that he represented the Urlinie in *Mw* 2 as an interruption, in which case $\hat{5}$ appears only in the position of a fifth above I.

[4] In discussing Schenker's organicism, Solie focuses on the botanical moment within this metaphor and overlooks the purposive moment; see Ruth A. Solie, "The Living Work: Organicism and Musical Analysis," 153.

fourths that Strauss failed to project. For if the motives of Mozart's symphony are participants in a drama, the character responsible for their situation is none other than Mozart. It is Mozart who "reshapes" the motive and "rends it in twain," whose manner is "vehement," and whose mental state is "most frenzied." Schenker is very careful, however, to avoid giving the impression that he is describing the actual state of Mozart's spirit at the time that he wrote the passage, for he marks not one but both psychological interpretants with the expression "as it were" (*gleichsam*). The rhetorical force of this expression is the subject of this chapter.

Before examining the positive effect of this "as it were," let us consider Schenker's views on inferring composer's moods from their works. Preparing composers to make informed selections, says Schenker, ought to begin with training in counterpoint. It is there that musical apprentices become acquainted with the core of the purely musical and get their first glimpse into the world of absolute effects that attend various arrangements of tones. Strict composition prepares composers for the real world of free composition by teaching them how to configure tones in ways that will satisfy a restricted set of compositional desires. Schenker's training manual is unique in that it offers the student insight into what lies outside that restricted sphere, for it is replete with examples of proscribed tonal configurations (and their attendant effects) that could only satisfy desires arising within the world of free composition. For example, after setting out the prescription for strict composition that dissonant tones must be approached and left by step, Schenker makes this revealing comment on the relation between strict and free composition:

All the other treatments that leap into or out of the dissonance – and conceivably there is an infinite number of such treatments – must be declared completely unsuited for strict composition (for the stage of the exercise, that is). They are instead reserved for free composition, which, in contrast to strict and in precise accord with the compositional mood [*Stimmung*], can simultaneously provide and make good the psychological reasons for any more individual kind of treatment. (*Kp1* 241/179)

From the interpretive point of view, the question is: are such "psychological reasons" or "compositional moods" inferable from the configurations of free compositions?

Schenker's basic position seems to be this: as long as the desire in question is the achievement of a specific effect, he is confident we can reasonably infer what the content of that desire was, namely, the observed effect. Desires for a specific effect may also be instrumental in serving other desires; so long as the latter are musical effects, they are also inferable; but if the purpose served is psychological or programmatic, then Schenker thinks such a desire cannot be securely inferred from tones and effects in themselves (of course, composers may use other means to indicate their psychological reasons or compositional moods). In chapter 2 we saw how Schenker drew a limit to the interpretation of compositional *Geist* in allowing deduction of the logical structure of effects but not their actual, historical genesis. To that we can add a limit between the particular "interest" in an effect and the general climate of desire in which that interest arises and whose purposes it serves. He first articulated this limit in "The *Geist* of Musical Technique":

Every prescription and proscription, fundamentally relative, supports a certain *musical appeal* [*Reiz*] – nothing more and nothing less – and so it upholds that appeal so long as the more intense interest of another is not in play. The less intense interest of the one then yields to the more intense interest of the other. The sum of all these interests forms the piece. Above the sum of interests, of course, hovers the spirit of the mood [*der Geist der Stimmung*], yet the interest of the composer is demonstrable to everyone, while the mood must be appropriated by each in his own way. This is a very essential distinction. (*EK* 142)

Schenker is clearly interested in restricting interpretation to what is demonstrable, namely, to the interests synthesized by the composer. But as we will see, he does not live by the letter of this restriction.

Twenty-five years later, his position remained unchanged. When writing of the third movement of Beethoven's op. 101, Schenker demonstrated that the Adagio has the effect of repeating the first movement's principal motive and inferred that the concealed repetition was intentional, but when it came to inferring Beethoven's motivation for literally quoting the first movement's motive following the Adagio, Schenker drew his interpretation of Beethoven's *Geist* to a halt:

If the musician has seen the likeness between the motives of the Adagio and the first move-ment, he will probably also find this quotation quite natural, even if he disregards whatever psychological-programmatic reasons may perhaps have led the master in this case. Even with all due respect to a programmatic motivation (so long as its execution does not violate the musical art), the re-creative musician simply ought never to forget the musical connec-tions in searching for programmatic elements, no more than the composer, if he is a master like Beethoven, neglects musical connections [when pursuing] the programmatic. I there-fore like to leave the unfruitful solution of such puzzles to others ... (*LfS101* 46^{2}58)

Though he does not say here what would constitute a solution to the psychologi-cal-programmatic puzzle, he probably has in mind the sort he encountered in such writers as Wilhelm von Lenz and Paul Bekker, whose writings, along with several others, are critiqued in a separate "Literature" section. Lenz, in particular, wonders whether the quotation is "the triumph in the composer of the artistic soul over the man who feels unhappy" and whether the Allegro that follows, dubbed "the deed" by Beethoven,[5] is "the thought to which the heart is entitled," a thought that shows "nothing of the infirmity of hypersensitivity" but instead was the perfect picture of psychological health: "All health of soul, dignity of the undefiled genius" (quoted in *LfS101* 74). Such speculation lies beyond the pale of a demonstrable relation to tonal content and for that reason lies outside the strict confines of Schenker's inter-pretive practice.

---

[5] According to Lenz, Schindler attributed the following designations of the sonata's movements to Beethoven: "1. Träumerisches Gefühle. 2. Aufforderung zur Tat. 3. Rückkehr der träumerischen Gefühle. 4. Der Tat" (quoted in *LfS101* 72). These designations do not appear in Schindler's biography, but may have been reported elsewhere.

It will be instructive to observe the point at which Schenker holds himself to those confines in this case. Here is how he continues along "the path of purely musical representation":

With the filled-out dominant in bar 20, the motivic connection between the Adagio and the quotation also brings to fruition the effect of an antecedent phrase, in contrast to which the quotation is intended to lay claim almost to the character of a consequent phrase. And yet at the very moment when the consequent entered in the first piece (bar 5), a fermata now suddenly brings the quotation to a standstill: it serves to clarify a change of heart [*Sinnesänderung*] on the author's part. (*LfS101* 46²58)

It may seem as if Schenker is about to enter into the realm of psychological reasons that he has declared off limits, but actually "change of heart" betokens no more than Beethoven's decision, obviously realized in the tonal content of the sonata, not to follow through with a verbatim repetition of the first movement. This is quite clearly a decision that has a musical effect as its object. Beyond that there is no "hermeneutic divination," as Schenker is wont to call it in his critiques of Lenz and company, that can fathom the composer's *Geist*. And so Schenker continues:

To what this relates programmatically is, as was just said above, not discoverable; however, it is possible to say all the more specifically that for which it aims, from a purely musical point of view. A glance at the motive's conclusions in bars 22, 24, 28 and bar 1 of the Allegro will bring us to the puzzle's solution:

Ex. 3.3. *LfS101* fig. 43

It must be gathered from this illustration that an answer to the first two figures under *a* and *b* is furnished by the last one under *c*; the former both remain fixed in the dominant and manifest only a difference in the altered interval (the step of a second in *b* for the step of a third in *a*). The "answer" character is expressed above all by the change of Stufen, V–I; and consequently the last figure is not just a settlement of the two preceding half-cadential figures; in a far greater sense it is the sign that the last movement of the sonata in general answers the first, insofar, that is, as the figures under *a* and *b*, as quotations of the first movement, may readily be taken now as *pars pro toto*. (*LfS101* 46²58)

Again, what is demonstrable is an idea with a specifically musical content – a question and answer that concern not words or ideas, but tones and effects: the dominant of the half close is, as it were, the copula, left incomplete in the half-close but completed by tonic in the answering passage.[6] As a general rule, Schenker demands that the objects of desire, the goals of motion, the content of "propositions," and so

---

[6] In *Hl* 291/219 Schenker likens the half-close to grammatical signs of incompletion: commas, semicolons, and question marks (the association was of long standing among German theorists, dating back at least a century to Heinrich Koch).

forth be tones. That is a demand Schenker places upon the rhetoric of interpretation.

And now to return to Schenker's comment on Mozart and the effect of "as it were." If, as the "as it were"s seem to indicate, the attribution of a mood to Mozart is beyond the pale of the demonstrable, then Schenker seems to have ventured where he would have others fear to tread. If we are at all charitably disposed toward him, we should try to invent a reason why it seemed to him desirable to transgress his own rule. The reason, I suggest, is rhetorical. When it comes to writing an effective sentence that uses psychological terms to communicate the synthesis of effects in this passage, it becomes necessary to attach the mental states to a subject, either explicitly or by implication. To do so is, in Marion Guck's terms, to create an analytical fiction.[7] As the agent ultimately responsible for musical effects, the composer is a natural subject, though as we have seen tonal entities may also be drawn into the fiction.

It is the function of expressions like "as if" and "as it were" to mark this step into the fictional. And the purpose of this step, typically, is to convey the synthesis of effects in a passage. What, then, did Schenker mean by "synthesis?"

During the foment of the early 1920s, when the concept of the Urlinie and its transformation at once vastly increased the depth of interpretation and also, because of its novelty, threatened to distract readers from the essential contribution of more familiar factors such as repetition and harmony, Schenker stressed more than ever the synthetic breadth of the musical artwork, giving the Urlinie an honored but partial role within the overall synthesis.[8] The various descriptions of synthesis dating from this period – which are the most explicit to be found anywhere in his writings – have in common a listing of several interacting yet independent "forces." So, for example, in the commentary on op. 101 (1921) he writes:

A piece of music comes into the world alive, woven out of Urlinie, Stufen, and voice leading. All of these basic humours and forces (motive and melody issue forth from the Urlinie) constantly interweave and interact, so the method of observation – [viz.] that one must become aware of each one of them individually at first – should not deceive. Not even the nature of man, for example, as a whole mysteriously woven together out of a thousand-fold forces, is in any way neutralized by the fact that knowledge of it can only be obtained by studies of its particular aspects (for example, anatomy, physiology, etc.). By this I mean to say that [the same] may, indeed must, be said of the Urlinie above all, if it works together with and is inseparable from the other forces in the artwork's play of forces. (*LfS101* 22²8)

Forces interweaving, creating a multi-dimensional texture: that is synthesis. A particular moment in such a texture, like that in the development section of Mozart's

---

[7] See Marion A. Guck, "Analytical Fictions," *MTS* 16 (2) (1994), 217–30.

[8] Schenker writes about synthesis in the introduction to *LfS101* (quoted at length in *Tw* 1: 23–25) and at the conclusion of several of the longest analytical essays in *Tw*: *Tw* 2: 17–19, on Mozart's Piano Sonata in A minor (K. 310); *Tw* 2: 36, on Beethoven's Piano Sonata in F minor op. 2, no. 1; *Tw* 3: 17–20, on Haydn's Piano Sonata in E♭ major; *Tw* 7: 21, on Beethoven's Piano Sonata in F minor op. 57. In later writings he often refers to these passages when broaching the topic of synthesis.

symphony, is highly individual by virtue of its situation, its embeddedness in a multiplicity of processes. Reflective understanding apprehends the elements of artistic synthesis analytically, through observation of individual aspects and contexts, but the act of perception, in which the interweaving and interaction is sensed and thereby understood, is synthetic. Synthesis resists straightforward description. Schenker's rhetorical practice reflects this divide between what can be stated and what can only be felt. The sound of synthesis exceeds the grasp of Schenker's method of observation but still lies within the reach of words. "As if" and "as it were"'s mark the contents of that region of excess.

Schenker's account of synthesis at the conclusion of his essay on Beethoven's Piano Sonata op. 57 (1924) begins tersely:

German synthesis – Synthesis altogether!
The binding together of a tonal whole through diatony in all its forms. (*Tw* 7: 21)[9]

The opening statement is incomplete, not just in the obvious grammatical sense of an elided copula that joins the two lines, but more significantly in the suppression of a subject for the nominalized verb *Bindung*, "binding together," the subject whose creative or interpretive act binds tones into a whole. Given that Schenker's agenda is to probe compositional *Geist*, the obvious candidate for this role is the genius-composer, who alone has a knack for placing tones into a multiplicity of independent relations and configuring them in such a way that they could (Schenker would say must) be interpreted in an appropriately manifold way by a person with the right interpretive disposition. When Schenker pauses in *Der freie Satz* to inform composers of the significance of the Ursatz for their craft, he does so in terms of binding:

Anyone whose tonal sense is not mature enough to be able to bind tones together into Züge and to lead off [more] Züge from [the first] Züge, that person obviously lacks musical farsightedness and procreative love: only living love composes, leads to Züge and connection [*Zusammenhang*]. (*FS* 20/160)[10]

If tones are the elements that composers bind together into a living entity, so to speak, the "forms of diatony" are categories of relation into which the tones are made to enter, their forms of life, as it were. In the essay on op. 57 he lists the following forms:

Binding through tonal lineage [*Tongeschlecht*] . . .
Binding through the Urlinie as a key [*Tonart*] in the horizontal dimension . . .
Binding through Ursatz, prolongation, Stufen, diminution . . .
Binding through registers, through low and high . . . (*Tw* 7: 21)

---

[9] "Deutsche Synthese – Synthese überhaupt! / Bindung eines Ton-Ganzen durch die Diatonie in allen ihren Formen."

[10] Schenker plays on the assonance of Zug and Zusammenhang, perhaps aware that the latter word is an expanded, prolonged form of the former: Zu–[sammenhan]–g, and thus in a figurative sense exemplifies the very compositional skill he describes.

Each item in the list is followed with a brief description of how it is realized in op. 57. Two points require explanation. "Tonal lineage" recalls a form of life presented in *Harmonielehre*. The identity of the individual Stufe is understood as its relation within a system of relations generated by a tonic Stufe; each Stufe traces its lineage back to that tonic (except IV, which represents, as it were, the grandsire of the system) (*Hl* 52–54/38–39). Even tonicization, which effectively emancipates the dependent Stufe, does not eradicate the lineal relation to the tonic. The second point that requires comment is the absence of that most basic form of tonal life, repetition. I suggest that it is to be found in this list under the terms Urlinie and diminution. During the first few years of its life, the concept of the Urlinie bore within it the idea of repetition; indeed, Schenker's Urlinie for the first movement of op. 57 is saturated with repetitions of a neighboring motion. Only during the course of the next few years did Schenker gradually remove repetitions from the Urlinie, until he had reduced its content to a single entity, a Zug. By that point, repetition became solely a by-product of diminution, independent in the sense that there is nothing in the concept of diminution that would require the production of similar configurations from separate diminutions.[11]

Another aspect of synthesis is communicated by the terms "force" and "causality." In material based on a passage from the first book of *Kontrapunkt* and drafted in 1917 for the conclusion of *Der freie Satz* (OC 51/1378–91), Schenker attempted to summarize the various principles articulated in the text: from the simplest principles of consonance and dissonance, intervals, the various species of passing (sevenths, accented passing tones, anticipations, neighbor notes, suspensions), through the more complex principles of flowing line, Stufen, mixture, modulation, and chromatics, to the most complex effects of thematics and form. All of these he brought under the concept of "musical causality":

Under causality one has to imagine a drive, a compulsion, which legitimizes the tone as a living, logically thinking being, as it were, therefore as a logical motor like the one we grant analogously to our language (see *Kp1* 376/291). (OC 51/1378)

The compulsion that he has in mind drives forward from the present into a future, like the effect of a dissonant suspension drawn ineluctably toward the future of its resolution. The musical artwork is a synthesis of causal forces, each of which propels into the future along its own trajectory, until coming to rest at the end of the composition.

Synthesis is above all the composer's perceptive and creative ability. But Schenker invites noncomposers to cultivate an interpretive knack for synthesis. Sometimes the invitation is only implied, as when mention of the compositional agent is suppressed in the description of synthesis; and sometimes, as in the following passage, Schenker issues a more explicit invitation:

---

[11] See, for example, his essay on the Largo of Bach's Sonata no. 3 for solo violin in *Mw* 1, where he describes successive levels of diminution and the motives that belong to each level.

The consonant relation of two tones establishes between them a logical relation that un-doubtedly influences the coming and going of the tones. For if one knows what effect belongs to this relation, then this same effect is often the one that is or must be striven for. The Idea of this effect then comes first in the composer's mind in order to steer the tones hither and thither, thus to produce something for which the thinking man must be pre-pared. (OC 51/1378–79)

Schenker helps "the thinking man" prepare himself by analyzing effects and by crafting analytical fictions designed to synthesize analytical observations.

To display Schenker's use of analytical fictions to convey synthesis, I present three cases. Synthesis, by its very nature, engages complex musical situations and conse-quently quite a bit of analytical stage setting is required. The first example, which I will treat at some length, is once again the finale of Beethoven's Piano Sonata op. 110. I selected this example to be the first, because the content of Schenker's inter-pretation is authorized by the composer through verbal annotations that are incor-porated into the work's authentic text. By way of contrast, the second case, a highly charged, "chaotic" moment in the second movement of Beethoven's Piano Sonata op. 109, presents an interpretation of synthesis that is entirely of Schenker's own invention. The third example, taken from Schenker's commentary on the first movement of Beethoven's Third Symphony, displays Schenker's use of imagery to convey the effects of rhythmic and voice-leading transformations. As in chapter 2, I have chosen examples that date both from Schenker's earlier period and from his later period: the essays on op. 110 and op. 109 were published in 1914 and 1913, respectively, while the essay on Beethoven's Third Symphony appeared in 1930.

II

Beethoven, Piano Sonata op. 110, third movement

Schenker's interpretation of the movement is this: Beethoven's expression of victory over weakness and depression. Primary evidence for the content of this program is found in notations that Beethoven entered into the text of the sonata; the most relevant markings are given in table 3.1 (to these could be added the "neutral" key signature of the Recitativo and first Arioso and the implicit verbal association of these sections). Secondary evidence is provided by the musical effects, which sup-port the inferred sequence of programmatic events. And the proposition that this is Beethoven's surmounted suffering follows from conjoining both the programmatic intention and the musical effects to the assumption that only a composer "whom fate has destined to suffer much and who therefore knows from his own experience how torment and suffering are expressed in the body, in gestures, and in the ca-dences of speech" is capable of arranging for there to be such effects (*LfS110* 66[2]98). This assumption also indicates the basis upon which Schenker elaborates the pro-gram: a similitude between the movements of the body and speech and the move-ments of tones. As a general rule, Schenker selects from among the imaginings mandated by the program those aspects that have a dynamic quality.

Table 3.1

Bar	Annotation	Location
4	Recitativo	Adagio
5	*cantabile*	
9	Arioso dolente. (Klagender Gesang.)	Arioso (1)
26	[key signature of A♭ major]	Fugue: Exposition
31	*sempre piano*	
116	Perdendo le forze, dolente. (Ermattet klagend.)	Arioso (2)
136	L'istesso tempo della Fuga.	Fugue: Modulatory Section
	poi a poi di nuovo viventi / nach und nach wiedger auflebend	
136	*sempre una corda*	
165	*poi a poi tutte le corde*	
168	Meno allegro. Etwas langsamer.	
172	*poi a poi più moto / nach und nach wieder geschwinder*	
174	[key signature of A♭ major]	Fugue: Closing Section

Fig. 3.1

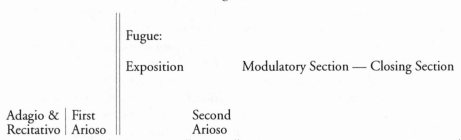

As I described in chapter 2, Schenker interprets the movement as structured around the fugue. The basic plan of the movement, according to Schenker, arises from the intention to present the fugue in two separate parts. Because the fugue consists of three sections (exposition, modulatory section, and closing section), there were two natural possibilities for the binary division: 1+2 or 2+1 sections. Either choice results in a proportional imbalance; the first also lacks the effect of parallelism between the two parts. Beethoven nevertheless chose the first and, as Schenker tells it, hit upon unprecedented solutions to each of the problems. The bipartition is effected by means of inserting an Arioso passage after the fugue's exposition. A similar Arioso is also placed before the exposition, thereby integrating the Arioso idea with the binary plan. An Adagio and Recitativo effect a transition from the purely instrumental world of the second movement to the vocal and lyrical world of the first Arioso. The resulting form has four main parts (fig. 3.1). Schenker accordingly organized his commentary into four sections, each headed by a general description of Beethoven's plan and followed by more detailed commentary on the plan's realization, discussion of the sketches and manuscripts in light of the final version, and recommendations for rendering the work in performance. Description of the musical effects whose synthesis is conveyed by the program is scattered among the various sections and subsections, so to represent it I have had to knit together remarks from a wide variety of contexts.

The program unfolds in four phases that correspond to the movement's four parts. The exclamatory recitative merges into the more coherent lament of an Arioso. The lament gives way to a more stable, healthier fugue. But then the movement lapses back into "an even deeper weakness and depression" in the second Arioso. The modulatory section of the fugue marks a gradual attainment of health ("poi a poi di nuovo vivente") and the closing section its exuberant affirmation.

Adagio and Recitativo

The Adagio (bars 1–3) presents three "compact" cadences that Schenker recommends rendering "with some certainty" admixed with "as much uncertainty as is required to express the sense, as it were, of groping and searching in the modulations" (54^269–70). The immediate musical object of the search is the stability of a key in which the lament will occur, A♭ minor. And although that key is reached and sustained in the subsequent Recitativo, the first strains of the recitative continue to project an unsettled, indecisive state (*Schwebezustand*). This state is produced, in the first place, by the unstable meter of the Recitativo: in contrast to the regular, well-projected 4/4 meter of bars 1–3, bar 4 unfolds in seven quarters, bar 5 in eight quarters less two thirty-seconds, and bar 6 in five quarters. Were it not for the pattern established in the Adagio and the radically different characters of bars 4, 5, and 6, there would be no cause to speak of them as metrical units.

Schenker singles out bar 5 for special attention (see ex. 3.4a), mainly because copyists and editors, seeing that the notes fall one sixteenth short of the full sum of eight quarters, remedied the deficit rather than impute to Beethoven an intention to realize an effect by means of the irregular notation (as usual, Schenker errs on the side of charity toward the composer). In the earliest editions, the initial appoggiatura is rewritten as a normal thirty-second note (thus as part of the bar and not as an embellishment within the first dotted eighth). That emendation did not entirely solve the problem, for it still left the bar one thirty-second short of eight quarters. Bülow left the appoggiatura in place and instead added a sixteenth just before the dotted sixteenth. Either emendation, says Schenker, destroys effects that support the program: a metrical uncertainty and a rhythmic instability produced by a series of syncopations. As ex. 3.4b shows, the first several syncopations identified by Schenker are quite straightforward; each a^2 is attacked on a metrical time point that is weaker than a later time point within its duration. Less straightforward, however, is the syncopation that includes the pairs of thirty-seconds. Here, says Schenker, where the attacks now come on strong parts of the bar (on the sixteenths), a much broader syncopation effect takes hold, for the series of paired thirty-seconds begins on a weak part of the bar (the third beat of the first half-bar) and is carried over into a stronger part (the first beat of the second half-bar). The left hand's chord in the first

Ex. 3.4. Beethoven, Piano Sonata op. 110, III: (*a*) bar 5 (Schenker's edition);
(*b*) based on *LfS110* fig. 84–85 (²83–84)

autograph is clearly positioned beneath the third-to-last pair of thirty-seconds; in fact, there is even a trace of an erased barline in the first autograph; because the first half of the bar sums to four quarters and the final three beats of the second half are clearly notated in quarters, the lapse must occur in the fifth quarter note.

Schenker also observes a rhythmic effect within the series of syncopations, namely, a striking of the tone at increasingly smaller intervals: three sixteenths, twice two sixteenths, twice one-and-a-half sixteenths, and nine times one sixteenth.

Schenker uses the image of "agitation" to describe the synthesis of the metrical lapse, syncopations, tone repetitions, rhythmic contraction, and dynamic curve: "Beethoven's intended impression of a tone at once palpitating according to the natural laws of a genuinely human passion in great agitation and also swelling and subsiding according to the laws of a highly stylized vocal art" (53²67).

The first Arioso

Two things distinguish the Arioso from the Adagio and Recitativo. First, it has a more determinate form, resulting from metrical normality, regular phrasing, and a rational progression of Stufen. And second, in that it appears to have a "will to modulate" away from A♭ minor (to C♭ major), it also manifests a vitality greater than that of the Recitativo. While both these features contribute to a sense of definiteness in the Arioso, they are restrained and counteracted by the halting rhythms of the melodic line, which Schenker interprets in terms of its deviation from a rhythmically "normal" melody. He suggests, for example, that players rehearse the melody of the first Arioso "in its stable outlines" (57²78) (see ex. 3.5). What he proposes is far more modest than the rhythmic interpretations we encountered in chapters 1 and 2.

Ex. 3.5. Beethoven, Piano Sonata op. 110, III: (*a*) *LfS110*, fig. 110 (²109);
(*b*) bars 9–12 (right hand)

Here Schenker stabilizes only the tones syncopated forward, leaving intact the suspensions of bars 10 and 12 and not at all attempting to interpret the actual melody in terms of its deviations from a rhythmically balanced line. Nevertheless, the intent is the same: he interprets a presented configuration in terms of its deviation from a normally structured configuration. Schenker even goes so far as to suggest that the anticipatory syncopations can be intensified if the player deviates slightly from the meter. If strict adherence to the meter is the appropriate means for expressing rhythmically normal phenomena, then it is inappropriate, he says, for the expression of abnormal rhythmic events such as these. Instead, a metrical give-and-take is required. The sensitive performer will usually respond to this type of situation by stretching the tempo slightly, causing the d♭² in bar 9, say, to fall later than it would under normal circumstances. By contrast, Schenker recommends the opposite: attack the d♭² in bar 9 prematurely, for that is a more effective association with the effect of the tone: anticipation. The left hand should assist in this effect by accelerating slightly as the d♭² approaches.

To help fix in the performer's mind the rhythmic effects he seeks (while declaring that without his own supervision the intended goal may not be realized), he draws upon a physical experience, one clearly associated with the programmatic content:

Anyone who has noticed how physical fatigue and frailty are sometimes expressed by involuntarily letting oneself fall down (which quite prematurely furnishes the position required for rest) will agree with my suggestion that in like manner the accompaniment in bar 9, instead of slowing, on the contrary ought to swoon [*hinsinken*], as it were, toward d♭² in order to rest a little just beyond d♭². . . . After having in this manner rendered vivid the anticipatory rhythmic shift as such, one should proceed but wearily to the end of the bar. (58²79)

The image of a person swooning is hardly mandated directly by any of the annotations shown in table 3.1, but it is consistent with them. And that seems sufficient for Schenker to make use of it in adumbrating this synthesis of rhythmic and metric effects.

The fact that the entire melody is characterized by such shifts is one of several reasons Schenker is led to extend the idea of physical weakness to the entire Arioso and to pull the preceding passages into the picture as well. Schenker's characterization is worth quoting at length, to illustrate how he weaves together attributions of musical and programmatic effects:

Arioso dolente. Both autographs also explicitly bear the German designation "klagender Gesang" [plaintive song]. The cloud of the recitative has condensed and now all the mourning, instead of continuing to vent itself merely in exclamations, already assumes more determinate form, without, however, stepping beyond those bounds that are placed upon a corporeal weakness [*Ohnmacht*] for purely physical reasons. For if it is understood that the impetus toward the incorporation of newer and newer ideas in an associative sense presumes, so to speak, an activity of health and consequently signifies the expenditure of a healthy drive ever striving for more distant goals, then it will be understood immediately that merely a tiny spark of life, by contrast, cannot as effectively fuel the blaze of newer and newer ideas. So, then, in our case, too, the (programmatically hypothesized) wretched corporeal constitution of the author naturally restricts the scope of the form, and what could perhaps be interpreted in it as a will toward modulation (from A♭ minor to C♭ major), and therefore at the same time, too, as a symptom of an initial victory over impotence, is instead again brought closer to the image of an actual impotence by wracking the tones of the melody forward in most cases from the rhythmically stronger positions, as though broken and worn out. This very state of hovering between a psychical brokenness in the tones and their yearning for a form still so modest and so clear, this very state of hovering constitutes the character of the *Arioso.* (55²72)

This passage is also noteworthy for Schenker's parenthetical indication that the attribution of the psychological program to Beethoven is hypothetical. The effect of the parenthetical is identical to that of *gleichsam* in the remarks on the diminished fourths in Mozart's symphony. It permits Schenker all the rhetorical force of the attribution while avoiding the implication that the relation between the program's content and Beethoven's actual physical condition is any firmer than a plausible hypothesis.

How, then, are we to understand the Arioso hypothetically in terms of a "wretched corporeal constitution"? A weak view would run as follows: Beethoven composed an arrangement of tones that an appropriately backgrounded listener may take as an expression of weakness and depression. This weak view, I suggest, is what Schenker holds for freely invented interpretants of the sort encountered in his comment on Mozart's symphony. Here, however, where so many annotations in the text of op. 110 point to an intended psychological program, Schenker would hold a stronger, yet still modest view: Beethoven composed an arrangement of tones intending that an appropriately backgrounded listener would recognize it as an expression of weakness and depression. This modest view, I suggest, is what Schenker holds when programmatic content is specified by the composer, either through a title, a program, or through annotations in the score. In the case of op. 110, however, Schenker promotes an even stronger view of expression, for he appears to hold the view that Beethoven composed this arrangement of tones intending that an appropriately backgrounded listener would interpret it as an expression of weakness and depression actually experienced by the composer. Schenker draws the following conclusion after the long paragraph quoted above:

In this way we taste Beethoven's pain in the Arioso. What a god, who surrenders his own pain to others merely for [their] enjoyment! I daresay no one could actually share in his pain, because (as I have already stated elsewhere) reading the great book of his heroic life was even more difficult than reading his works, so he lamented his pain in tones, and now, only in sounding do they entice people to enjoyment! (55²72)

Even this account, however, remains hypothetical. What makes it plausible is the psychological nature of the program and the generally known fact that Beethoven suffered much in his life.

Fugue: exposition

If the plaint of the Arioso took place within a "palpitating, trembling atmosphere," an atmosphere of hovering between psychical weakness and yearning for health, the first taste of escaping the cause for lamentation and satisfying that yearning is expressed in the exposition of the fugue (57²76, 65²96–97).

The binary division of the fugue into 1+2 sections creates a proportional imbalance between the two parts, which Beethoven rectifies by expanding the content of the exposition, presenting not one but three sets of thematic entries separated by relatively long episodes. Schenker describes the overall effect of the exposition as "a peculiarly quiet, indeed reserved seriousness that leans strongly toward solemnity without quite achieving it" (65²96). "Reserved behavior" characterizes the synthesis of its tonal and dynamic aspects, for all but one of the nine thematic entries appears in either the tonic or dominant triad of A♭ major and most of the entries share a common dynamic state (*sempre piano*). The effect of bringing the section to a close is signaled by the one exceptional entry (in D♭ major) and completed by means of stretti and a pedal point (59²82). Despite the *sempre piano*, there are a number of *fortes* notated within the exposition; these are to be taken, Schenker says, *cum grano salis*, as inflections within the general *piano* and not as full-bodied *fortes*. In bar 70, for example, he states that "the *f* has to be understood less in its absolute, physical sense [i.e., as a degree of loudness] and more in the sense of a psychical agitation that is intensified here as if merely involuntarily and by means of which the motive of the episode is placed increasingly higher" (65²96). The *forte*, then, along with the increasing height of the episode's motive and the extension of this episode beyond the limits set for previous episodes, together – that is, synthetically – have an effect akin to "agitation," a state of activity temporarily out of control, out of keeping with the more normal, reserved behavior of the exposition. The *fortissimo* in bars 73 ff., to cite another example, comes right after a *piano* in bar 72 and is "all the more surprising" because it appears precisely when one should expect a thematic entry in *piano*; it is a "sudden contrast," both in terms of its dynamic and its content (a false entry), that "serves as a preparation for further contrastive effects in the episode" (65²96).

Ex. 3.6. Beethoven, Piano Sonata op. 110, III: (*a*) *LfS110*, fig. 110 (²109) (transposed);
(*b*) bars 9–12 (transposed); (*c*) bars 116–21

The second Arioso

The effects whose synthesis is characterized in terms of the program as a "relapse
into the lament" and into a "state of even deeper weakness and depression" are based
on repetition and contrast (65–66²96–97). The second Arioso repeats the harmonic
motion, modulatory plan, and melodic line of the first, but deviates more intensely
from a rhythmically normal melody (ex. 3.6). Schenker interprets this more intense
deviation as if it were the expression of a more serious psychological crisis:

In the second Arioso we see the suffering bodied forth, as it were; we see clearly how the
sufferer [i.e., Beethoven, hypothetically] stammers, how he labors and breaks down, strug-
gles up and sinks – in short, how the tones nearly become lines and how the piece nearly
becomes an actual likeness of misery. In order to bring about this effect, . . . Beethoven
mainly uses a type of abbreviation. (66²98)

By "abbreviation," Schenker means that what had been a longer note value in the
original version of a motive is replaced with a shorter note value and subsequent
rest. The effect is akin to stammering: "the original fullness is sheltered in the shortened, stammered tone exactly as it had been in the longer, unbroken tone" (66²99).
The melody of the second Arioso presents numerous abbreviations (compare ex.
3.6*b* and *c*) as well as a greater number of anticipations and anticipatory rhythmic
shifts (see the lines between *b* and *c*).

In his commentary on bars 116, 118, and 119 (see ex. 3.6), Schenker gauges the
musical effects by imagining the second Arioso as a fictional singer's attempt at a
second rendition of the first Arioso. The designation "Arioso" alone is sufficient to
warrant interpreting the melody as if it were actually sung, and in point of fact

Schenker approached all melody, from the Urlinie to the tune hammered out in the most extreme register of the piano, as if it were vocally conceived (*Erl, FS* 30/10 and 175/107, *LfS109* 32–33^{2}17–18); but the presence of an imaginary singer would normally go unremarked, whereas here the program warrants its mention. Schenker attributes the increased rhythmic complexity of the second Arioso to the singer's increased difficulty with breath control, a difficulty presumably due to the onset of an even deeper depression:

Where before (i.e., in the first Arioso) the breath had always extended long enough, here (in the second Arioso) it is now shortened; yet because it lacks endurance, it suddenly breaks off and must begin a second time and repeats the tone that it cannot sustain, still expressly striving as if for clarity. ... Quite incomparable in figurative gesture are the abbreviations in bars 120–21: the breath, for which strength seems to stream in from a mysterious source, can already carry the tone longer, but it also is deceived – one hears it clearly – quite near to the tone that it wants to achieve – it suddenly breaks off there in the last possible moment and looks toward the goal that nevertheless seems so certain to it. In vain, then, does the tone b♭^{1} in bar 120 struggle toward the tone c^2, c^2 toward d^2 in bar 121 and so forth. (67^{2}99–100)

The effect of melodic disintegration is promoted by the accompaniment as well. In the first Arioso, the left hand had been relatively free of rhythmic abnormalities. The second begins in the same fashion, but in the second half (bar 123 ff.) it "manifests an analogous disintegration in the form of suspensions and anticipations."

As in the first Arioso, the fourth and final phrase is rounded out with a brief appendix, the content of which echoes the concluding two tones of that phrase's melody ($\hat{2}$–$\hat{1}$), sounding in octaves in the lower register. But suddenly, in the upbeat of bar 132, where that two-tone motive is expected to conclude, the third appears in place of the root; and not the minor third that would be consistent with the mode of the Arioso, but instead the major third. And that, together with the "gradual swelling" of the cadential harmony (G major), "expresses a presentiment of the future harmony of health [i.e., the major key of the fugue] that will actively stride forth and fashion deeds" (67^{2}101).

Fugue: modulatory section

The "program of binary division" obliges Beethoven to fashion the beginning of the modulatory section as a parallel to the exposition, "as if the fugue had not been interrupted, that is, as if it only began right here" (67^{2}101). Beethoven's solution is to resume the fugue in the key of the second Arioso (G minor) and reintroduce the voices one by one using an inversion of the theme. The programmatic process of a gradual return to health conveys the combined effects of the gradual reentry of the voices, the gradual resumption of the fugue, the gradual retransition to the harmony that signifies health (A♭ major), and the gradual return to normal (uninverted) thematic behavior. Moreover, as in the exposition, the program incorporates the effect of the dynamic shadings: a gradual increase from the implied *pianissimo* of the *sempre una corda* in bar 136, through a *crescendo* beginning in bar 160 and reaching *piano* in bar 168, another *crescendo* starting in bar 172, and then, in the first bar of the closing section, the attainment of an actual *forte*.

Another component in the synthesis is a complex process of acceleration. First, a thematic acceleration is accomplished by introducing the subject in diminution (eighths) in bar 152, though the accelerating effect is initially offset by a statement of the theme in augmentation beginning in bar 153. While that statement unfolds, the eighths of the counterpoint gradually give way to sixteenths. A single pair of sixteenths appears in the downbeat of bar 153, and again in the downbeats of bars 154, 155, and 156. Then, in bar 157, a pair of sixteenths in both downbeat and upbeat. The pace increases yet one more increment as two pairs of sixteenths appear in the downbeat of bar 158, and then, from the upbeat of bar 159, a continuous stream of sixteenths, "an intensification which in itself signifies not only the unfolding of an increasingly improving life ('poi a poi di nuovo vivente') but also the first announcement of a higher intensification" (68^2103). The next stage of intensification begins in bar 168, where the counterpoint is now refashioned from a "double diminution that, because it consists exclusively of sixteenths and thirty-seconds, naturally necessitates an uninterrupted motion of sixteenths" (69^2105). This acceleration, too, is somewhat restrained, in that the slightly slower pace of *meno allegro* indicated in bar 168 "urges the player to restrain somewhat the prevailing tempo on account of the thematic significance of these sixteenths" (70^2108). Only with an accelerando beginning in bar 172 does the movement approach an uninterrupted motion of sixteenths in the original tempo; Schenker recommends that the acceleration culminate in bar 174, where the sixteenths lose their thematic significance and instead of expressing a single voice in sixteenths now have the effect of compounding two voices moving in eighths.

Fugue: closing section

With the coincidence of the return to *allegro* and the attainment of a true *forte*, the closing section of the fugue commences. It culminates in an exhilarating statement of the fugal theme in the highest reaches of the piano above a thundering tonic pedal, a pedal that can be interpreted as a sign of stability and, given the program, as a sign of restored health (see ex. 3.7). Now is the time of "that future harmony of health" in which deeds are fueled by a tonic pedal point that "draws to itself all the hitherto accumulated energy" (73^2113). As the theme above the pedal nears its conclusion in bar 203, it breaks from its appointed path, just after reaching its peak at the tone f^3. Instead of returning from there to close below on the tonic $a\flat^2$, the line surpasses its peak, climbing first to $g\flat^3$ in bar 204. After that tone falls back to f^3, the melody climbs still higher, to $a\flat^3$ in bar 206; again it falls back a step. But once again it climbs upward, to $b\flat^3$ in bar 208. And then, instead of falling back to $a\flat^3$, the line lights upon c^4:[12]

---

[12] In short, the line executes a series of what Schenker would later bring under the technical concept of reaching-over (*Übergreifen*).

Ex. 3.7. Beethoven, Piano Sonata op. 110, III, bars 200–213

Yet see the immense passion that the final tones develop just in order to be able to carry out their assumed role [i.e., in the program], see that immense passion rise to exuberance as if nourished by itself alone, so that they at first fly beyond their real goal (which is what the tone a♭³ seems to be); and so in bar 209, as if they could not bridle their passion as suddenly as required, they bring instead of the expected tone a♭³ its higher third c⁴! As a mark of just this type of untamed and overexcited passion, the harmony remains in *ff* for four bars, becoming intoxicated with itself, as it were, in its own boisterousness. (73²113)

In the final bar of the fugue and of the sonata c⁴ yields to a♭³, which Schenker interprets as an invitation to an even grander programmatic interpretation: "Whoever so desires may find therein a passionately affirmative answer to the fundamental question [*Urfrage*] that the first bar of the first movement seems to raise" (73²114).

The program of op. 110 is mandated by indications that are a matter of record. When such indications take the form of notations entered into the text of the work, and not, say, programmatic interpretations recorded in a diary or private correspondence, Schenker seems to consider the programmatic content as belonging to the work in question. If so, it forms part of "the purely factual" basis on which Schenker grounded his interpretations. Why, then, instead of stating programmatic content in the indicative mood, does he persist in using the subjunctive and the conjectural *gleichsam*? My guess is that without the constant reminder of "as if"s and "as it were"s, Schenker thought we might be tempted to regard the sound as a mere signifier, a vehicle, and concentrate our attention on a signified, a meaning, thereby exchanging word for tone as the object of our attention. Instead, Schenker wants to keep attention firmly fixed on the sensible tonal object and its effects.

The "as if"s and "as it were"s serve that desire by robbing the ideas in the program of their substantive vehicle. There is no body swooning in bar 9 of the *Arioso dolente*. There is only swooning. Swooning is not what bar 9 means, as if the tones somehow pointed to the concept of swooning. Quite the contrary: "swooning" points to the tones and the complexion of their effects. Schenker's qualification of the physical imagery with "as it were" sets off the analytical fiction from the reality of tones and effects. I suggest that this is how Schenker indicates, without saying so, that the purpose of the fictional is to elucidate the tonal. It is a vehicle and practical aid, and not the consummation of meaning. Corroborating this is the fact that he always embeds analytical fictions firmly and inextricably within representation of musical effects; never, in fact, does he offer a programmatic interpretation without the support of such a representation. After all, not to provide a representation of the musical effects that support the programmatic would violate his most basic rule of interpretation (see the Introduction).

The type of programmatic content that most attracts Schenker is the dynamic process: psychical vicissitude in op. 110 and, as we will see, unpredictable, chaotic behavior in Beethoven's op. 109. He expresses this preference for dynamic qualities several times in the introduction to *Der freie Satz*, including the following passage:

In its Züge music reflects the human soul in all its movements and changes – "everything passing is but a likeness" – and yet how differently does today's idol, the machine [reflect the soul]: with its effect, it too in fact dissembles an organic [entity], but since its components are each appointed a partial goal, a partial achievement, it leads as a totality only to an aggregate that has nothing in common with the human soul! (*FS* 6/xxiii–xxiv)[13]

Schenker is careful not to say that the Züge mimic or refer to the human soul; rather, they "reflect" the soul, and not even every aspect of it but only its "movements and changes." An object has a reflected image only if it is first brought before a mirror and observed. This is crucial. It is Schenker who created the setting, who placed the

---

[13] Oster mistakenly renders "anders" as an adjective and thereby partially obscures Schenker's comparison between how music and the machine reflect (or fail to reflect) the human soul.

soul before the surface of the tones and observed its reflection. As with real mirrors, the reflection created and observed by Schenker is partial. Strikingly, what it does not reflect, according to Schenker, are its feeling states and moods.[14] Or at least not directly, for if music is an art of movement, the representation of a state is beyond its means, except insofar as a state can be expressed in movement. For example, when the program of op. 110 involved physical and mental states (in the two Ariosos and in the culmination of the fugue), Schenker sought to interpret the tones in terms of how such states might be expressed in bodily movements and the cadences of speech, the latter leading naturally to interpretation in terms of the stylized expression of a vocal lament.

III

Beethoven, Piano Sonata op. 109, second movement, development section

Schenker's interpretation of the development section focuses on a single motive, originally presented as the bass counterpoint in the first thematic idea of the exposition (ex. 3.8). The basic content of the motive is an evenly paced, four-tone, stepwise descent (what he would later call a Zug), whose third tone is "inflected" by the skip of a third in the direction of the passing motion. The motive is repeated in varied form in bars 5–8, but then does not reappear until bars 66–69 (see ex. 3.9), where it functions as a rhetorical "apostrophe," invoking the absent thematic entity in a flourish within the final cadence of the exposition. This apostrophe prepares for the development section, which is suffused with repetitions of the motive.

A canonic pattern of imitations presented by two upper voices above a bass tremolo starts the development (ex. 3.9). The imitations are led by the lower of the two upper voices. The motives in each voice are chained together to form even longer descending lines. These continue without interruption until bar 80, where the uppermost, imitating voice, rather than proceeding on the downward path, instead repeats its last statement (with chromatic alterations that tonicize the C-major triad). The first tone of this restatement is placed an octave lower, so that it appears also as a retention of the pitch from which the lower voice departed just two bars earlier. When it returns to the higher register across bars 80/81, the lower voice also ascends (see the arrows). As a result, the content of bars 81–82

appears involuntarily as an inversion of bars 79–80 (*pace* a♭ and a♮!) and dissembles what seems to be a newly derived, two-bar motive. (*LfS109* 38²30)

Schenker then tries to capture the synthesis of these effects:

If one considers that the point of departure for the rhythmic operations has been the four-bar quality of the development's motive, then one will notice in the three-bar quality of bars

---

[14] See Guck, "Questions of Interpretation in Musical Analysis" (paper presented at the conference on Music and Meaning held at the University of Cincinnati, December 1993).

Ex. 3.8. Beethoven, Piano Sonata op. 109, II, bars 1–4

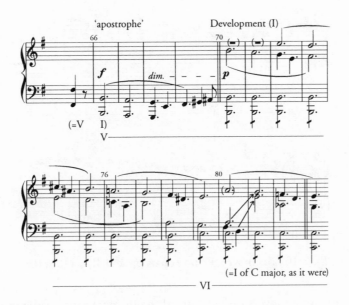

Ex. 3.9. Beethoven, Piano Sonata op. 109, II, bars 66–83

78–80 (see the lower voice!) and the two-bar quality of bars 81–82 (upper and lower voices!) the association of a world (of imitations) collapsing into itself, as it were! (38²30)

The result of this catastrophe is "chaos."

If, as suggested, we measure the effects of the development in terms of the motive's content, the following musical effects arise in the wake of the catastrophe. A switch from the original descending form of the motive to its inversion marks a divide between the two halves of the development. The second half (ex. 3.10) begins by apparently renewing the imitative play in inversion, but now without the stabilizing influence of the bass tremolo and with a variety of disruptions. What seems as if it will be the first statement of the inverted motive in the bass of bar 83 ff. shows no inflection in its third bar; the inflection does appear, by contrast, in the imitating voice (bar 87), but is then stretched into the next bar. Meanwhile, a third voice enters in bar 87, only to break off before reaching the third-inflection in its third bar. A fourth voice enters in bar 89, apparently in imitation of the third, but it

Ex. 3.10. Beethoven, Piano Sonata op. 109, II, bars 83–108

turns out to be not an inversion but instead the original form of the motive; at the same time, the ascending bass is pulled back into the lower octave (see the arrow). Anticipatory tones in the bass in bars 87–88 obscure the registral shift with a misplaced inflection. Despite being the voice that inaugurated the second half of the development, the bass does not manifest the inflection within a motivic statement until bar 91. Schenker describes the synthesis from the vantage point of bar 91:

And now, suddenly, all the riddles of the preceding events become fully clear! Only now and from here on do we grasp in retrospect why Beethoven upset the structure of the imitations and created, as it were, a chaos; why, further, he at first spread a mist ("sul una corda"!) over bars 83–86 and let such strange voices emerge from it in the right hand, wandering ghostlike (voices which of course, in another respect, are supposed to substitute for the previous tremolo in the left hand); why, finally, he suppressed for so long the third-figure in the inverted motive in the lowest voice! All this was aimed only at the one goal of concealing in darkness for as long as possible the artistic intent and staving off full acknowledgment of the inversion technique for the sake of tension! (39²32)

The third-inflection is a distinguishing mark in the otherwise stepwise motive and, by always appearing in the third of the motive's four bars, clearly orients the listener to the motive's time span, which is why its failure to appear in the bass voice is so significant, for without it the passage is disoriented ("wandering"). The upper line's imitative entries are barely discernible ("ghostlike"), and overall there is a great deal of uncertainty about whether we are in fact dealing with the motive and whether an instance begins here or there ("chaos"). This programmatic effect and also the contrast of the inversion serve the purpose of making the reprise sound fresh, even though it begins with the very same motive.

The third-inflection in bar 91 is the turning point from chaos to order. The upper voice's complete statement of the original form of the motive and the registral shifts in bars 89 and 93 produce a return to the four-bar quality of the motive. But as the upper voice completes its statement of the original motive in bar 92, the bass voice strays, turning to d♯ instead of e and then dropping in bar 93 to E instead of stepping up to e. In bar 93, the upper voice again presents the motive in its original descending form against the inverted form of the bass – but again, the third bar of the motive defies expectations, as each voice inflects the third in the opposite direction; these inverted inflections produce the effect of switching in midstream from one form of the motive to the other. The outer lines of bars 93–96 are exchanged in bars 97–100. To interpret the synthesis of these effects, Schenker shifts imagery from chaos and darkness to a more human image, that of uncooperative tones who are induced to return to their original path. In doing so, he may be picking up an implication of his earlier statement about the involuntary truncation of motives:

In the lower line, which as before remains the decisive one, the first two dotted halves already pull [*ziehen*] downward, hence in a manner that corresponds to the original, while the third and fourth tones in bars 99–100 (dragging with them, as it were, the bad fruit of the figure in bar 95!) still proceed in the [manner of the] inversion. As if it were now a matter of breaking the impediment of unruly tones, Beethoven endeavors in bars 101–2 to bring the last two tones (like the first and second tones) back onto the track [*Geleise*] of the original. Only after this last impression of the original type of motion does the bass line finally regain, as it were, its awareness of the original version, and in fact the original in bar 105 ff. of the reprise stretches its limbs with all the force they originally possessed! (39²32)[15]

The movement closes with another instance of a motive's defiance overcome. The closing section begins with four repeated tones, but when repeated in a brief coda-like passage, the same tones, originally notated as ♩⁷ and played *forte*, are now notated as ♩. and played *piano*:

Notated thus, and pulled into *piano* and legato besides, the closing idea at last appears subdued in last recess of its original defiance, as it were. (40²34)

Where the opposite operation, abbreviation, had the effect in op. 110 of compressing and concentrating the force of a tone within a briefer span of time, here the effect, predictably, is the reverse: a dilution of force.

---

[15] Because of their connection with the direct passing motion of the motive, the words *ziehen* and *Geleise* in this passage have the same interpretive force as the related term *Zug*.

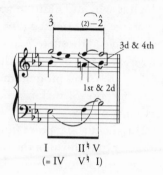

Ex. 3.11. Beethoven, Symphony no. 3, I (based on *Mw* 3, fig. 2)

IV

Beethoven, Symphony no. 3, first movement, exposition

Schenker's essay on Beethoven's Third Symphony, issued in 1930, was to become the last text in the series of "independent literature appendices" that accompanied *Neue musikalische Theorien und Phantasien*.[16]

Within the extraordinarily rich analysis of effects provided for the first movement, Schenker invents a program. Like the program invented for op. 109, it does not take in the entirety of the movement. Two rhetorical veins converge in Schenker's program: the greater contribution comes from imagery that he built into his theory (for example, the tone's procreative urge, its desire for emancipation, and the behavior of executing a Zug); the lesser contribution stems from Beethoven's inscription on the title page of the work, "Sinfonia eroica, composta per festeggiare il souvenir di un grand' Uomo . . ." The invented program that emerges from these two sources centers on the youthful acts of a hero.

The basic premise (*Ursatz*) of Schenker's interpretation of the first movement's exposition is given in example 3.11. The point I want to concentrate on is the first-order Zug that unfolds a descending fifth from scale degree $\hat{2}$ and provides the transitory V with a closural effect. In point of fact, $\hat{2}$ is the point of departure for not one but *four* executions of the descending fifth-Zug. And consequently, the question that weighed on Schenker's mind concerned how Beethoven postpones full realization of the Zug's closural effect until the fourth and final execution. What do the first three executions lack that, in effect, "drives the action onward"?

The first pair of executions connects the anticipatory $\hat{2}$ with the inner voice's b♭, while the second pair composes out the fifth-space within the V Stufe (see the

[16] The appendices are continued beyond the third yearbook of *Mw* with the issuance in 1932 of *FUT*, a second volume of which was planned but never issued. As much is indicated by Schenker in the foreword to *FUT*, where he writes that the present work was published as a result of the encouraging response to his Urlinie graphs of Beethoven's Third. He goes on to say, with perhaps unintentional hyperbole, that "the presentation in graphic form has now developed to the point that makes an explanatory text unnecessary."

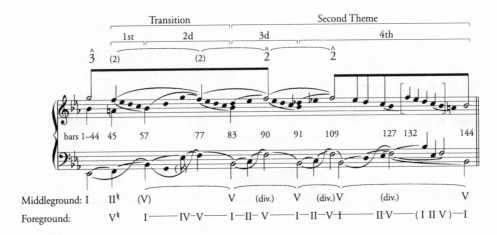

Ex. 3.12. Beethoven, Symphony no. 3, I, bars 1–144 (based on *Mw* 3, Urlinie-Tafel)

brackets in ex. 3.12). The first pair thus belongs to the transition section and the second pair to the second theme. The four executions of the Zug are shown in greater detail in example 3.12. Each execution furnishes the basic melodic content for a thematic unit (i.e., the Zug is the interpretive measure of the melodic content in each unit). The units span bars 45–57, 57–83, 83–91, and 91–144. Schenker divides his discussion according to these units and at the conclusion of each he comments on the synthesis of effects in the passage. It is this interpretive path that I will follow.

The first fifth-Zug (bars 44–57) is presented in two versions, one slowly unfolding over the entire span and one hurriedly executed in the concluding bars (see ex. 3.13). A texture saturated with motivic repetitions projects a four-bar hypermeter and provides a temporal rule by which to measure and compare the pace of the entwined executions. The seeds of Schenker's programmatic interpretation are sown in a comment on the bass counterpoint:

At the end, namely, at c^3 in the last quarter of bar 56, both versions of the first falling fifth-Zug are entwined; one which glides over the peak tones of the first flute and one which is more accelerated in bars 55–57.

The bass sets only the bare fall of a fifth (= B♭:V–I) against the first falling fifth-Zug of bars 45–57, without rendering its individual tones self-sufficient by making them consonant in some contrapuntal fashion. (*Mw* 3: 33)

The language of the last sentence is reminiscent of the image Schenker uses to portray tonal relations in *Harmonielehre*. There he underscored the essential moments of his harmonic theory by means of "biological" metaphors.[17] To underscore

---

[17] Schenker has in mind not biology as a science, but in a wider sense as the study of life, in this case the life of tones (*Tonleben*); among the "biological moments" of music presented in *Hl* one finds not only physical metaphors (e.g., procreation), but also social and legal analogies (family relations, constitutions, social contracts, etc.).

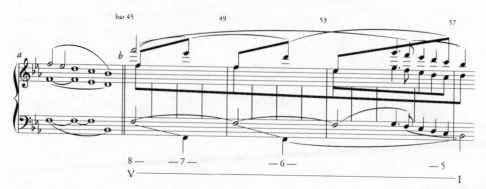

Ex. 3.13. Beethoven, Symphony no. 3, I, bars 45–57 (based on *Mw* 3, Urlinie-Tafel)

the axiomatic status of the triad, Schenker presents it in terms of the most basic and natural biological relation that can obtain between two individuals, a relation that arises from the fundamental biological impulse of the individual to procreate. The procreative urge is the first manifestation of the tone's natural egoism. One of the analogy's virtues is that it conveys the internal differentiation within the triadic entity: (1) one entity is the source of the others, (2) the generated individuals are dependent upon the source entity for their identity, and (3) the dependants are ranked, with one (the fifth) enjoying the rights of primogeniture. The generated tones, however, are also endowed with the same natural egoism, the exercise of which leads to the dissolution of the first family and the establishment of new triadic units.

The same image is applied here to the dissonant passing tone, which is emancipated when a counterpointing voice enters into a consonant relation with it.[18] In the case of a Zug, the bond that is sublated through this emancipation is the bond between the passing tone(s) and the initiating head-tone (*Kopfton*). Without that emancipation, the head-tone remains in force even at the completion of the Zug, keeping the effect of coming to rest from emerging fully.[19]

If the next thematic unit (bars 57–83) is interpreted in terms of the melodic Zug, the initial tone has the effect of being delayed. The line gradually wends its way back to f^3, using a pair of reaching-over motives (the first executed in two registers) to scale the arpeggiation $bb^{[1]2}–d^{[2]3}–f^{[2]3}$ (see ex. 3.14). Accompanying the doubled execution of the first reaching-over motive are two presentations of a variation on the hurried fifth-progression from bars 55–57 (the motivic variation noted by

---

[18] This is not to be confused with the emancipated (*emanzipiert*) passing tone described in *Kp1* 248/284. The term used here is a form of the verb *verselbständigen*, a word used in legal contexts for the emancipation of a child from its first family; see, for example, Hegel, *Elements of the Philosophy of Right*, ed. Allen H. Wood, trans. H. B. Nisbet (Cambridge: Cambridge University Press, 1991), 214–15.

[19] Compare Schenker's remarks in *FS* on the effect of a third-Zug above a stationary bass: "The third-Zug $e^2–d^2–c^2$, supported merely by the root of the I Stufe, would only express the one tone e^2 and not yet the Urlinie-Zug 3–2–1: the bass lacks the arpeggiation and thus any movement whatsoever" (*FS* 43/19).

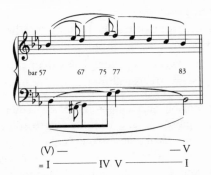

Ex. 3.14. Beethoven, Symphony no. 3, I, bars 57–83 (based on *Mw* 3, Urlinie-Tafel)

Ex. 3.15 Beethoven, Symphony no. 3, I, bars 55–68 (based on *Mw* 3, Urlinie-Tafel)

Schenker, shown here beneath the score in ex. 3.15, is concealed within a more obvious variation of the same motive, which I have bracketed in the bass line of the example). These motivic statements, says Schenker, seem "as if [they] wanted to make amends after the fact for their earlier rhythmic and harmonic haste" (34). But the repetitions by themselves cannot make the necessary amends, nor can the more elaborate bass line in bars 57–77. And, in the end, the bass accompanying the execution of the fifth-Zug again fails to emancipate the passing tones, for the upper line reaches the Zug's starting point only after the motivic enrichment of the bass is finished. It reaches its starting tone just as the bass reaches the dominant (bar 77) and, after momentarily holding that tone suspended above the dominant, it plunges through the Zug at a pace even more precipitous than that of the first. Schenker's closing remarks on this passage are as follows:

And yet, despite all this undeniable enrichment of the bass's counterpoint, the falling fifth-Zug in bars 78–83, which is mostly what it comes down to, still does not have a counter-point that would render the individual tones [of the Zug] independent. Once again the bare leap of a fifth (V–I) is all there is! A singable diminution [in the upper voice], however, does not appear in the present course of events and arpeggiations prevail instead (though of course, besides the parallelisms in the arpeggiations, the conduct of the bass takes care of their organic effect). This ought to be looked upon perhaps as something programmatic: it is as if the arpeggiations are used to express a seizing done at first without consideration, to express a youthful unaffectedness and lack of concern. (34)

The invented program (note the precautionary "perhaps" and the subjunctive mood) synthesizes three effects. (1) As before, the bass lacks tones that would eman-cipate the passing tones of the Zug and leaves them in a youthful condition. (2) Without the slower version of the Zug and with the increased pace (now eighths instead of quarters), the execution of the Zug is all the more hasty and rash. And (3) arpeggiations in the upper line (bars 65–68) are not further elaborated into a sing-able line and are thus immature as melody.

The program invented by Schenker is strikingly indeterminate. Its content is represented by a nominalized verb – *Zugreifen*, "seizing" – and an attributive phrase that describes its manner, but there is no mention of either agent or object. Whose seizing is it? What is it that is seized? Schenker crafts his words to avoid answering such questions. What stands center stage is the manner of the behavior, the dynamic quality itself. If there is an agent whose seizing this is, it is perhaps "the hero," not a specific person but a type, a concept. This much is authorized by Beethoven's title, about which Schenker writes the following:

No appearance of a hero, be it ever so overwhelming, no program, be it ever so vividly preconceived, could have enabled Beethoven [to write] such a work, had not his original, ingenious predisposition and the artistic experiences he had collected since his youth al-ready risen to the point of finally impelling a musically heroic expression. The readiness of the master for such a new and intensified music is what in the first place evokes the plan of the heroic symphony; the reverse is inconceivable. Thus Beethoven's celebration of the hero far sooner comes down to heroically celebrating the art of tone through his work and ultimately, of course, himself as its heroic mediator!

This simple observation disposes of all the legends that want to recognize the head of a specific hero – Napoleon or Nelson – in the noteheads of the symphony. (85)

If there is a hero whose youthful character is chronicled in this movement, it is likely Beethoven, for Schenker's essay bears the dedication "Beethoven dem Helden" – To

Beethoven, the hero. But establishing the identity of the hero is ancillary to Schenker's programmatic interpretation and its purpose, adumbrating the sound of synthesis.

The content of the third thematic unit (see examples 1.26 and 1.27) resembles the second, in that the initiation of the Zug is delayed by a motion from an inner voice elaborated with reaching-over motives (there it was an arpeggiation, here an ascending third-Zug). As I stated in chapter 1, there is nothing in Schenker's theory that attaches an effect to the synthesis of a protracted preparation and a Zug hastily executed with the barest of harmonic support, but he nevertheless reaches for a description, which he couches in programmatic terms:

The falling fifth-Zug in bars 90–91, which is now the third fifth-Zug . . . , also still remains without any contrapuntal emancipation of its individual tones. So despite the gravitation towards speech and song, as must be manifested in the repetition of tones, [there] continues [to be] an almost programmatic restriction of the bass prolongations in the end at the critical juncture! But this is also what drives the action [*Handlung*] onward; we sense, indeed we know, that the bass of the falling fifth-Zug, too, must eventually receive its contrapuntal due, and we all the more eagerly await the progress of the action. (36)

Only in the extended consequent phrase that follows, where the Zug is finally worked out, twice, above a contrapuntal bass (see ex. 3.12), is there satisfaction to be found: for the bass, for the Zug, for the hero, and now, more explicitly, for those who participate in the drama as witnesses:

So, then, in the consequent phrase, the initiating tone of the fifth-Zug appears for the first time on the I Stufe; this now announces the long-due working through of the fifth-Zug . . . the hastening to the I Stufe [of B♭ major] under the $\hat{2}$ constitutes the main distinction between antecedent and consequent. (37)

In the swifter progress of the small fifth-Zug built inside [the larger] is echoed the all-too-swift ebb [*Ablauf*] of the first three fifth-Züge falling from $f^{3(2)}$. (42)

The programmatic interpretation extends beyond the transition section and ultimately ties together all four executions of the fifth-Zug. In fact, it is probably his inclination to treat motivic history as the development of character and the identity of the Zug as the unifying trait of the transition and second theme that leads Schenker to invent what amounts to a dramatic plot, the early scenes of which are suffused with the expectation that the callowness of youth will give way to maturity.

One resource for inventing this interpretation of synthesis lay at hand within the words of Schenker's theory of effects, both in the names he invented for effects and in the imagery he used to convey them. Adverbial qualifications of the term Zug, for example, conveyed the contributions made by other tones and effects in the context. Such an interpretive move keeps readers mindful of the metaphorical resonances that make a term like Zug apt for certain tonal configurations.

The term Zug, as noted in chapter 2, draws upon a diverse set of ideas:

- a trait or characteristic (as in a motive)
- the physical arrangement of discrete entities into a linear series
- the action of pulling
- an uninterrupted, unimpeded motion
- the more complex motion of a train, departing, traversing intermediate points, arriving at a destination.

Since one of the dimensions in which the Zug is drawn is time, the line of a Zug is subject to interpretation as a process, a directed motion from one place to another. One domain of Schenker's interpretive extension of the Zug concept rests on interpreting the line as a path (*Weg*) and the process of its execution as path-taking. And as soon as he speaks of these, he can speak of the intention to travel a certain path and thence the manifold ways in which the intention can be actualized, frustrated, fulfilled, and so forth.

The content of the Zug *qua* intention has three components: a *goal* that lies elsewhere within the known terrain,[20] a *path* to the goal that is the most direct imaginable, and a *pace* of regular, measured steps by which the path will be traveled. Interpreting the Zug in itself as the content of an intention and its traversal as the execution of that intention obviously accords with Schenker's practice of interpreting tonal content as the composer's realization of intended effects. The following list provides a sample of qualifiers that Schenker uses to convey manner of realization:

- kinds of path taking: steps, skips, leaps[21]
- directions: up, down, from the outside in, from the inside out, climbing, etc.
- pace and manner: hesitant, storming, gliding, hastening, tumbling, dragging, etc.
- protraction of path taking: delays, setbacks, detours.[22]

Schenker's aesthetic preference for fulfillment and satisfaction is clearly revealed in the priority assigned to the goal. No matter what resistance is experienced in the taking of the path, it is always overcome: the pleasure of the path can be extended, protracted, but not in the end voided. One reason Schenker gives for preferring goal-oriented movement is that he can thereby find in art what is rarely found in life, namely, the experience of fulfillment that comes with attainment of a desired goal (FS 9/xxiv). It may be that Schenker strongly desired the artistic experience of fulfillment because the pain of nonfulfillment was all too real in his own life – little

---

[20] In this light, a neighbor motion is indecisive, like the tensing of one's body in anticipation of moving, followed by a release back into a state of rest in the same location.

[21] Given the usual concept of a Zug as a complete step motion connecting two consonant tones, it seems impossible that the Zug could proceed in any way but by step, but Schenker's practice is not so rigid. An arpeggiated Zug, for instance, is exemplified in *Mw* 1: 193/107, fig. 5, where presumably the middle term of the arpeggiation has a passing effect (recall in this connection the emancipation of the passing event from the law of stepwise motion in free composition). Skips are also possible, as exemplified by the first fourth-Zug in ex. 2.4d. The pictures of the first bass prolongation in *FS* fig. 14 include the possibility of "leaping over" (*Überspringen*) one or more of the passing tones (note that in order to leap over the tone, it must be there in some sense and be a part of one's conception of the tonal space).

[22] *Tw* 8/9: 47, FS 18/5.

or no professional recognition, certainly no institutional or financial reward for his labors, few friends, no offspring. In any event, it is true that he saw pain, loss, and nonfulfillment as temporary conditions in art worthy of the name.

V

Schenker achieved rhetorical brevity and vividness by grammatically transforming the relation between tonal entities and effects. As we have already observed on several occasions, it is characteristic of Schenker's interpretive practice that any tonal entity, be it a tone, a motive, or the tonal complex of a thematic unit, can be treated as if it were a person. This was the case, for example, with "the $\hat{5}$" in Mozart's symphony. In op. 109, just a few lines after saying that the tones of the inverted motive "pull downward," Schenker treated the motives as persons, calling them "unruly," as if they refused to behave in accordance with the motivic rules of conduct. And in the Third Symphony, it was the entire tonal content of a thematic unity that was one of the implied agents of "seizing." Besides opening the door to a variety of interpretive complexes such as drama, psychical states, and actions, such conferrals of subjectivity also purchase rhetorical brevity and at the same time serve Schenker's pedagogical purpose.

The rhetorical transformation of entities into subjects involves suppressing mention of real agents (composers, performers, and listeners) and the placement of tonal entities in the grammatical position of subjects. A full statement of the musical effects produced by a given configuration includes, as we have seen, reconstruction of the composer's intentions and the implicit assumption of a listener or performer who shares with the composer the interpretive skill of bringing a range of paradigms (tones and their associated effects) to bear upon the given configuration. In chapter 2 I suggested that Schenker often uses passive constructions as a way of keeping the composing agent implicitly in play while foregrounding the content of the composer's intention, namely musical effects. Schenker's suppression of the interpreting listener and performer serves a similar purpose. Listeners and performers have been conspicuously absent in my account of Schenker's interpretive practice. And, from Schenker's point of view, that is as it should be. Schenker's project is directed toward cultivating interpretive skill in noncomposers to the point where it becomes second nature, as instinctive as the composer's inventive skill. Constantly training the reader's attention on the mechanism of that skill would deflect attention away from the mental content that is the product of rightly exercising the skill. A colleague of mine once remarked that telling singers how to correct a particular aspect of their physiology often backfires because the student becomes too involved with that aspect and ends up distorting the overall physiological set. The challenge is to find indirect ways of concentrating the student's attention. Schenker's conferral of subjectivity on tonal entities is just such a technique, encouraging us to focus on what tones do (their movements and effects) and not on how it is we know what they are doing.

To illustrate the rhetorical economization and its desirability, consider the following ways of formulating the overall effect of a simple and familiar configuration.

(1) To the properly backgrounded listener, the series of tones F–E–D will (must) be heard as producing (giving, presenting, having) the effect of passing through a consonant space.

This account of an interpretive judgment could be filled out with descriptions of the requisite disposition (knowledge of the paradigms for consonant and dissonant effects), the required skill (an ability to interpret presented sounds in terms of those paradigms), and also an enumeration of the first- and second-order effects that are synthesized in the final interpretive judgment. Clearly it would be cumbersome for Schenker to invoke all the terms of this formulation every time he wanted to mention an effect, much less include the composer who intended and arranged for the effect. It is not surprising, then, that he routinely omits mention of the listener altogether, stating only that

(2) F–E–D produces (gives, presents, has) the effect of passing through a consonant space.

Even this formulation is cumbersome if the rhetorical point is not the relation between the configuration and its effect. So Schenker often reduces the formulation still further:

(3) E is a passing [tone] within the third F–D.

The most economical formulation that Schenker uses is one that calls least attention to the relation between configurations and effects. In this formulation, the passive copula is transformed into an active verb. The semantic source of this new verb is the effect, and the agent of the verb is an entity within the configuration:

(4) E passes within the third F–D.

Schenker himself makes the connection between formulations that describe the listener's exercise of interpretive skill and those that invest tonal entities with subjectivity. At the beginning of the section on tonicization in *Harmonielehre*, he writes: "Every Stufe has the tendency to impersonate [*vorzustellen*] tonic whenever possible or, to speak anthropocentrically, we ourselves have the inclination to attribute the highest possible value to a Stufe, i.e., that of tonic" (*Hl* 336/254). The order in which he presents these formulations and the qualification of the second as a manner of speaking are telling: the formulation most congenial to Schenker is that in which the tonal configuration is an active agent.[23]

Schenker cares deeply about the art of tonal music and individual musical works, and so he found it fitting to craft his rhetoric so as to express that feeling. His personification of tonal entities places music and works in a rhetorical position that

---

[23] Bent makes this point in "History of Music Theory: Margin or Center?" 13–14.

accords with the value music obviously had in his life. And this perhaps explains why he thought it desirable to acquire the habit of seeing tones as creatures. As Stanley Cavell writes,

Objects of art not merely interest and absorb, they move us; we are not merely involved with them, but concerned with them, and care about them; we treat them in special ways, invest them with a value which normal people otherwise reserve only for other people.[24]

The habit of investing tonal entities with subjectivity has the effect of investing music with a value akin to the value of personhood. And that places musicians – composers and noncomposers alike – in an ethical relation to tones, tones whose social relations and laws have to be respected and observed. There is also an ideo-logical purpose served by this investiture: it minimizes the role of the perceiver's subjectivity in constituting content and thereby promotes the illusion that content is out there in the world, objective, eternal, immutable (see chapter 4).

In a paragraph placed toward the end of the introductory material in *Der freie Satz*, Schenker draws out this connection by reinscribing one of the procreation images of *Harmonielehre* in terms of human subjectivity:

Music is not an object of theoretical observation alone; it is a subject just as we ourselves are subjects. Indeed, the octave, fifth, and third of the overtone series are an organic function of the tone *qua* subject just as man's drives are organic. (*FS* 27/9)

Kevin Korsyn takes this passage as evidence of a parallel between Schenker's view of the unified musical artwork and Kant's view of the unified subject: "Music is subject because its unity parallels that of a cognitive subject. It is this analogy to the structure of our minds that enables us . . . to have, in Buber's terms, an I–Thou relationship with music. Schenker's theory explains why music matters so intensely to us."[25] Korsyn is right to fix on "unity" (*Einheit*) as the basis of the parallel. Music is a subject because its entities (for example, the root of a triad) can be rhetorically invested with subjectivity. But the further parallel between mind and work is dubi-ous. The interpretive move from tonal entity to person alone is sufficient to ground the I–Thou relationship. One need not (and Schenker does not) assert "the struc-ture of the mind" as the ground of the analogy. By Schenker's lights, the content of the musical work is infused with the composer's subjectivity (see chapter 2), giving rise to a different I–Thou relation. Quite possibly it is the force of Schenker's habit of portraying tones as creatures (subject to laws and forces) that led Korsyn to claim that "the organic composition is a correlate of Kant's cognitive subject" and that "the Ursatz is the transcendental consciousness of the piece, its 'I think'."[26] I doubt that Schenker, who was aware that his portrayal of tones as creatures was just that, a manner of speaking, would have affirmed a correlation between the incommensu-rable notions of a synthetic, interpretive act and a property of the artwork. Korsyn is

[24] *Must We Mean What We Say?* (Cambridge: Cambridge University Press, 1976), 197–98.
[25] "Schenker and Kantian Epistemology," 39.
[26] *Ibid.*, 35.

on surer ground when he notes a similarity between Schenker's description of how a Zug is perceived (the mental retention of the initiating tone) and Kant's notion of synthesis as a mental, memorative act of interpretation combining a manifold of mental representation.[27] On the other hand, Schenker's theory does not explain what Korsyn claims it does; if anything it is the very opposite: the fact that music matters so intensely to Schenker explains why his theory is couched in rhetoric that invests music with subjectivity. It is this rhetorical move that bespeaks an I–Thou relation prior to writing and is intended to promote the reader's cultivation of an I–Thou relation subsequent to reading. This brings us to the point of Schenker's interpretive practice, which is not just the appropriation of analytical understanding but, beyond that, the synthesis of that understanding in musical experience:

Musical connection [*Zusammenhang*] is only to be achieved through an Ursatz in the background and its transformations in the middleground and foreground.

. . .

Indeed, as a traversal of several planes, as a binding together [*Verbindung*] of two points separated in space and mind, every connection represents a path that is just as real as any sort of path we "walk" with our feet. A connection must accordingly be "walked," must be *thought*, and this most certainly requires real time. (*FS* 20–21/6)

The assonance and typography of Schenker's formulation escape translation:

Ein Zusammenhang is demnach wirklich zu be–"gehen," zu be*denken*.

The parallelism between *begehen* and *bedenken* is striking for its implication about the nature of musical experience, namely, that the musical experience is at once visceral and mental.

VI

Schenker encouraged readers to feel their way through all the connections and to avoid giving in to the desire for hasty satisfaction, a desire he saw as endemic to modern culture and exemplified in the masses' obsession with the airplane's ability to "fly over" great distances. But as his ability to analyze connections increased, he seems to have grown less interested in the interconnections of effects. Nothing in his later writings, for example, matches the interpretations of synthesis seen in the essays on op. 109 and op. 110.

The shift in attention occurred in the 1920s. Once Schenker began to interpret the full span of a movement or work in terms of an Ursatz and its effects, sorting out tonal effects into conceptually ordered layers (a quintessentially "analytic" move), he devoted less and less attention to impressions made by combinations of effects. So

---

[27] See Korsyn's "Schenker and Kantian Epistemology," 19–43, esp. pp. 30–31. Jamie Croy Kassler makes a similar comparison between music and consciousness in her essay, "Heinrich Schenker's Epistemology and Philosophy of Music," in *The Wider Domain of Evolutionary Thought*, ed. David Oldroyd and Ian Langham (Dordrecht: D. Reidel, 1983), 247.

even though he talks more than ever about "synthesis" in later years, there is far less verbal representation of it. Having analytically resolved a passage or movement into its constituent effects, he would often simply cease his representation of content. That alone is not sufficient reason to claim he had narrowed his conception of interpretation, but there are indications that he was tempted to think that the analytical resolution of effects exhausted the interpretation of content.

Schenker gives in to this temptation in his criticism of Ernst Kurth's *Grundlagen des Linearen Kontrapunkts.* [28] What rankled with Schenker was the same fault that he detected in the older hermeneutic critics like Kretzschmar, namely, failure to demonstrate a relation between the configuration of tones and the terms of interpretation. Schenker's critique of Kurth (*Mw* 1: 93–98/50–53) appears in his review of the secondary literature on two of Bach's works for solo violin, both the subject of interpretation in the first yearbook of *Das Meisterwerk*; accordingly, Schenker begins by singling out apparently irresponsible statements that Kurth makes about these two works. About the opening bars of the Largo of Bach's third sonata (see ex. 2.7), Kurth writes,

First a rising and then a falling span of motion [*Bewegungszug*] in the theme; the spinning-forth leads the latter further down to a nadir (d¹), and from there pushes on toward the high register in new developments of tension. [29]

Schenker complains about Kurth's imprecise use of the words "rising," "falling," "motion," "spinning-forth," and "new developments of tension":

No mention is made of the goal toward which all this motion strives; why it adheres to precisely these limits; why the content of the first three quarters in bar 1 is elevated to the status of a theme; why precisely d¹ functions as a nadir ... (*Mw* 1: 94/51)

Having thus disparaged Kurth's interpretation of the two violin works, Schenker expands the scope of his critique to include the basic tenet of Kurth's book. The interpretive responsibility that Kurth allegedly fails to fulfill is the same one that Kretzschmar allegedly shirked in his interpretation of Beethoven's Ninth Symphony, now translated into Hegelian terms:

What is the use, then, of making such a show of the identification of movement above all as the allegedly unique driving force of music? Is the task not rather to exhibit the movements expressed in all human activities in their particularity – that is, in their specific manifestation, how every material demands a different manner [of realization]? (*Mw* 1: 95/52)

[28] Bern: Drechsel, 1917; 3rd edn, Bern: Krumpholz, 1948. Portions of *Grundlagen* are translated in *Ernst Kurth: Selected Writings*, ed. and trans. Lee A. Rothfarb (Cambridge: Cambridge University Press, 1991). For an introduction to Kurth's views, see Lee A. Rothfarb, *Ernst Kurth as Theorist and Analyst* (Philadelphia: University of Pennsylvania Press, 1988). From what Rothfarb has to say about things Schenker may have picked up from reading and critiquing Kurth (such as the term *Zug* and the concept of "superordinate lines"), it is tempting to think that the smoke generated by Schenker's public critique is meant to hide his indebtedness to one of his contemporaries.

[29] Kurth, *Grundlagen*, 229.

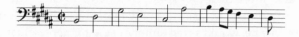

Ex. 3.16. Bach, Fugue in B major, *Well-Tempered Clavier* (bk. 2), bars 1–4

The problem, from Schenker's point of view, is that Kurth lacks a robust theory of the musical idea of movement. He has some vague inherited concepts like "spinning-forth" and some newfangled but empty concepts like "span of motion," but he does not say how such species of motion are realized in tones.

Schenker caps his argument by setting against one of Kurth's faulty interpretations one of his own that fulfills the stated obligation. It is here, I think, that Schenker overstates his achievement and at the same time undervalues Kurth's interpretive abilities. The passage in question is the fugue theme shown in example 3.16. Kurth interprets the theme as a motion through the octave, B–b, that gains intensity until the pent-up energy is discharged, the goal attained:

The formal sense of this theme lies in its steep and precipitous, upwardly directed energy of motion. It already provides the basis for the first linear phase, which peaks with the tone g♯, a motivic shape that in the thrust of its movement spans an ambitious arc; the same motivic shape is repeated with a renewed impulse in the next two bars, driving upward to the octave above the starting tone, b. The energy of the total thematic thrust of motion, which presses forward to this apex note in a twice-enacted impulse, thus acquires, with the culmination of the overall intensification in the leading-tone character (extended over half a bar) of the tone a♯, such a concentration of melodic intensity and a sharpening of the upwardly directed tension of movement that the abrupt discharge into the apex of the theme seems to radiate like a gleaming summit. [30]

Schenker counters this interpretation with a set of voice-leading models (ex. 3.17) and a paragraph slightly briefer and at first glance more precise than Kurth's:

Here lies before us a fulfillment of the major triad of B (see *a*). On this occasion it pleases Bach to lead the compositional execution [of the triad] along the paths of an obbligato three-voice setting, as the illustration shows in *b*. The upper voice traverses the space of the triad's fourth from f♯ to b – the space of the fourth is something altogether determinate, a larger voice-leading entity that contains within it Kurth's "leading-tone span," and the lower voice travels over the third-Zug B–d♯. To bring about agreement between the four tones of the fourth-Zug and the three tones of the third-Zug along the way [*im Durchgang*] and to avoid the consecutive fifths that threaten because of the similar motion of the two Züge, a 5–6 exchange is called upon. (*Mw* 1: 97/52)

By resolving the theme into three ascending lines that navigate spaces created by a four-voice tonic triad in close position, Schenker satisfies the desire left unfulfilled by Kurth, namely, the desire for a specification of how the concept of movement is

---

[30] *Ibid.*, 229.

Ex. 3.17. *Mw* 1: 97/52, fig. 3

determinately actualized in tones. The interpretation of the three passing lines is further determined by other aspects of the theory, such as a preference for reusing the same concept (i.e., for hearing repetitions), a preference for avoiding perceptions of consecutive fifths, and a repertory of patterns to call upon when such situations arise. If each line is to end at the same time as the others (i.e., if they are to be agreed in their purpose), some rhythmic adjustments are required along the way, partly because the lines differ with respect to the number of tones involved and partly in order to avoid consecutive fifths (by using the repeated 5–6 pattern). The third stage in Schenker's illustration shows the path traced by the theme through the three-voice complex. Here is where Schenker seems at a loss, in that the effect of such a path lies outside the repertory of purely musical effects. Aside from empty rhetorical posturing *vis-à-vis* Kurth, Schenker says nothing at all about the character of the melodic motion that he has charted, hardly even mentioning the idea that it has the effect of "unfolding" the succession of vertical sonorities shown in the second stage. In other words, he does not describe the effect of the line created by an unfolding of the contrapuntal complex, that synthesis of the effects of sustained harmony, passing motions, and unfolding (i.e., compound or polyphonic melody), to say nothing of the omission of the first fifth, or the accelerated effect of the second 5–6 motion coming after the first, protracted 5–6, or the abrupt change in surface rhythm in bar 4, or the change from leaps to steps across bars 3/4.

Ordinarily I would argue that this is not so much a failure as an oversight or simply the result of a limited purpose. But not here, where the content of the thematic line is precisely what is at issue in his critique of Kurth. What does it sound like for the keyboard instrument to play now a note from this line, now a note from that line? What is the sound of just this particular selection of tones and times? A quite plausible interpretation of the synthesis, I suggest, is provided by Kurth. And it is an answer that is unusually compatible with Schenker's understanding of instrumental lines in general and of this theme in particular, so much so that it leads me to wonder whether it was the risk of sounding too much like Kurth that made Schenker stop short of saying anything about effects arising in the third stage of his analysis. The two "impulses" nearly match the two upward slurs in Schenker's example: B–g♯ and c♯–a♯. But whereas Kurth neatly distinguishes between the effect of the upward and downward motions, Schenker's slurs do not. Schenker could have done so had he distinguished the effects of upward and downward motion in the line, for as I have remarked before, he conceived all melody, including instrumental melody, as vocal. Here, then, he should have been sympathetic to Kurth's interpretation of the initial upward motion as an intensification and the subsequent descent as a relaxation, followed by another pattern of intensification and relaxation that crests at the b in bar 4. Moreover, is it not true, given Schenker's general notion of passing events, that the first ascent gains forward thrust because it reaches up to an ascending passing tone (g♯) and that the second ascent is even more intensely directed because the passing tone through which it reaches is also a leading tone and because it picks up the pace of the motion toward the goal?

Unlike the treatment of Kretzschmar we read in the Introduction, Schenker slips from accusing Kurth of not demonstrating how his concepts relate to the material facts to insinuating that he uses concepts that would fail any such demonstration. That was an unfortunate misstep. For it helped make what was arguably a shift in emphasis – as Schenker took less interest in verbally representing the overall character of complex configurations (their synthesis) and concentrated instead on refining his conceptual resolutions of a work's effects (an activity that is properly called analysis) – seem to be a rejection of alternatives. The reduction of Schenker's interpretive practice to analysis of effects was helped along posthumously by the fact that Schenker's last word, *Der freie Satz*, precisely because it became his last word, was regarded as a definitive formulation of his interpretive approach and the fact that the verbal representations of synthesis so often encountered in his earlier writings could be largely ignored, mostly because the bulk of Schenker's interpretive writing went untranslated.

4

PARTICIPATION

> Schenker once labeled his theory among other things as "a securing of instinct." How keenly, therefore, he must have felt that that instinct had begun to fade in a serious way. But also how very much he must have been aware of his mission, which now lay in the *salvation of the instinct that still existed*.[1]

The practice of interpreting artworks is a social phenomenon, a form of culture. It thrives only if other minds, other generations participate. When the interpreter of a musical artwork asks herself "What do I hear?" she engages in the activity of reporting to herself; even if her self-reporting is not made public, it still depends upon a social practice for its forms of representation, for just as there can be no private language, there can be no private interpretive practice. When reports do take the form of public expression, they can initiate a social exchange that centers about the question "Do you hear what I hear?" Whether one finds them in the studio, the lecture hall, in the pages of books and journals, or in snatches of conversation, whether they take the form of words, musical notation, a gesture, a dance, or even more music, public interpretive expressions are often motivated by a desire for a shared musical experience, a desire for the meaningful affirmation of "Yes, I do hear what you hear." What is called musical analysis or criticism is but one form of this social practice, albeit focused and highly developed.[2]

"What many music theorists do when they analyse a composition," writes Kendall Walton, is "spell out the intensional objects of their musical experiences." This reporting may well spell out the intensional objects of the experiences of others, "to the extent that others experience the music in similar ways – or come to do so under the influence of the analysis."[3] Later Walton draws explicit attention to the basic desire underlying the social exchange: "analyses are usually meant to induce the recognition or acknowledgment that constitutes *understanding* of that way of

---

[1] Felix Salzer, "Die historische Sendung Heinrich Schenkers," *Der Dreiklang* 1 (1937), 9. Salzer's was the lead essay in the short-lived, eulogistic periodical that he and Oswald Jonas founded shortly after Schenker's death.

[2] Not all who participate in this practice have been able to do so without communicating a sense of detachment from the lively engagement that motivates the practice; see Marion A. Guck, "A Woman's (Theoretical) Work," *PNM* 32 (1) (1994), 28–43.

[3] Kendall Walton, "Understanding Humour and Understanding Music," in *The Interpretation of Music*, ed. Michael Krausz (Oxford: Clarendon Press, 1993), 265.

hearing, understanding that goes beyond accepting what the analysis says and involves exercising one's own musical intuitions." For the desired exchange to take place, participants must share, in large measure, assumptions, vocabularies, and principles. The practice of music theory, including Schenker's, is largely that of spreading, revising, and expanding the representational media that make such exchanges possible.

In the autumn of 1910, Schenker decided against delivering his lectures on Beethoven's Ninth Symphony, because he doubted that his desire for shared musical understanding would be satisfied. Looking back twenty years later, he reflected on the difficulties posed by that form of participation:

How gladly I would have accepted many an invitation issued to me and addressed myself to musicians over the most direct path in open speech, if it had not been the case at that time (in contrast to the other arts and intellectual disciplines, where at least common words and concepts unite the lowest and highest schools) that a complete disparity between hearing music and comprehending it in words had not still separated us in such a fashion that any communication over a direct path must for the time being seem impossible. (*Mw* 3: 21–22)

As we will see, the lack of a common discourse was only one of many problems Schenker felt he confronted as he struggled to participate in the evolving social practice of musical interpretation.

Although Schenker fervently desired that musicians would assimilate his words and thereby train their musical intuition and understanding, he regarded this social bond with his readers as secondary and derived. The primary spiritual bond he sought, and that which he commended to his readers, was a bond formed with the master composers. The object of his interpretive practice was composerly intention realized in tone, and the question that spurred his reflection was "Do I hear what the master heard?" He presents his reports of musical understanding not principally as accounts of his own hearing, but rather as descriptions of the composer's intuitive and imaginative rapprochement with tones. And he apparently assumed his descriptions were accurate: the title of his text on Beethoven's Third Symphony, for example, is "Beethoven's Third Symphony Represented for the First Time in its True Content." He clearly believed that what he found in himself was a reflection of what the master invested in the masterwork. Thus the question posed over and over by his writings is "Do you hear what we – the master and I – hear?"

To fuel his readers' desires to participate in this spiritual union, Schenker opened *Der freie Satz* by naming the fruits of participation in an epigraph, the final couplet of Hofmannsthal's *The Death of Titian*.

> But those who are like the master – they go forth,
> And beauty and sense appear where'er they gaze.[4]

With these words, one of Titian's disciples concludes a litany of conjectures about

---

[4] Hugo von Hofmannsthal, *Der Tod des Tizian: Bruchstück* (1892).

what life would be like had he and his fellows not learned from their departed master, a litany in which the disciple speculates:

> We would live in twilight,
> And our life would have no sense . . .

As Schorske writes, Hofmannsthal

senses danger and, even in this most "aesthetic" of his works, gives the danger voice: for the orthodox of the religion of art, the interpretation of life as beauty brings a terrible dependency. The genius can always see beauty; to him every moment brings fulfillment. But those who know not how to create must helplessly await the "revelation" of the genius. Meanwhile life is drained of vitality: "Our present is all void and dreariness / If consecration comes not from without."[5]

Of that consecration there is no promise. It was not a fact for Titian's disciple any more than it was for Schenker that he was like the master. Another of Titian's disciples puts the point on the dilemma when he asks,

> Who will say whether we are artists?

The disciple's doubt arose from an insecurity of instinct. It was Schenker's mission to provide, for his own art form, a means for disciples of the masters to secure their instinct and thereby assure the continuation of the tradition, even after the death of its greatest masters. At the same time, however, the novelty of his ideas and language, coupled with his bitter and excessive attacks on the aspects of contemporary musical practice that, in his view, threatened the success of his mission, repelled many readers. In this chapter I consider aspects of Schenker's social outlook and agenda that compromise his attempts to fuel his readers' desires to commune with the masters and then look briefly at the nature of the communion that was the object of his interpretive practice.

I

Schenker divided the world into two groups of people: those who, for want of time, energy, or spirit, have no ear for music, and those who do (see figure 4.1). Among those who do have an ear for the art of tone, he distinguished a small circle of creative artists and a far larger group of re-creative musicians, who lack the power of invention but not the power of interpretation. Schenker makes a further distinction between musicians who can render the works of the creative artist and those who merely receive them as listeners. Orthogonal to these distinctions is the dimension of skill, for being a musician of any sort involves the exercise of instinctive musical skill, the content of which is spelled out in Schenker's interpretive theory.

In an ideal musical culture, interpretation complements composition. The principles by which composers form and execute intentions have counterparts in the principles by which noncomposers interpret the composer's tonal configurations.

---

[5] Carl E. Schorske, *Fin-de-siècle Vienna* (New York: Vintage Books, 1981), 16–17.

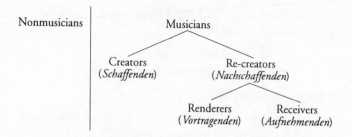

Fig. 4.1

Thus, what the master composer intended to realize in tone (and succeeded) is what the noncomposer interprets from the tones. Schenker expresses this complementary relationship by referring to the composer as creative (*schaffend*) and the non-composer as re-creative (*nachschaffend*). To both groups he declared that "tones arranged in such and such a manner produce this particular effect and no other. ... One can predict this effect; it must come about!" (*Kp1* 21/14). His contrapuntal teaching is a collection of rules that say if one configures notes in a particular way, such-and-such an effect will appear to the right-minded interpreter. Such rules form an essential part of the composer's productive instinct and the re-creative musician's interpretive instinct. The goal of Schenker's activity was to help composers and noncomposers alike develop that interpretive faculty. It is a goal adumbrated in the title of *Neue musikalischen Theorien und Phantasien*, if one takes "theory" to be description of the principles whereby tones are observed and interpreted and "phantasy" to be the imaginative, creative mind of composers; what is perhaps "new" is Schenker's understanding of rules as prescribing effects (given a configuration) and not as prescribing what configurations to write (based on the assumption that only some effects are desirable).[6]

The idea that re-creative listeners and performers have to possess the same rule book as the composer if they are to understand or perform the composer's works is a theme that Schenker sounded throughout his career. In an early essay entitled "Das Hören in der Musik" he writes that "The process by which it comes to be in the composer must find a replica in the listener" (*EK* 102). To achieve such replication, re-creative musicians must acquire and then use a "'habituation' to the artwork and the laws that belong to it" (*EK* 102). In fact, the essay bears an epigraph by Goethe that captures the ideal relation that Schenker envisions between creative and re-creative musicians:

> Selbst erfinden ist schön; doch glücklich von Andern Gefundnes
> Fröhlich erkannt und geschätzt, nennst Du das weniger Dein?

---

[6] For this formulation of Schenker's revolutionary conception of rules, see Dubiel, "'When You are a Beethoven'," 295.

> To invent on one's own is good; yet what is found by others with delight,
> gladly known and appreciated, dost thou call that any less thine? (*EK* 96)

The complementarity of listening and composing in music, says Schenker, is analogous to the reading and writing of poetry: "so many a mystery of the effect of a poetic work rests precisely on the fact that the observer can attempt not only to walk with the poet step by step but, poetically co-creating [*mitschaffend*] at the same time, to sense ahead in advance, to construct what is yet to come in the piece" (*EK* 99). In an ideal culture, re-creative musicians exercise their interpretive abilities extemporaneously, just as composers practice their inventive art.

Desire for complementarity between creative and interpretive instinct is also expressed several decades later in a similarly titled essay, "Die Kunst zu Hören." In this essay, Schenker reproduces (or invents?) a conversation he had with a fellow musician about the interpretation of linear and harmonic effects in a Bach prelude. From the reported exchange it can be gathered that Schenker preferred his interpretation as the correct one because it brought into play a greater number of basic laws than his companion's interpretation. The standard of correctness, however, is stated to be "the sense of the master." He says to his companion:

I must tirelessly point out that perception and reproduction would lose nothing of their intrinsic value if the series of tones were also correctly grasped in the sense of the master, no more than the master himself forfeited his personal feeling when he launched the series of tones into the world in the way that I read it. Again and again it must be stressed ... that it is high time to guide the ear toward better hearing. Just as a field needs manure, so too must today's completely barren ear be supplied with fertilizer, so to speak, in order to improve its productive capacity. And what could be better suited to this end than to guide the ear down those paths on which our great masters have created such novel and ingenious varieties and prolongations of the basic laws? (*Tw* 3: 23)

The sense of the masters is something Schenker felt he had a grip on, not because he felt capable of similarly novel and ingenious creations (he did not), but because he felt that he was a member of their spiritual community. In *Harmonielehre*, for example, he depicted himself as one who could disclose to his fellow artists the secrets of their musical instinct. In a discussion of the so-called overtone series in §8, Schenker claims that the artist has an instinctual familiarity with the *Naturklang* but generally lacks theoretical understanding of it. Acousticians, by contrast, grasp the phenomenon intellectually but have no instinct for how to use it as a source of imaginative artistic activity. Each group lacks what the other possesses. Schenker then presents himself as an artist who possesses both instinct and intellect:

I will now attempt to interpret the instinct of artists and to show what they have unconsciously used and still use from the proposals of Nature. ... Now, if these discussions are intended, in the first place, to make the artist henceforth fully conscious of his instinct, which in such a mysterious manner dominates his praxis and accommodates Nature, and if they are also destined to enlighten the entire musical public about the relationship of Nature and Art with respect to the system, then it might not perhaps be unwelcome also to acousticians and theorists to learn how, from the midst of the artists' circle, one with intuition judges what his fellow men have sensed intuitively for centuries. (*Hl* 33/21)

In the second yearbook of *Das Meisterwerk*, he again describes the ideal of an extemporaneous complementarity between invention and interpretation, drawing a parallel between the genius's ability to compose on the fly (*Stegreif-Fantasie*) and the ideal listener's ability to fly along (*Mitflug*) (*Mw* 2: 51). For both composer and noncomposer, the ideal is to so assimilate the knowledge of music's laws that they become second nature, instinctual. As he wrote of J. S. Bach later in the same yearbook, "Bach's know-how [*Wissen*] is comparable, to cite an example from daily life, to the know-how of a man who in every situation hits upon what is right without spending hours in soliloquy examining the philosophical argumentation of a Spinoza or Kant, or even the stipulations of the penal code in its application to the given case" (*Mw* 2: 92). All musicians, says Schenker, should aspire to such instinctual knowledge of musical laws.

Schenker crafted his interpretive practice with the aim of cultivating this ideal society. If such a society was healthy, an interpretive practice like Schenker's could be used to pass the tradition on from one generation to another or to inculcate it in those who do not already possess it in full. But while it could be useful, it would not be necessary. After all, for more than a century, training in the discipline of species counterpoint and in the practical arts of figured bass and improvisation had apparently been sufficient to train the greatest composers and performers. What made a practice such as his necessary, in his mind, was a serious breakdown in the process of cultural transmission. Those who were now teachers and so-called masters of the art were, in his eyes, bunglers and traitors. Teachers and the authors of textbooks, histories, practical manuals and theoretical treatises simplified, distorted, or suppressed the ideas and principles that were the lifeblood of the German tradition. As a result, the composers and noncomposers of his day were far from the ideal. "We lie a long way off," he writes, "from the happy state where all musicians and hearers would instinctively grasp tonal events vividly like Bach" (*Mw* 2: 93). Schenker's mission, in light of this, was to reform musical instincts and to bring them into line with the instincts and habits that permitted a Bach to compose masterworks. If he had any hope of succeeding, it rested principally with readers who already had an inkling of the ideal:

I am very well aware *that my teaching*, as something derived from the genius's artistic practice, *is itself also an art and must remain one*; thus it can never become an "intellectual discipline." My teaching – obviously far removed from the desire to pursue the breeding of genius – is therefore addressed above all to the practical musician, and at that, only to the most gifted among them. Although it is suited as well for liberating the theory, history, aesthetics and philosophy of music from centuries-old errors, it is nevertheless addressed only to such representatives of these branches of knowledge as have an artistic sensibility cultivated in accordance with the genius's art. (*Mw* 3: 22)

Schenker's reform of musical culture, then, was to begin with those who were most directly connected to the transmission of the art from one person to another, the performers, to continue with those whose business it is to speak and write about music, and, through them, to reach the wider musical public.

II

Schenker's most complete pronouncement on the psychological state of present musical culture is found in the preface to the first book of *Kontrapunkt* (1910).[7] At the very outset of the preface, he states that music, like the once-great cities of Herculaneum and Pompeii, lies in ruins (*Kp1* vii/xvii). The import of this remark, as Dubiel glosses it, is that "no one . . . has the right attributive theory [i.e., instinct] any more; so not only can no one compose, but no one can perform or listen either."[8] Schenker accuses all the groups that constitute musical culture with a failure of instincts. Performers are barely literate. They can read the notes but do not understand what they mean. "They do not pay attention to the fact that the notational signs in reality conceal more than they reveal and that strictly speaking even nowadays the signs mean scarcely more than mere neumes, behind which a world all its own looms deep and wide, a true nether side, as it were, of the artist's soul" (*Kp1* viii/xxvi). "Inferior instinct and (often) complete lack of secure knowledge on the part of today's performing musicians are the reasons that the masterworks – how bitter a truth! – have not been heard in our time in their authentic shape!" (*Kp1* ix/ xviii). Without proper instincts for music, without a mindset for the laws of tonal effect, performers cannot provide access to the world of human experience that Schenker sensed in the masterworks: "performances often sound as though a Japanese or Chinese were to pick up a text by Goethe without sufficient knowledge of the German language" (*Kp1* ix/xviii).

   The layman, says Schenker, considers his natural, untaught instinct the measure of things musical, when the fact of the matter is that his instincts are no more than mediocre. Laymen affected a professional air but were unable to back it up in practice. Rothgeb and Thym even go so far as to render Schenker's term, *der Laie*, as "dilettante," even though the term itself more properly, and less pejoratively, means simply a nonprofessional member of a community. Schenker, after all, is not out to

---

[7] In *Hl* (vii/xxvi) Schenker promised an essay "On the Decline of Compositional Art – A Technical-Critical Investigation," but never fulfilled that promise, perhaps because his publisher, Emil Hertzka, who published scores by composers Schenker despised (e.g., Mahler, Strauss, Reger, Schoenberg), refused to publish such an inflammatory tract. A long typescript copy of the essay (117 pp.) is found in OC 31/28–153. In order to distance himself from Schenker's polemics and negative assessment of modern music, Hertzka set up separate publishing ventures for *Tw* and *Mw* and allowed Schenker to publish his more objectionable tracts in those periodicals; for instance, Schenker had originally wanted to publish "Von der Sendung der deutschen Genie" in *Kp2* which would bear the imprint of Universal Edition, but Hertzka forced him to place it in *Tw* (*NTB* 31, 33).

[8] "'When You are a Beethoven'," 304.

tell his contemporaries how to be proper dilettantes, but rather to tell them that, in their misbegotten state, they are dilettantish laymen. As evidence for the mediocrity of the musical public, Schenker cites the fact that composers of mediocre talent are celebrated right alongside acknowledged masters; a musical public capable of distinguishing the moderately from the expertly skilled presumably would respect the difference. The layman's mediocrity is not an irremediable predicament and could be altered if one could just convince him that listening is as much a skill as composing or performing; however, "in an era so confused in its spiritual and social outlook, it is . . . difficult to get across to him that the uncorrupted instincts of which he is so proud have no value whatever for art itself as long as they remain untrained, unrefined, and unable to move on the same level as the artistic instincts of the masters, who alone have true artistic instincts in the first place" (*Kp1* xi/xix). The layman's instincts are likely to remain in their mediocre state, not because some external force, political or cultural or social, keeps the layman from improving them, but simply because mediocrity tends to spread itself like an infectious disease.[9] Thus, at the beginning of his plaint about the layman he states that "a serious organic relation to art remains foreign to him forever," and at the conclusion he states woefully, "Alas, what a curse hangs over the mediocre person: to be forced to partake, without even being *able* to partake!" (*Kp1* x/xviii, xiv/xx).

Composers are also at fault. They lack a technique that is grounded in an instinct for synthesis. They revel in empty sonorities (*Klänge*) and lack the ability to bind sonorities together as elaborations of a single chord, though they try to compensate for their inability by "stuffing their sonorities with the excelsior of passing tones" (*Kp1* xvii/xxii).[10] Like performers, contemporary composers lack an intuitive understanding of the inner complexity of the masterworks. A composer like Richard Strauss, he says, is consequently unable to compose works whose depth and complexity are comparable to Haydn's (*Kp1* xvi/xxi–xxii). Instead, says Schenker, Strauss tries to disguise the primitive simplicity of his designs with heavy orchestration, with noise and gesticulation, with so-called polyphony and cacophony; and instead of relying on passing and other techniques of synthesis, he resorts to the extramusical solutions of programs and drama to solve problems of musical continuation.

Schenker positions himself in this ailing culture as one who both perceives the

---

[9] "The leveling force to which average people are subject is never imposed upon them by political or, in a broader sense, spiritual dictators; it is, rather, like an infection that passes from one average person to another" (*FS* 8/159).

[10] A similar charge was brought against Reger in *Harmonielehre*, where Schenker cites the opening bars of Reger's Quintet op. 64 in a footnote to §89 (220–26n; this note is omitted from the English edition). After searching in vain for a sensible *Stufengang* in the allegedly projected key of C minor, Schenker concludes that Reger lacked artistic instincts. Schenker makes an example of Reger in order to bemoan those laymen and cultural leaders who would hail Reger as a great composer: "And such an author, who is abandoned by all instincts for music, is going to be celebrated seriously in German lands as a 'Master of Music' – a few years after the death of a Brahms – oh, what indolence of the German public, what cowardice of writers and of the musical power brokers!" (223–24n).

external grace and inner complexity of the masterworks and is able to represent it.
But other writers, wittingly or not, made a compromise with dilettantish laymen,
pandering to their lackadaisical musical spirit by offering them oversimplified theories or representations of content and by commending the easy act of believing
instead of the arduous task of understanding. Such writers model themselves, so to
speak, after Aaron rather than Moses:[11]

But that is just it: under the word "understand" the dear world understands simply this –
believing, accepting without effort! What, if anything, have people "understood" since the
creation of the earth, when they in truth understood nothing, but rather only believed
everything! They demonstrate an inclination toward error, which merely needs believing,
and a turning away from truth, a truth which, most unfortunately, wants really to be understood! Hence they prefer to go – yes, we see it every day – with the priest instead of Christ,
with the rabbi instead of Moses, with Bülow instead of Beethoven . . . (*Kp1* xx/xxiii)

The typical writer on music is a professional priest who dilutes the truth of art for
the sake of the laity, a view that is repeated in the second yearbook of *Das Meisterwerk*:

The masses need mediators not only to God, but also to genius. Even in art, the churches of
genius could not be dispensed with, churches in which the masses had to be preached to if
one wanted to bring them to art, if only in the loosest connection. However, on its way via
the mediators, the truth is for the most part lost; what the masses get to hear from them is no
longer the original. As it was, so it is, and so shall it also remain. (*Mw* 2: 81–82)

By the 1920s, Schenker believed the damage done to the social fabric of music was
virtually irreparable, damage so serious that the very existence of the tradition was at
stake.

What disillusioned him, above all, was the renouncing of German culture that
followed in the wake of Germany's defeat in the World War. If in *Harmonielehre* and
the first book of *Kontrapunkt* there was evidence that Schenker thought the musicians of his day would be receptive to his revelations, by the end of the World War it
is clear that he altogether despaired of this: as it was, so it is and ever shall be. Greater
Germany had suffered the ignominy of the treaties of Versailles and St.-Germain,
losing her position of leadership in the world, and Schenker suffered for lack of
professional recognition, unable to secure an academic position that would affirm
his intellectual leadership. In the face of these national and personal tragedies, the
embittered Schenker grew pessimistic about the possibility of cultural renewal in his
own time. The issues of *Der Tonwille*, published on the heels of the treaties of Versailles and St.-Germain, are littered with complaints about the unfair treatment of
Austro-Germany and the dire consequences of allowing German culture to be
supplanted by that of her conquerors.[12] The biblical cadence of the passages quoted

[11] For discussion of Aaronic and Mosaic imagery in Schenker's writings, see Ian Bent, "Heinrich Schenker e la
missione del genio germanico," *Rivista Italiana di Musicologia* 26 (1) (1991), 3–34.
[12] See especially the opening essay of the first pamphlet, "Von der Sendung der deutschen Genie"; on the content
of this essay, see Bent, "Heinrich Schenker e la missione del genio germanico."

below evokes the image of a biblical prophet decrying the captivity of the chosen people. Notice, too, that Schenker again proclaims himself the first to possess sufficient intellectual insight into the artist's instincts to be able to present an accurate image of them in words.

To the captor nations he writes:

...But do you know who I am? I will tell you:

That I am not Sebastian Bach, not Handel, not Beethoven, Haydn, Mozart, not Schubert, Mendelssohn, Schumann, Brahms – that I know better than all of you. Before them I am dust, not worthy of the wind that carries it off. What all of you, each and every one of you, do not know, but what I know very well, is that to create even the likes of me has not been given unto you, nor will it ever be given.

Favored by the grace of our greatest ones, I hold a mirror to the art of tones as no philosopher of antiquity, the Middle Ages, or of modern times, nor any of the musicians, music historians, aestheticians, nor all these together, have been able to. I am the first to show music's own laws, wherein its own life obtains, I show the German masters' soaring ear, their improvisatory capacity, their synthesis. I show their boldness in the dimension of the ear, such as man has experienced it till now only in the dimensions of the other senses. I have, as it were, for the first time opened the dimension of the ear to word and communication, according to our masters, and thereby enriched the existence of man with a new dimension. (*Tw* 5: 54–55)

What will be left to man, then, but to content himself within the bounds that eye and hand set for him? When there is nothing more to rob, then, nothing more to steal, O, then you will crave to learn from the Germans how to hear – and then you will have to turn to the German particle of dust, to me. (*Tw* 5: 55)

Therefore I say unto you: as your life, your deeds, so shall you be. As those are vulgar, so shall you be vulgar and common! And to all your disdain I say: just as all your imperialisms, your money-bags, enterprises, trusts, businesses, armies, presidents, statesmen, all your fathers and children are nothing before a small, nay smallest, prelude by Sebastian Bach, so you are nothing before the one who for the first time heard and imparted the prelude. All of you, each and every one of you, are nothing before me, a German particle of dust! (*Tw* 5: 56)

Now that the chosen nation Germany, which had produced the likes of Bach and Schenker, had fallen and forsaken its artistic heritage, Schenker's mission shifted away from the possibly imminent redemption envisioned in *Harmonielehre* and the first book of *Kontrapunkt*. He deplored the fact that the German people wanted to install Franck, Berlioz, Debussy, and Ravel in the temple of Bach, Mozart, and Beethoven (*Tw* 4: 24) and warned that "the danger is exceedingly great that the German musician is utterly forfeiting music, since today he almost makes no distinction any more between, for example, Moussorgsky and Mozart, Stravinsky and Bach, Ravel and Handel" (*Mw* 1: 60/30).

As the publications of the early 1920s clearly attest, his hopes shifted toward a future rejuvenation of musical culture, a future that he did not expect to live to see. Every issue of *Der Tonwille*, for instance, is dedicated "to a new youth," and in the second book of *Kontrapunkt* we read the following:

If my theories (like all my other works) have from the outset borne the stamp, as it were, of rescue work (insofar as it was a matter of protecting the tonal art against the centuries-old errors of theory and historicism), my obligation has increased all the more, as the intervening World War has loosed all the forces of destruction that have totally extinguished the tonal art in the West. Today it is more a matter of transmitting the essence of music to more distant times, since we cannot expect it to be restored in the near future. (*Kp2* vii–viii/xii)

His contemporaries' betrayal of their German culture was in his eyes "a falling away from genius (an apostasy) and from the solutions to mankind's problems that have long been seen by the genius," "an extreme evaporation of all the invariable concepts that were already established, a complete breach of knowledge and ethics right down to the ultimate condition of lost spirit and morality" (*Tw* 1: 3). He implored them not to forsake their heritage in this troubled time, but rather to cling to it as their best hope of recovering what had been stolen from them by the western democracies. The part he chose to play in this mission of redemption was "to discuss the proper conditions for the creation and reception of an ingenious artwork and to prescribe the single path leading to this goal" (*Tw* 1: 3). If German musical culture were rejuvenated, it might then be possible for genius to reappear:

It is impossible, I fear, for the present generation to rouse itself again to the level of ingenuity that is undoubtedly due – *semper idem, sed non eodem modo* – to seeking and finding ever new prosperity [*Heil*] in the Ever-same [*im Ewig-demselben*] . . .

The task of redemption awaits a new generation. Once again a pillar of fire will travel thither before men, again a Prometheus must appear, a genius, to proclaim and empower anew the Ever-same. (*Tw* 1: 20)

However, Schenker's unforgiving critiques of how participants in his musical culture fail to live up to the masterworks, critiques occasioned by the moral outrage he felt toward those who were satisfied with anything less than his ideal, undermined his redemptive mission. Schenker recorded a conversation in his diary (16 and 24 April 1920) in which Wilhelm Furtwängler put his finger on the problem:

Once again there is talk of my polemics, and I notice that F. has once again changed his stance; it sounds as if he feels that he too is implicated, and that makes me still more irritated: I plead and defend my right to polemics, passionately as usual, and, as we enter the cafe, I let myself be carried away so far as to say that I have the obligation to annihilate my opponents.

"There you have it," F. says, "why should you be amazed that they put up a fight?" (*NTB* 112)

Furtwängler's retort suggests he believed that quashing one's opponents, rather than bringing them to see the error of their ways, will have just the opposite effect: it will put them on the defensive, entrenching them still deeper in their position. If Furtwängler, Schenker's long-time advocate, saw himself as the victim of Schenker's critique, there can be no doubt that others also felt its sting. William Mitchell, for example, having read Schenker's remark that "only the genius is endowed with a feeling for tone space" – and knowing well that a feeling for tone space, after all, is necessary if one is going to be able to follow along the paths and detours of a masterwork – concluded that Schenker "is either flattering many of us beyond our deserts or . . . he is posting a despairing limit to participation in the 'Great Tradition'."[13]

Schenker rightly portrays the arts of listening, performing, and composing as a complex of skills and dispositions. Because composing, performing, hearing, and reporting such experiences require the intelligent exercise of skill, not everyone will be willing or able to achieve the same degree of mastery. Realistically, then, Schenker admits that most musicians would never be more than modestly skilled and that attaining his ideal would only be possible for one who, like himself, could devote a lifetime to art (see FS 29/9). A quotation from Lessing at the outset of the Ninth Symphony monograph puts it aptly: "True connoisseurs of poetry have at all times and in all places been just as rare as true poets themselves" (NS v/3). As it was, so it is and ever shall be.

In this he can be compared to the nineteenth-century novelist Adalbert Stifter, whom Schenker admired.[14] In his novel Der Nachsommer (1857), Stifter "projected an ideal of life that implied a social withdrawal and a cultural élitism ultimately incompatible with his redemptive intent."[15] The educational mission of Der Nachsommer was, in Stifter's own words, an outgrowth of a pessimistic assessment of his world: "I have probably made the work on account of the rottenness which in general and with a few exceptions prevails in the political conditions of the world, in its moral life and in the literary arts. I wanted to contrapose a great, simple, ethical force against the wretched degeneration [of the times]."[16] The main character of Stifter's Bildungsroman, Heinrich Drendorf, passes from the commercial world of his merchant father into "the utopia of the mid-century Austrian middle class" and from there into the life of a country gentleman.[17] The novel's main focus is this last phase. Its central symbol is a country estate, the Rosenhaus, where Heinrich meets his surrogate father, Freiherr von Risach, and enters a spiritual aristocracy. Together they dedicate their lives – like Schenker – to recovering and preserving the arts and crafts of the past.

III

Like Stifter's Drendorf or the musical archaeologists who stood "before a Herculaneum and Pompeii of music!" (Kp1 vii/xvii), participation in the tradition had been reduced, at least for the foreseeable future, to preserving the artifacts of a culture no longer thriving. Schenker worked on the assumption that such participa-

[13] William J. Mitchell, "Review of Harmony, by Heinrich Schenker," Musical Quarterly 41 (2) (1955), 259.
[14] Schenker's Nachlass contains only a few items related to literature, but among these are extensive notes on Stifter's works (OC 12/176–248), including Der Nachsommer, as well as a summary of and commentary on Goethe's famous Bildungsroman, Wilhelm Meister (JC 21 f. 4).
[15] Schorske, Fin-de-siècle Vienna, 295.
[16] Ibid., 283.
[17] Ibid., 287.

tion was a necessary condition of the tradition's continuation. Artworks created by the master composers have a fixed and determinate content that musicians re-create or rediscover. Yet if re-creative musicians have an essential role to play in sustaining the tradition and its artifacts, there is the danger that they might fail and consequently that the artworks and their tradition might pass away. Schenker felt that danger so keenly that, in addition to desiring that the content of musical artworks be stable and immutable, he sometimes wished that re-creative musicians had no role in sustaining them and thus were incapable of destroying them. It is these conflicting views of what musicians can and cannot do *vis-à-vis* participation in the tradition and its works that are discussed in this section.

If a work's content is neither tones in themselves nor the notation but rather the effects produced by the tones and indicated by the notation, then content must be a product of interpretation. The proposition that a tradition is sustained by the constant renewal and re-creation of an artistic *Geist* is in fact what drove Schenker's interpretive practice. For to sustain the existence of the masterworks and their artistic tradition, listeners and performers must be trained so as to acquire the mindset of that tradition. As long as there is a properly disposed listener who attributes the work's effects to the acoustical material (real or imagined) or a performer who produces acoustical material that does not interfere with the effects, the work exists.[18] Because its existence is sustained by a social practice of interpretation, it may (and usually does) outlast the life of its creator. Schenker notes this longevity in the introduction to the first book of *Kontrapunkt*: "art exists not for him [the layman] but for its own sake … compositions (which seemingly belong to a transcendental world) often have a far longer life than human generations, and that, therefore, they have to be understood almost as animate creatures, just as human beings themselves" (*Kp1* x/xix).

Even when he castigates the inadequate participation of his contemporaries, he usually does not deny the dependence of the tradition and its works on participation. So, for example, in the second issue of *Der Tonwille* he tries to describe what it means to be part of the German tradition:

The invention of synthesis from the Urlinie and total-melody is German, prototypically German … and generates from the depth and breadth of German spirit…

But of course, how difficult it is to *be* German in the company of our great German masters! The musician still does not find his way in their counterpoint [*Satz*], their form, or their melody, because he feels his way around synthesis only with petty concepts of melody. And one who starts off from metaphysics and seeks synthesis in rhythm, melody, and God knows what else, passes deafly by the Urlinie, and yet the Urlinie is the epitome [*Inbegriff*] of metaphysics. And then there is the mediocre person! One says to him: race upon race sinks into the grave, but the line of tones [*Tonlinie*] continues to live as on the first day – he does not lay hold of it. One meets him and says: capital is self-acting and likewise also the tonal

---

[18] This view of performance is expressed, among other places, in *Kp1* vii–x/xviii, *Tw* 8/9:47–48, and *FS* 24–25/8.

line – he does not grasp it. He knows only this one question: Where is all that? It stands in the noteheads, not in your heads! (*Tw* 2: 6)

One could read the close of this passage as denying the interpretive status of the tonal line, instead reifying it "in the noteheads," but if we are mindful of the historical context that Schenker invokes – the failure of musicians here, now, in greater Germany to participate in the tradition – we should read it as denying the culturally mediocre person's ability to get into his own head what the composer has put into the noteheads. Fortunately, Schenker would have us believe, as long as there are heads like his, the line of tones lives on. Schenker makes this explicit in the introduction to *Der freie Satz* (6–8) when he addresses problems in the transmission of the work of genius to the listener.[19] He likens the music that reached its zenith with the German masters to a star whose light shines upon an uninterested humanity:

Nebular spirals condense into stars – born from its original irrationality as from a nebular spiral, and made ever more dense through diminutions, music grew into a star in the heaven of Spirit. But how strange: mankind has more interest in the most distant stars of the firmament than in the star of music in the heaven of Spirit! Oh, may the light of this sweet star yet shine on. Its light is still captured well and protected in my eyes, but what will happen when my eyes have closed for ever? (*FS* 7/158)[20]

Though starlight shines upon the just and unjust alike and exists regardless of whether it is perceived by earth's inhabitants, Schenker worries that the light might go unnoticed. He gives us to believe that perception of the starlight is essential to its continued existence (else what would be the point of capturing and protecting it?). Toward the end of the section he states explicitly that the life of music depends upon right reception by listeners:

Protecting [*Pflege*] genius is never somehow romantic or "living in the past." Rather, it is a blessed cherishing [*Hegen*] of a contemporaneity above and beyond the time that separates, a sincere belief in the absolute of art and its skilled masters [*Meisterkönner*]. If, after centuries pass, there should be but one who is able to hear music again in the spirit of its coherence, then even in that one shall music be again resurrected in its absoluteness. (*FS* 8/xxiv)

This is the spirit in which he announces his mission in *Der freie Satz*: "My time has come . . . to proclaim the new concept of organic coherence and thereby give the fullest possible expression to what the music of the masters was and must continue to be if we wish to keep it alive" (*FS* 2/xxii). But note that as the Indian summer of *fin-de-siècle* Vienna turned into the postwar winter of Schenker's discontent, his hopes for the appearance of another genius had apparently withered, for the hope

---

[19] Jonas and Oster substantially reordered and condensed the material of Schenker's introduction (*Vorwort*). The fifth of the introduction's seven sections, for example, begins with the first two paragraphs on p. xxiv of the translation, continues with passage A in the Fourth Appendix (pp. 158–59), and concludes with three more paragraphs: the second and third paragraphs from the end of p. xxiv, in reverse order, and then the first paragraph of passage B in the appendix (p. 159).

[20] There is at least a hint here of John 1.5: "And the light shineth in darkness; and the darkness comprehended it not" ("Und das Licht scheint in der Finsternis, und die Finsternisse haben es nicht begriffen"). See also Isa. 9.2.

expressed in *Der Tonwille* that genius would one day reappear and reinvigorate the Austro-German tradition with new masterworks is here reduced to the hope that the tradition might continue as a living museum dedicated to preserving masterworks from the past.

What results from the envisioned participation is the renewal of a fixed and unchanging content. In Schenker's view, the artwork's content does not change over time. The object of interpretation, after all, is the artwork as intended by the genius-composer. Its content is given, deposited in the tones, and the terms Schenker used for his practice reflect this: a "mirror" held up to the art of tones, "representations" and "elucidations" that bring content to light. He avoided "interpretation," probably because it had been co-opted by the hermeneuts to mean "invent in one's head" rather than "decipher the noteheads" and because he wanted to draw a line between the excessive and irresponsible hermeneutics of Kretzschmar and his own hermeneutics, which he regarded as proper exegesis of what was already in the tonal text. He was most certainly not of the opinion that cultural artifacts are "open to interpretation." For despite the fact that in several instances he published conflicting interpretations of one and the same work, he held that there was only one correct interpretation. It is important to keep in mind that this does not mean that he denied the interpretive conflicts that arise from an event having different effects that are on the face of it incompatible but in fact arise from situating the event in different contexts (see chapter 1, section VII). What Schenker denies on the whole are ambiguities of effect within a single context. An obvious case is the Urlinie of an entire work. One of the files in his Nachlass is a collection of references to compositions for which he had not settled on an Urlinie interpretation. On a scrap of paper in this file there is a draft of a paragraph apparently intended to follow the discussion of the three Urlinie forms in *Der freie Satz*:

§47 $\hat{8}$–$\hat{5}$–$\hat{3}$

In all the preceding paragraphs, a $\hat{3}$, $\hat{5}$, or $\hat{8}$ is assumed, but seen from the foreground it is not unusual for there to be difficulties deciding whether $\hat{3}$, $\hat{5}$, or $\hat{8}$ is at issue. There can be no doubt, however, that *only one solution* is always the correct one, but feeling one's way to it demands an extremely intense, inspirational sense of rapport from the background to the foreground and vice versa. (OC 38/215)

Schenker could not admit the possibility that a composer might intentionally craft a composition that was capable of sustaining incompatible interpretations. Interpretive closure was a *sine qua non* of his practice.

For content to be immutable, not only must one assume that unresolvable interpretive ambiguities of this sort are impossible, one must also hold that the laws of interpretation whereby effects are caused by tonal configurations are unchangeable.[21] Schenker may have admitted that different cultures invented and interpreted

---

[21] Were a score understood to underdetermine an Urlinie (that is, were it to be plausibly understood under more than one Urlinie interpretation), there would obviously be a great deal of difference in the effects that one understood the tones as producing. So much so, that we might have to speak not of one but of two works,

music by different principles, but he also held that there was but one table of law worth having. The epitaph he wrote as an addendum to his last will attests to the Mosaic image he created for himself: "Here rests one who, like no other before him, understood the soul of music and proclaimed its laws in the sense of the great ones" (20 May 1934; *NTB* 37 n. 56). He explicitly adopts the mantle of Moses the law-giver in a passage withheld from the translation of *Der freie Satz*:

By confessing, both in its creation and in its finished state, only *one prime cause* in the background, a work is arranged *monotheistically*. In that case, so-called heathens are those who, whether creative or re-creative, consider only the foreground of the work and lose themselves in its particulars, while confessors of a true divinity are those who worship the background. In the artwork, too, the one prime cause remains immutable in the background, and deviating toward the cravings of the foreground heathens is a sin against the spirit of monotheism. Shall I therefore proclaim my monotheistic doctrine of art from a Mount Sinai and thereby seek to win confessors of it? Am I to perform a miracle? Now, miracles will indeed occur, for belief in coherence will sooner or later cause musicians to hear, though even that belief will never be able to make talents of the ungifted. (*FS* 5)[22]

Every issue of *Der Tonwille* declares itself a "testimony to the immutable laws of music." And the immutability of musical laws is what is at issue in the first part of his motto "*semper idem* sed non eodem modo," prominently inscribed beneath the title of each major division of the second book of *Kontrapunkt* and on the title page of *Der freie Satz*. If Schenker was so immersed in the musical world he discovered as a youth that he could imagine no other, he was mistaken in thinking that the interpretive principles which constitute the tradition do not change as new works shape and reshape the perception of older works. We could readily dismiss him were it not that he thereby purchased an intensity of imagination that was and continues to be so richly productive of musical experiences within that tradition.

Musical laws are subject to change within a tradition. Since at least the eleventh century, for example, western European composers were in the habit of arranging for there to be two different tones sounding at the same time. Written records confirm what is inferable from the compositional record, namely, that musicians ascribed different effects to spacings of simultaneously sounding tones (so-called vertical intervals). The measurement of intervals and the basic categories of interval-lic effects remain substantially unchanged from the eleventh through the nineteenth centuries. What shifts over time, in some instances dramatically, is the *correlation* between intervals and effects, in other words, the law of interpretation governing their relation. Thus it is legitimate to say, for example, that the tonal distances termed *ditonus* and *diatessaron* by Guido d'Arezzo writing in the first half of the eleventh century, and likewise by Johannes de Garlandia some two centuries later, are identi-

---

whose contents share all the same tones but not all the same effects (no doubt many foreground effects would be shared).

[22] Other instances of Schenker's Mosaic aspirations are cited in my "Schenker's Senses of Concealment," 111–13; see also the draft of a letter to Baron Alphonse von Rothschild dated February 1911, *NTB* 24 (JC 5 f. 34).

cal with the *terza maggiore* and *quarta* described by Zarlino in the mid-sixteenth century and with Schenker's *die große Terz* and *die Quart*.[23] Furthermore, all four authors classified vertical intervals according to the concepts of consonance and dissonance. Where they part company is in what interpretive law they invented by sorting the intervals into these two categories. Guido included the diatessaron but not the ditonus under the term *symphonia*. Johannes de Garlandia included both among the *concordantiae*. Zarlino also included the *terza maggiore* and *quarta* among the *consonanze*, but acknowledged that practicing musicians consider the *quarta* one of the *dissonanze*. Finally, Schenker classed both *die große Terz* and *die Quart* among *die Konsonanzen*, but allowed that the latter must generally be regarded as a *Dissonanz*.[24] It is true that various explanations for the correlation between vertical intervals and consonant and dissonant sounds have been offered over the centuries. Guido glosses the meaning of *symphonia* as "smooth unions of notes." Johannes de Garlandia believed that *concordantia* obtained "when two sounds are joined at the same time so that one can be heard as compatible with the other." Both Zarlino and Schenker define consonance with reference to small number ratios. Zarlino uses an arithmetic rule: "the ratio of the proportions that form the consonance . . . are the ones contained among the parts of the senary number [i.e. the integers 1 through 6]"; Schenker uses an acoustical rule: "only those intervals that can be reduced to the simple proportions 1, 2, 3, and 5 in the overtone series."[25] But despite these various explanations, there is arguably a common sense in which the two tones forming a consonance sound compatible with one another.

Each of the authors cited also saw the consonant intervals as the basis for the music that they wrote about. To Guido, for instance, the symphonia are "the laws that hold for diaphonies, i.e. organa," and to Schenker, consonance is the wellspring of strict counterpoint and thence free composition.[26] If the sounds of intervallic arrangements changed over time, the change must be attributed to a change in the laws of interpretation governing their effects. The musical laws are culturally relative and alterable. They exist as a tradition in a community of minds. They can be learned. They can be forgotten. They can become so habitual as to work almost unbidden, unconsciously.

Interpretive laws are relative to musical practices. The sound of intervals in a Noh

---

[23] Guido d'Arezzo, *Micrologus*, ed. Jos. Smits van Waesberghe (n.p.: American Institute of Musicology, 1955); English translation by Warren Babb in *Hucbald, Guido, and John on Music*, ed. Claude V. Palisca (New Haven, Conn.: Yale University Press, 1978), 57–83. Johannes de Garlandia, *Johannes de Garlandia: De mensurabili musica*, translated by Erich Reimer in *Beihefte zum Archiv für Musikwissenschaft* (1972), 10; translated by Stanley H. Birnbaum as *Concerning Measured Music* (Colorado Springs: Colorado College Music Press, 1978). Gioseffo Zarlino, *Istitutioni Harmoniche*, facs edn (Ridgewood, N.J.: Gregg Press, 1966); part III translated by Guy Marco and Claude V. Palisca as *The Art of Counterpoint* (New Haven, Conn.: Yale University Press, 1968).

[24] *Micrologus*, 116/63; *De mensurabili musica*, 67–68/15–16; *Istitutioni Harmonische*, 176–78/10–15; *Kp1* 155/112.

[25] *Micrologus*, 116/63; *De mensurabili musica*, 67/15; *Istitutioni Harmonische*, 36/8n4; *Hl* 174/131.

[26] *Micrologus*, 116/63; the translator obscures the legal trope by rendering "diaphoniæ, id est, organi iura possident" as "the basis of diaphony, that is, organum." *Kp1* 152–55/110–12; the conclusion of the passage revolves around a proclamation ("In the beginning is consonance!") that Schenker reshapes and recycles two years later in *NS* as "In the beginning was content!."

ageuta, a Mozart aria, and a Babbitt quartet, for example, are radically different sounds because each is measured using a different construction of tonal space. I can imagine participating in one or another such practice, perhaps testing my imagination by using acoustical material to help me play at hearing vertical thirds now as dissonant, now as consonant, now as not a third but an ic4. If a vertical major third just simply "sounds" consonant to me, it is no doubt because I have trained myself or acquired by experience a disposition to attribute consonance to vertical major thirds when I believe I am presented with acoustical material that will repay that attribution. If, when so disposed, I hear a particular acoustical presentation as tones a major third apart (and not, say, a diminished fourth), the tones sound consonant to me. The effect is my response, my attribution of an effect. Given a law and an arrangement of tones, the effect necessarily follows, but the law itself is contingent and subject to change. Two or more musical practices can exist together, not just within the same time period but even within one cultural milieu as was the case in Schenker's Vienna and is now the postmodern condition. We can move easily between such practices and often do so without confusing the laws of one with those of another (confusions generally arise when it comes to verbalizing about one practice with terms and concepts originally designed for another).

Even though his view of what constitutes "tonal material" (*Kp1* vii/xvii) is such that the "material" – the ability to ascribe what he considered the right effects to tones – was capable of passing out of existence, Schenker was unwilling to assent to the contingency of musical laws. And even though he premises his interpretive practice on the notion that musicians constitute the content of a work anew each time they produce or listen to the work's tonal configurations, his despair at times gets the better of him and he asserts that the content of musical artworks is independent of the continued participation of re-creative musicians.

Schenker acted in several ways to forestall the destruction of his interpretive practice. In the Ninth Symphony monograph, for example, he spells out three main lines of his defense: "to reveal the musical *content* of the work," "to set forth the accordingly re-conceived *performance canon*," and "to verify the result of the analysis and forestall misunderstandings, so that . . . the Beethoven work itself should be insulated against any possible future errors" (*NS* vi/3–4). The first defends content against the danger that listeners themselves will fail to be properly disposed toward the acoustical material and that they will therefore not know how to interpret its effects. The second defends against the danger that performers will misunderstand the notation of the work and consequently garble the acoustical material so badly that not even a properly disposed listener could grasp the sense of the work. The third defends against false representations of the work's content that might mislead listeners and performers. And as we saw in section I, Schenker did not expect his mission to succeed in the foreseeable future. Left with only the hope that the masterworks would live for a few individuals scattered here and there in the coming centuries, Schenker at times seems compelled to view the work's very existence as immune to the misdeeds of listeners and performers, denying that the participation of re-creative musicians is what sustains the existence of the musical artwork. This is nowhere more clearly stated than in the introduction to his essay on Mozart's G-minor Symphony. He opens the essay with a rhetorical question, "What has Mozart been to the world until today?" And in reply he states that mankind does not have an actual relation to Mozart's masterwork, no matter how much it may promote its external existence (through performances and critical acclamation). The members of high society who attend its performances are not connected to it, nor are the theorists who posit entities that cannot be found in the work, nor performers who allow the connections of notes to pass unnoticed:

The work of genius remains removed from the races and their ebb and flow. All the strivings deposited in the work live as they did on the first day, nourished by the stream of forces that drive from the background through the middleground and on toward the foreground. Were I to say that mankind has no part in the work of genius, then it would also be said at the same time that mankind lacks the power to pronounce it dead, to kill it – the work of genius lives by the force of the one who fashioned it, not by the grace of its re-creators [*Nachschaffenden*]. (*Mw* 2: 108–9)

In fact, Schenker presents his Mozart essay as "a testimony" to the idea "that Mozart lives and will ever live" (*Mw* 2: 109).

　　Expressions of the idea that the masterworks live on eternally in their own world are woven into the very same texts that seek to protect it from the dangerous influences of ignorance and incompetence among listeners and performers. In *Der freie Satz*, for example, in pointed contrast to the passage cited at the beginning of this section, Schenker speaks mystically of the masterwork possessing its own means of protection:

Thus it is also true that given in the secret of the Ursatz is a sort of natural protection [*Naturschutz*] against an all-too-quick annihilation at the hands of the masses ... (*FS* 29/9)

As they move toward the foreground, the transformation levels are actually bearers of developments and are, at the same time, repetitions or parallelisms in the most elevated sense – if we permit ourselves to use the word "repetition" to describe the movement from transformation level to transformation level. The mysterious concealment of such repetitions is an almost biological means of protection [*Schutzmittel*]: repetitions thrive better in secret than in the full light of consciousness. (*FS* 42/18)

The contradiction between the innate protection ascribed in these passages and the external protection offered by Schenker for the starlight of genius may well reflect the different contexts in which we find these passages in *Der freie Satz*. In the earlier passage, Schenker writes about the value of his "new doctrine" and so is intent on securing a place for himself in the picture of how the new doctrine related to the existence of music. In writing of the masterwork's natural protection, Schenker addresses the use of his doctrine in educating the masses and so is intent on making sure that the failure of the masses to understand the relation between his new doctrine and the masterworks would not impugn the doctrine. Similarly, in writing about concealed repetitions much later in *Der freie Satz*, Schenker is concerned with the perception of repetitions and with making sure that the failure of listeners, and even the composers themselves, to acknowledge the repetitions would not be grounds for denying their existence (and thus would also not be grounds for impugning Schenker's assertion that they exist as part of the masterwork's content):

Although these new types [of repetition] seem to lie just as clearly before eye and ear as the repetitions that occurred within the imitative forms, they remained less accessible because they did not offer creator and listener the same ease of perception. They were fully as effective as the simpler repetitions; they, too, sprang only from the blood relationship of statement and variant, almost beyond the composer's volition – but they remained concealed. Yet it was precisely these concealed repetitions which freed music from the narrowness of strict imitation and pointed the way to the widest spans and most distant goals; thus even very extended tonal structures could be based on repetition!

In these concealed repetitions lie the seed and flowering of German creative genius. (FS 162/99)

One explanation for Schenker's ontological ambivalence, then, may be this: when concerned with securing a place for himself in the life of the masterworks, Schenker stresses the idea that listeners like himself play a role in sustaining the existence of the masterworks, but when faced with the fact that few listeners and performers could or would succeed in sustaining the masterworks, he stresses the idea that the masterworks are safe none the less. The one horn of Schenker's dilemma guided his interpretive practice, while the other undermined its very purpose.

IV

To participate is to exercise a skill that is not simply a way of thinking about tones but is, in fact, a way of experiencing those tones. The experience that Schenker's words and illustrations were intended to facilitate is, as I noted in chapter 3, at once visceral and mental. I quote again the relevant passage:

Indeed, as a traversal of several planes, as a binding together [*Verbindung*] of two points separated in space and mind, every connection [*Zusammenhang*] represents a path that is just as real as any sort of path we "walk" with our feet. A connection must accordingly be "walked," must be *thought*, and this most certainly requires real time. (FS 21/6)

An analytical interpretation of a musical artwork is not merely a set of propositions whose truth values one must assess; rather, it is a set of propositions and verbal and notational nudges that are meant to guide the manner of our musical experience. Take, for example, the way Schenker introduces the passing effect in *Kontrapunkt*:

E, as a second between F and D, forms a bridge, as it were, upon which these two tones meet to make the effect of a third. (*Kp1* 116/83)

There is no concrete bridge between F and D, nor even a bridge made of tone. We are not to think of the idea of a bridge each time we attribute the passing effect to a tonal entity, much less think of the words "bridge" or "passing." And most assuredly the E between F and D does not mean "passing" or "bridge" in anything like the way the words "passing" and "bridge" mean what they mean. Rather, "passing" is what Schenker called a *Wirkung,* a word ambiguous between effect and response, between objective and subjective. It is, in one sense, something that E does between F and D, but it is also something we do as F is succeeded in turn by E and D. What we ought to do with E, so I infer from Schenker's writings, is have a psycho-physical response – an experience that we can describe as spanning between then and not yet, as being neither here nor there but somewhere in between and on the way (*durchgehend*). Schenker's mention of an imaginary bridge is a way of inducing just this response to a particular type of tonal configuration.

There are no doubt other means one could use to induce this experience in oneself. In an ancient Sanskrit text devoted to instructions for reaching various psycho-physical states, the following exercise is commended:

Center on the sound *a-u-m* without any *a* or *m*.[27]

I suggest that the "as if"'s and the "as it were"'s that qualify so much of the language that Schenker uses to represent synthesis have the same effect: they turn the verbal imagery into just such an exercise. The interpretive image is a vehicle and practical aid, and not the consummation of meaning. This is, after all, the point of Schenker's interpretive practice: not the appropriation of analytical understanding but rather the synthesis of such understanding in a musical experience, be it creative or re-creative.

In his commentary on the program of Beethoven's op. 110, Schenker is not interested primarily in our being informed of Beethoven's surmounted suffering, as if the sonata were a report, nor is he interested merely in our being informed that there is a sequence of musical effects whose dynamic quality is akin to Beethoven's life experience. What Schenker wants us to want when we make the music of op. 110's finale is not the information about its musical effects conveyed in the words of the program; rather, what he wants is for us to want to be informed about those effects in the psycho-physical mode of appropriation we call our sense of hearing. As Daniel Dennett writes of another aesthetic experience,

What we want when we sip a great wine is not, indeed, the information about its chemical contents; what we want is to be informed about its contents in our favorite way.[28]

The scored sonata and Schenker's commentary invite our imaginative participation. What we participate in is akin to the experience of surmounted suffering, akin to its dynamic. But it is not surmounted suffering itself that we experience. Why, then, should Beethoven and Schenker conspire to give the musical experience of op. 110 a name that on the face of it has nothing to do with the experience of tones? Perhaps it was because the most similar nonmusical experience that Beethoven or

---

[27] *Zen Flesh, Zen Bones,* comp. Paul Reps (Tokyo: Tuttle, 1957), 203.
[28] *Consciousness Explained,* 384.

Schenker could imagine and put into words was surmounted suffering. The point of their drawing such a connection is to help induce a musical experience that is like their own, and so extend the circle of those who would participate in their musical tradition and in the making of what we call op. 110. That is what Schenker means, I suggest, when he says

We taste Beethoven's pain in the Arioso. What a god, who surrenders his own pain to others merely for [their] enjoyment! I daresay no one could actually share in his pain, because . . . reading the great book of his heroic life was even more difficult than reading his works, so he lamented his pain in tones, and now, only in sounding do they entice people to enjoyment! (*LfS110* 55²72)

We taste it, savor it, partake of it, make it our own. Both tones and words are vehicles pointing to that one end.

In the conclusion of his critical commentary on theme and variations op. 109, Schenker describes an empathetic participation, in which we hear ourselves join in performing the dramatic role of the theme:

For the sake of resolution, the theme enters again. The repetitions drop away, as do the luxuriant arpeggios in bars 5 and 13. More shadowy in substance, as it were, and with a peacefully purified soul, the theme takes its leave of us and slips back into that dreamland from which it descended for a while in order to let us take part in its changes and ordeals . . . (*LfS109* 48²54)

The ellipsis points at the end are in the original. The absence of a period suggests that the completion of the sentence, indeed of the entire monograph, lies beyond discourse, in the activity pointed to in the concluding words: the reader's participation. The role of Schenker's text is that of invitation: an utterance aimed at getting the reader to join him in imaginative re-creation of the masterwork.

This view of the role of text in criticism is elegantly expressed by Paul Claudel:

The written utterance is employed to two ends: either we want to produce in the mind of the reader a state of knowing, or a state of delight. . . . In the second case, by using words as the painter uses colors and the musician uses notes, we want to constitute a kind of equivalent or soluble space in the mind out of a spectacle or an emotion or even an abstract idea. . . . We inform the reader, we cause him to participate in our creative or *poetic* action, we place in the hidden mouth of his mind an utterance of a certain object or a certain sentiment that is at the same time agreeable to his thought and to his physical organ of expression.[29]

"Nous plaçons dans la bouche secrète . . .": Claudel voices a belief that the aim of his criticism is to invite readers to appropriate for themselves the ideas of the writer, to reach a manner of agreement with the author by saying the same thing together. This is what is meant by the placing of an enunciation, an utterance, a way of expressing something, in the secret mouth of the reader's mind. What could this

---

[29] Paul Claudel, "Reflexions et propositions sur le vers français," in *Positions et propositions*, part 1. Vol. 15 of *Œuvres complètes de Paul Claudel* (Paris: Gallimard, 1959), 10–11.

enunciation be unless it were a script, produced by an author and consumed by a reader? And what else could the end of such writing be than for it to be consumed by the reader, to be taken in and made part of her, to be appropriated as her own, to be uttered by her as if she herself had been the writer? But the consumption of the text is not the end of writing, for the consumption is a nourishment, a stimulation of one's fancy that leads, in Schenker's case, through the terms of the text toward the making of music. This is one end to which Schenker strove in creating descriptions of musical works: the appropriation of his creative or poetic action by a reader, sharing listening experiences by means of moving between hearing and writing and back again, mutually re-creating the musical artworks of the Austro-German tradition.

The desire that spurred Schenker's interpretive practice is ultimately a desire for the participation of minds and bodies in that tradition. If he offended in his overly zealous and defensive polemics, it was none the less a worthy desire, and if his writings are not always as lucid and articulate, and thus as helpful, as one might hope, they nevertheless served that desire well, so much so that I have little doubt that, stripped of its negative overtones, it is true that

> ... those who are like the master – they go forth
> And beauty and sense appear where'er they gaze.

BIBLIOGRAPHY OF
SECONDARY LITERATURE

Babbitt, Milton. Review of *Structural Hearing*, by Felix Salzer. *Journal of the American Musico-logical Society* 5 (1952), 260–65.

    Words about Music. Ed. Stephen Dembski and Joseph N. Straus. Madison: University of Wisconsin Press, 1987.

Bach, C. P. E. *Versuch über die wahre Art, das Clavier zu spielen*. Facsimile edition. Leipzig: Breitkopf and Härtel, 1957.

    Essay on the True Art of Playing Keyboard Instruments. Trans. William J. Mitchell. New York: Norton, 1949.

Baker, Nancy Kovaleff, and Thomas Christensen, eds. *Aesthetics and the Art of Musical Compo-sition in the German Enlightenment: Selected Writings of Johann Georg Sulzer and Heinrich Christoph Koch*. Cambridge: Cambridge University Press, 1995.

Baxandall, Michael. *Patterns of Intention: On the Historical Explanation of Pictures*. New Haven, Conn.: Yale University Press, 1985.

    "The Language of Art Criticism." In *The Language of Art History*, ed. Salim Kemal and Ivan Gaskell. Cambridge: Cambridge University Press, 1991, 67–75.

Beach, David. "A Schenker Bibliography." *JMT* 13 (1) (1969), 2–37.

    "A Schenker Bibliography: 1969–1979." *JMT* 23 (2) (1979), 275–86.

    "The Current State of Schenkerian Research." *Acta Musicologica* 57 (1985), 275–307.

Beach, David, ed. *Aspects of Schenkerian Theory*. New Haven, Conn.: Yale University Press, 1983.

Benjamin, William E. "Schenker's Theory and the Future of Music." *JMT* 25 (1) (1981), 155–73.

Bent, Ian. "Heinrich Schenker, Chopin and Domenico Scarlatti." *MA* 5 (2–3) (1986), 131–49.

    Analysis. With a Glossary by William Drabkin. New York: Norton, 1987.

    "Heinrich Schenker e la missione del genio germanico." *Rivista Italiana di Musicologia* 26 (1) (1991), 3–34.

    "History of Music Theory: Margin or Center?" *Theoria* 6 (1992), 1–21.

Bettelheim, Bruno. *Freud and Man's Soul*. New York: Alfred A. Knopf, 1982; New York: Random House, Vintage Books, 1984.

Blasius, Leslie David. *Schenker's Argument and the Situation of Music Theory*. Cambridge Studies in Theory and Analysis, ed. Ian Bent. Cambridge: Cambridge University Press, 1996.

Boretz, Benjamin. *Meta-Variations: Studies in the Foundations of Musical Thought*. Vol. 1 of *Meta-Variations / Compose Yourself*. Red Hook, N.Y.: Open Space, 1995. Also published in installments in *PNM* 8 (1) (1969), 1–74; 8 (2) (1970), 49–111; 9 (1) (1970), 23–42; 9 (2) and 10 (1) (1973), 232–70; 11 (1) (1972), 146–223; 11 (2) (1973), 156–203.

    "Musical Cosmology." *PNM* 15 (2) (1977), 122–32.

    "What Lingers On (, When the Song is Ended)." *PNM* 16 (1977), 102–9.

    "The Logic of What?" *JMT* 33 (1) (1989), 107–16.

Burkhart, Charles. "Schenker's 'Motivic Parallelisms'." *JMT* 22 (2) (1978), 145–75.

Burnham, Scott. "The Criticism of Analysis and the Analysis of Criticism." *NCM* 16 (1) (1992), 70–79.

"Musical and Intellectual Values: Interpreting the History of Tonal Theory." *Current Musicology* 53 (1993), 76–88.

Cadwallader, Allen. "Motivic Unity and Integration of Structural Levels in Brahms's B Minor Intermezzo, Op. 119, No. 1." *TP* 8 (2) (1983), 5–24.

"Schenker's Unpublished Graphic Analysis of Brahms's Intermezzo Op. 117, No. 2." *MTS* 6 (1984), 1–13.

Cadwallader, Allen, ed. *Trends in Schenkerian Research.* New York: Schirmer, 1990.

Cadwallader, Allen, and William Pastille. "Schenker's High-Level Motives." *JMT* 36 (1) (1989), 119–48.

Cavell, Stanley. *Must We Mean What We Say?* Cambridge: Cambridge University Press, 1976.

Cherlin, Michael. "Hauptmann and Schenker: Two Adaptations of Hegelian Dialectics." *TP* 13 (1988), 115–31.

Citkowitz, Israel. "The Role of Heinrich Schenker." *Modern Music* 11 (1) (1933), 18–23. Reprinted in *TP* 10 (1–2) (1985), 17–22.

Clark, William. "Heinrich Schenker on the Nature of the Seventh Chord." *JMT* 26 (1982), 221–59.

Cohen, Ted. "Metaphor and the Cultivation of Intimacy." In *On Metaphor,* ed. Sheldon Sacks. Chicago: University of Chicago Press, 1979, 1–10.

Cohn, Richard. "The Autonomy of Motives in Schenkerian Accounts of Tonal Music." *MTS* 14 (2) (1992), 150–70.

Cone, Edward T. *The Composer's Voice.* Berkeley and Los Angeles: University of California Press, 1974.

Music: A View from Delft. Ed. Robert P. Morgan. Chicago: University of Chicago Press, 1989.

Cook, Nicholas. "Schenker's Theory of Music as Ethics." *Journal of Musicology* 7 (4) (1989), 415–39.

"Music Theory and 'Good Comparison': A Viennese Perspective." *JMT* 33 (1) (1989), 117–41.

"Heinrich Schenker, Polemicist: A Reading of the Ninth Symphony Monograph." *MA* 14 (1) (1995), 89–105.

Cumming, Naomi. "Music Analysis and the Perceiver: A Perspective from Functionalist Philosophy." *Current Musicology* 54 (1993), 38–53.

"Metaphor in Roger Scruton's Aesthetics of Music." In *Theory, Analysis and Meaning in Music,* ed. Anthony Pople. Cambridge: Cambridge University Press, 1994, 1–28.

Dahlhaus, Carl. Review of *Neue musikalische Theorien und Phantasien III: Der freie Satz* by Heinrich Schenker. *Die Musikforschung* 12 (4) (1959), 523–25.

"Schoenberg and Schenker." *Proceedings of the Royal Musical Association* 100 (1973–74), 209–15.

Dahlhaus, Carl, ed. *Beiträge zur musikalischen Hermeneutik.* Regensburg: Gustav Bosse, 1975.

Davidson, Donald. *Essays on Actions and Events.* Oxford: Clarendon Press, 1980.

Inquiries into Truth and Interpretation. Oxford: Clarendon Press, 1985.

"A Nice Derangement of Epitaphs." In *Truth and Interpretation: Perspectives on the Philosophy of Donald Davidson,* ed. E. LePore. Oxford: Basil Blackwell, 1986, 433–46.

Dennett, Daniel. *The Intentional Stance.* Cambridge, Mass.: MIT Press, 1987.

Consciousness Explained. Boston: Little, Brown, 1991.

Derrida, Jacques. "White Mythology: Metaphor in the Text of Philosophy." In *Margins of Philosophy,* trans. Alan Bass. Chicago: University of Chicago Press, 1982, 207–71.

Don, Gary W. "Goethe and Schenker." *ITO* 10 (8) (1988), 1–14.

Drabkin, William. "The New *Erläuterungsausgabe.*" *PNM* 12 (1973–74), 319–30.

"Felix-Eberhard von Cube and the North-German Tradition of Schenkerism." *Proceedings of the Royal Musical Association* 111 (1984–85), 180–207.

"A Lesson in Analysis from Heinrich Schenker: The C Major Prelude from Bach's Well-Tempered Clavier, Book I." *MA* 4 (3) (1985), 241–58.

Dubiel, Joseph. "A Schenker Analysis and Some of Schenker's Theories." Paper presented at the annual meeting of the Society for Music Theory, Philadelphia, Pennsylvania, 1984.

Review of *Introduction to Schenkerian Analysis*, by Allen Forte and Stephen E. Gilbert. *Musical Quarterly* 70 (1984), 269–78.

"'When You are a Beethoven': Kinds of Rules in Schenker's *Counterpoint.*" *JMT* 34 (2) (1990), 291–340.

"How Do You Know You Hear It That Way?" Paper presented at the annual meeting of the Society for Music Theory, Kansas City, Missouri, 1992.

"What Did Schenker Mean by Prolongation?" Paper presented at the conference Critical Perspectives on Schenker, University of Notre Dame, March 1994.

"Contradictory Criteria in a Work of Brahms." In *Brahms Studies*, Vol. 1, ed. David Brodbeck. Lincoln, Nbr.: University of Nebraska Press, 1994, 81–110.

"Function, Explanation, and Interpretation." Paper presented at the annual meeting of the Society for Music Theory, 1990.

Epstein, David. *Beyond Orpheus: Studies in Musical Structure.* Cambridge, Mass.: MIT Press, 1979.

"On Schenker's *Free Composition.*" *JMT* 25 (1) (1981), 143–53.

Federhofer, Hellmut. *Akkord und Stimmführung in den musiktheoretischen Systemen von Hugo Riemann, Ernst Kurth und Heinrich Schenker.* Vienna, 1981.

Forte, Allen. "Schenker's Conception of Musical Structure." *JMT* 3 (1) (1959), 1–30.

The Compositional Matrix. Monographs in Theory and Composition. Baldwin, N.Y.: Music Teachers National Association, 1961.

"Ernst Oster (1908–1977) In Memoriam." *JMT* 21 (2) (1977), 340–44.

Forte, Allen, and Steven E. Gilbert. *Introduction to Schenkerian Analysis.* New York: Norton, 1982.

Furtwängler, Wilhelm. *Ton und Wort.* 4th edn. Wiesbaden: F. A. Brockhaus, 1955.

Geertz, Clifford. *Works and Lives: The Anthropologist as Author.* Stanford: Stanford University Press, 1988.

Guck, Marion A. "Metaphors in Musical Discourse: The Contribution of Imagery to Analysis." Ph.D. diss., University of Michigan, 1981.

"A Flow of Energy: Density 21.5." *PNM* 23 (1) (1985), 334–47.

"Cognitive Alchemy: Transmuting Theoretical Vices into Analytical Virtues." Paper presented at the annual meeting of the Society for Music Theory, Rochester, New York, 1987.

"Beethoven as Dramatist." *CMS* 29 (1989), 8–18.

"Two Types of Metaphoric Transference." In *Metaphor – A Musical Dimension*, ed. Jamie C. Kassler. Vol. 1 of *Australian Studies in History, Philosophy, and Social Studies of Music*, ed. Margaret J. Kartomi. Davis, Calif.: Currency Press. 1991, 1–12.

"The Schenkerian Roots of Westergaard's Counterpoint." Paper presented at the annual meeting of the Society for Music Theory, Cincinnati, Ohio, 1991.

"Questions of Interpretation in Musical Analysis." Paper presented at the conference on Music and Meaning held at the University of Cincinnati, December 1993.

"Rehabilitating the Incorrigible." In *Theory, Analysis and Meaning in Music*, ed. Anthony Pople. Cambridge: Cambridge University Press, 1994, 57–73.

"Analytical Fictions." *MTS* 16 (2) (1994), 217–30.

"A Woman's (Theoretical) Work." *PNM* 32 (1) (1994), 28–43.

Musical Effects. In preparation.

Hatten, Robert S. *Musical Meaning in Beethoven: Markedness, Correlation, and Interpretation.* Bloomington, Ind.: Indiana University Press, 1994.

Hegel, G. W. F. *Reason in History: A General Introduction to the Philosophy of History.* Trans. Robert S. Hartman. Indianapolis, Ind.: Bobbs-Merrill, 1953.

The Philosophy of History. Trans. J. Sibree. New York, Dover, 1956.

Werke. 20 vols. Frankfurt am Main: Suhrkamp, 1970.

Hegel's Science of Logic. Trans. A. V. Miller. Atlantic Highlands, N. J.: Humanities Press International, 1989.

Elements of the Philosophy of Right. Ed. Allen H. Wood. Trans. H. B. Nisbet. Cambridge: Cambridge University Press, 1991.

Hubbs, Nadine M. "Schenker's Organicism." *TP* 16 (1991), 143–62.

Inwood, Michael. *A Hegel Dictionary.* Oxford: Blackwell, 1992.

Iser, Wolfgang. *The Act of Reading: A Theory of Aesthetic Response.* Baltimore: Johns Hopkins University Press, 1978.

Isenberg, Arnold. *Aesthetics and the Theory of Criticism.* Chicago: University of Chicago Press, 1973.

Janik, Allan, and Stephen Toulmin. *Wittgenstein's Vienna.* New York: Simon and Schuster, 1973.

Johnston, William M. *The Austrian Mind: An Intellectual and Social History, 1848–1938.* Berkeley and Los Angeles: University of California Press, 1972.

Jonas, Oswald. *Das Wesen des musikalisches Kunstwerkes.* Vienna: Universal Edition, 1934.

Einführung in die Lehre Heinrich Schenkers: Das Wesen des musikalischen Kunstwerkes. Rev. edn. Vienna: Universal Edition, 1972.

"Schenker, Heinrich." In *Die Musik in Geschichte und Gegenwart*, ed. Friedrich Blume. Kassel: Bärenreiter, 1963, 11: 1670–71.

"Heinrich Schenker und grosse Interpreten." *Österreichische Musikzeitschrift* 19 (12) (1964), 584–89.

Introduction to the Theory of Heinrich Schenker: The Nature of the Musical Work of Art. Trans. and ed. John Rothgeb. New York: Schirmer, 1982.

Kassler, Jamie Croy. "Heinrich Schenker's Epistemology and Philosophy of Music: An Essay on the Relations between Evolutionary Theory and Music Theory." In *The Wider Domain of Evolutionary Thought*, ed. David Oldroyd and Ian Langham. Dordrecht: D. Reidel, 1983, 221–60.

Katz, Adele T. "Heinrich Schenker's Method of Analysis." *Musical Quarterly* 221 (3) (1935), 311–29. Reprinted in *TP* 10 (1–2) (1985), 77–95.

Challenge to Musical Tradition: A New Concept of Tonality. New York: Alfred A. Knopf, 1945.

Keiler, Allan. "The Origins of Schenker's Thought: How Man is Musical." *JMT* 33 (2) (1989), 273–98.

"On Some Properties of Schenker's Pitch Derivations." *MP* 1 (2) (1983–84), 200–228.

"The Empiricist Illusion: Narmour's *Beyond Schenkerism.*" *PNM* 17 (1) (1978), 161–95.

"Music as Metalanguage: Rameau's Fundamental Bass." In *Music Theory: Special Topics*, ed. Richmond Browne. New York: Academic Press, 1981, 83–100.

Kerman, Joseph. *Contemplating Musicology: Challenges to Musicology.* Cambridge, Mass.: Harvard University Press, 1985.

Write All These Down: Essays on Music. Berkeley and Los Angeles: University of California Press, 1994.

Klonoski, Edward. "When Is a Line a Zug?" Paper presented at the annual meeting of Music Theory Midwest, Bloomington, Indiana, 1994.

Komar, Arthur. *Theory of Suspensions: A Study of Metrical and Pitch Relations in Tonal Music.* Princeton: Princeton University Press, 1971.

Korsyn, Kevin. "Schenker and Kantian Epistemology." *Theoria* 3 (1988), 1–58.

"Schenker's Organicism Reexamined." *Intégral* 7 (1993), 82–118.

Kramer, Lawrence. "Haydn's Chaos, Schenker's Order; or, Hermeneutics and Musical Analysis: Can They Mix?" *NCM* 16 (1) (1992), 3–17.

Krausz, Michael, ed. *The Interpretation of Music.* Oxford: Clarendon Press, 1993.

Kretzschmar, Hermann. *Führer durch den Concertsaal.* 1ste Abtheilung: Sinfonie und Suite. Leipzig: A. G. Liebekind, 1887.

Gesammelte Aufsätze. Leipzig: Breitkopf and Härtel, 1911.

Laskowski, Larry. *Heinrich Schenker: An Annotated Index to His Analyses of Musical Works.* New York: Pendragon Press, 1978.

Lerdahl, Fred, and Ray Jackendoff. *A Generative Theory of Tonal Music.* Cambridge, Mass.: MIT Press, 1983.

Levinson, Jerrold. *Music, Art, and Metaphysics.* Ithaca, N.Y.: Cornell University Press, 1990.

Lewin, David. "Music Theory, Phenomenology, and Modes of Perception." *MP* 3 (4) (1986), 327–92.

Lubben, Joseph. "Schenker the Progressive: Analytic Practice in *Der Tonwille*." *MTS* 15 (1) (1993), 59–75.

McCreless, Patrick. "Reading Schenker's *Kontrapunkt*." *Intégral* 3 (1989), 201–25.

Maus, Fred. "Music as Drama." *MTS* 10 (1988), 56–73.

"Agency in Instrumental Music and Song." *CMS* 29 (1989), 31–43.

"Self-Depiction in Writing about Music." Paper presented at the annual meeting of the Society for Music Theory, Oakland, California, 1990.

Mitchell, William J. Review of *Harmony*, by Heinrich Schenker. *Musical Quarterly* 41 (2) (1955), 256–60.

Morton, Frederic. *A Nervous Splendor: Vienna 1888/1889.* Harmondsworth: Penguin Books, 1980.

Thunder at Twilight: Vienna 1913/1914. New York: Collier Books, 1989.

Narmour, Eugene. *Beyond Schenkerism: The Need For Alternatives in Music Analysis.* Chicago: University of Chicago Press, 1977.

Nehamas, Alexander. "The Postulated Author: Critical Monism as a Regulative Ideal." *Critical Inquiry* 8 (1) (1981), 133–49.

Neumeyer, David. "The *Urlinie* from 8̂ as a Middleground Phenomenon." *ITO* 9 (5–6) (1987), 3–25.

"The Three-Part *Ursatz*." *ITO* 10 (1–2) (1987), 3–29.

"Fragile Octaves, Broken Lines: On Some Limitations in Schenkerian Theory and Practice." *ITO* 11 (3) (1989), 13–30.

Newcomb, Anthony. "Sound and Feeling." *Critical Inquiry* 10 (1984), 614–43.

Novack, Saul. "Foreground, Middleground, and Background: Their Significance in the History of Tonality." In *Schenker Studies*, ed. Hedi Siegel. Cambridge: Cambridge University Press, 1990, 60–71.

Oster, Ernst. "The *Fantaisie-Impromptu* – A Tribute to Beethoven." *Musicology* 1 (4) (1947), 407–29. Reprinted in *Aspects of Schenkerian Theory*, ed. David Beach. New Haven, Conn.: Yale University Press, 1983, 189–207.

"The Dramatic Character of the Egmont Overture." *Musicology* 2 (3) (1949), 269–85. Reprinted in *Aspects of Schenkerian Theory*, ed. David Beach. New Haven, Conn.: Yale University Press, 1983, 209–22.

"Re: A New Concept of Tonality." *JMT* 4 (1) (1960), 85–98.

"Register and the Large-Scale Connection." *JMT* 5 (1) (1961), 54–71.

Pastille, William A. "Heinrich Schenker, Anti-Organicist." *NCM* 8 (1) (1984), 29–36.

"Ursatz: The Musical Philosophy of Heinrich Schenker." Ph.D. diss., Cornell University, 1985.

"Music and Morphology: Goethe's Influence on Schenker's Thought." In *Schenker Studies*, ed. Hedi Siegel. Cambridge: Cambridge University Press, 1990, 29–44.

"The Development of the *Ursatz* in Schenker's Published Works." In *Trends in Schenkerian Research*, ed. Allen Cadwallader. New York: Schirmer, 1990, 71–85.

Peles, Stephen. "'Strength of Connection': On Some Extrahierarchical Aspects of Voice-Leading in Classically Tonal Music." Paper presented at the annual meeting of the Society for Music Theory, Cincinnati, Ohio, 1991.

Pierce, Alexandra. *Spanning: Essays on Music Theory, Performance, and Movement.*

Potter, Pamela. *German Musicology and Society from the Weimar Republic to the End of Hitler's Reich.* New Haven, Conn.: Yale University Press, forthcoming.

Proctor, Gregory. Review of *Free Composition* by Heinrich Schenker. *Notes* 36 (4) (1980), 879–81.

Proctor, Gregory, and Herbert Lee Riggins. "Levels and the Reordering of Chapters in Schenker's *Free Composition*." *MTS* 10 (1988), 102–26.

Randall, J. K. *Compose Yourself – A Manual for the Young.* Vol. 2 of *Meta-Variations / Compose Yourself.* Red Hook, N.Y.: Open Space, 1995.

"A Soundscroll." *PNM* 13 (2) (1975), 126–49.

Rast, Nicholas. "A Checklist of Essays and Reviews by Heinrich Schenker." *MA* 7 (2) (1988), 121–32.

Richter, Jean Paul. *Vorschule der Aesthetik.* In *Jean Paul's sämmtliche Werke*, 3rd edn. vols. 18–19. Berlin: G. Reimer, 1861.

Riezler-Stettin, Walter. "Die 'Urlinie'." *Die Musik* 12 (7) (1930), 502–10.

Rink, John. "Schenker and Improvisation." *JMT* 37 (1) (1993), 1–54.

Rothfarb, Lee. *Ernst Kurth as Theorist and Analyst.* Philadelphia: University of Pennsylvania Press, 1988.

Ernst Kurth: Selected Writings. Cambridge Studies in Theory and Analysis, ed. Ian Bent. Cambridge: Cambridge University Press, 1991.

Rothgeb, John. "Design as a Key to Structure in Tonal Music." *JMT* 15 (1971), 230–53.

"Strict Counterpoint and Tonal Theory." *JMT* 19 (2) (1975), 260–84.

"Thematic Content: A Schenkerian View." In *Aspects of Schenkerian Theory*, ed. David Beach. New Haven, Conn.: Yale University Press, 1983, 39–60.

"Translating Texts on Music Theory: Heinrich Schenker's *Kontrapunkt*." *TP* 9 (1–2) (1984), 71–75.

Rothstein, William. "Rhythm and the Theory of Structural Levels." Ph.D. diss., Yale University, 1981.

"The Americanization of Schenker." *ITO* 9 (1) (1986), 5–17. Reprinted in *Schenker Studies*, ed. Hedi Siegel. Cambridge: Cambridge University Press, 1990, 193–203.

Phrase Rhythm in Tonal Music. New York: Schirmer Books, 1989.

"On Implied Tones." *MA* 10 (3) (1991), 289–328.

Ryle, Gilbert. *The Concept of Mind.* Chicago: University of Chicago Press, 1949.

On Thinking. Ed. Konstantin Kolenda. Totowa, N.J.: Rowman and Littlefield, 1979.

Sacks, Sheldon, ed. *On Metaphor.* Chicago: University of Chicago Press, 1979.

Salzer, Felix. *Sinn und Wesen der abendländerischen Mehrstimmigkeit.* Vienna: Saturn-Verlag, 1935.

"Die historische Sendung Heinrich Schenkers." *Der Dreiklang* 1 (1937), 2–12.

Structural Hearing: Tonal Coherence in Music. 2 vols. New York: Charles Boni, 1952; reprint in 1 vol., New York: Dover, 1962.

Salzer, Felix, and Carl Schachter. *Counterpoint in Composition.* New York: McGraw-Hill, 1969; reprint, New York: Columbia University Press, 1989.

Schachter, Carl E. "A Commentary on Schenker's *Free Composition.*" *JMT* 25 (1) (1981), 115–42.

"Rhythm and Linear Analysis: A Preliminary Study." *MF* 4 (1976), 281–334.

"Rhythm and Linear Analysis: Durational Reduction." *MF* 5 (1979), 197–232.

"Rhythm and Linear Analysis: Aspects of Meter." *MF* 6 (1) (1987), 1–59.

"The Triad as Place and Action." *MTS* 17 (2) (1995), 149–69.

Schorske, Carl E. *Fin-de-siècle Vienna.* New York: Vintage Books, 1981.

Sessions, Roger. *Roger Sessions on Music: Collected Essays.* Ed. Edward T. Cone. Princeton, N.J.: Princeton University Press, 1979.

Siegel, Hedi, ed. *Schenker Studies.* Cambridge: Cambridge University Press, 1990.

Slatin, Sonia. "The Theories of Heinrich Schenker in Perspective." Ph.D. diss., Columbia University, 1967.

Snarrenberg, Robert. "Zen and the Way of Soundscroll." *PNM* 30 (1) (1992), 222–37.

"Schenker's Senses of Concealment." *Theoria* 6 (1992), 97–133.

"Competing Myths: The American Abandonment of Schenker's Organicism." In *Theory, Analysis and Meaning in Music,* ed. Anthony Pople. Cambridge: Cambridge University Press, 1994, 30–58.

Solie, Ruth A. "The Living Work: Organicism and Musical Analysis." *NCM* 4 (1980), 147–56.

"Beethoven as Secular Humanist: Ideology and the Ninth Symphony in Nineteenth-Century Criticism." In *Explorations in Music, the Arts, and Ideas: Essays in Honor of Leonard B. Meyer,* ed. Eugene Narmour and Ruth A. Solie. Stuyvesant, N.Y.: Pendragon Press, 1988, 1–42.

Steiner, George. *After Babel: Aspects of Language and Translation.* 2nd edn. Oxford: Oxford University Press, 1992.

Thaler, Lotte. *Organische Form in der Musiktheorie des 19. und beginnenden 20. Jahrhunderts.* Munich and Salzburg, 1984.

Treitler, Leo. 1989. *Music and the Historical Imagination.* Cambridge, Mass.: Harvard University Press.

"History and the Ontology of the Musical Work." *JAAC* 51 (3), 483–97.

"The Language of Musical Interpretation." Paper presented at the conference Music and Meaning held at the University of Cincinnati, December 1993.

Waldeck, Arthur, and Nathan Broder. "Musical Synthesis as Expounded by Heinrich Schenker." *Musical Mercury* 11 (4) (1935), 56–64. Reprinted in *TP* 10 (1–2) (1985), 65–73.

Walton, Kendall L. "What is Abstract about the Art of Music?" *JAAC* 46 (3) (1987), 351–64.

Mimesis as Make-Believe. Cambridge, Mass.: Harvard University Press, 1991.

"Understanding Humour and Understanding Music." In *The Interpretation of Music,* ed. Michael Krausz. Oxford: Clarendon Press, 1993, 259–69.

"Listening with Imagination: Is Music Representational?" *JAAC* 51 (2) (1994), 47–61.

Wason, Robert W. *Viennese Harmonic Theory from Albrechtsberger to Schenker and Schoenberg.* Ann Arbor, Mich.: UMI Research Press, 1985.

Weisse, Hans. "The Music Teacher's Dilemma." *Proceedings of the Music Teachers National Association* 1935: 122–37. Reprinted in *TP* 10 (1–2) (1985), 29–48.

Westergaard, Peter. "Some Problems in Rhythmic Theory and Analysis." *PNM* (1962). Reprinted in *Perspectives on Contemporary Music Theory,* ed. Benjamin Boretz and Edward T. Cone. New York: Norton, 1972, 226–37.

An Introduction to Tonal Theory. New York: Norton, 1975.

Wolf, Hans. "Schenkers Persönlichkeit in Unterricht." *Der Dreiklang* 7 (1937), 176–84. Reprint, Hildesheim: Georg Olms, 1989.

Whittall, Arnold. "Schenker and the Prospects for Analysis." *Musical Times* 121 (1980), 560–62.

Yeston, Maury. *The Stratification of Musical Rhythm.* New Haven, Conn.: Yale University Press, 1976.

Yeston, Maury, ed. *Readings in Schenker Analysis and Other Approaches.* New Haven, Conn.: Yale University Press, 1977.

Zuckerkandl, Victor. *Sound and Symbol: Music and the External World.* Trans. Willard R. Trask. Princeton, N. J.: Princeton University Press, 1956.

Man the Musician. Vol. 2 of *Sound and Symbol.* Trans. Norbert Guterman. Princeton, N. J.: Princeton University Press, 1973.

INDEX